THE INTERNET IN EVERYTHING

LAURA DENARDIS

The
Internet in
Everything

FREEDOM AND SECURITY

IN A WORLD WITH NO OFF SWITCH

Yale

UNIVERSITY PRESS

NEW HAVEN & LONDON

Published with assistance from the foundation established in memory of Philip Hamilton McMillan of the Class of 1894, Yale College.

Yale University Press books may be purchased in quantity for educational, business, or promotional use. For information, please e-mail sales.press@yale.edu (U.S. office) or sales@yaleup.co.uk (U.K. office).

Set in Times Roman type by IDS Infotech, Ltd.
Printed in the United States of America.

Library of Congress Control Number: 2019941081
ISBN 978-0-300-23307-0 (hardcover : alk. paper)

A catalogue record for this book is available from the British Library.

This paper meets the requirements of ANSI/NISO Z39.48-1992 (Permanence of Paper).

10 9 8 7 6 5 4 3 2 1

For Deborah R. Smith

CONTENTS

CONTENTS

ABBREVIATIONS

6Lo	IPv6 over Networks of Resource-Constrained Nodes
6LoWPAN	IPv6 over Low-Power Wireless Personal Area Networks
6TiSCH	IPv6 Time Slotted Channel Hopping
ACLU	American Civil Liberties Union
AI	Artificial Intelligence
AMQP	Advanced Message Queuing Protocol
ANSI	American National Standards Institute
AR	Augmented Reality
ARPA	Advanced Research Projects Agency
ARPANET	Advanced Research Projects Agency Network
AS	Autonomous System
ASA	Adaptive Security Appliance
ASN	Autonomous System Number
BGP	Border Gateway Protocol
BLE	Bluetooth Low Energy
CA	Certificate Authority
CARP	Channel Aware Routing Protocol
ccTLD	Country Code Top-Level Domain
CDA	Communications Decency Act
CDN	Content Delivery Network or Content Distribution Network
CDT	Center for Democracy & Technology
CERT	Computer Emergency Response Team

CFAA	Computer Fraud and Abuse Act
CIA	Central Intelligence Agency
CIGI	Centre for International Governance Innovation
CISO	Chief Information and Security Officer
CoAP	Constrained Application Protocol
COPPA	Children's Online Privacy Protection Act
CORPL	Cognitive RPL
CPS	Cyber-Physical System
CPU	Central Processing Unit
CVV	Card Verification Value
DARPA	Defense Advanced Research Projects Agency
DDoS	Distributed Denial of Service
DDS	Data Distribution Service
DECT	Digital Enhanced Cordless Telecommunications
DHS	Department of Homeland Security
DMCA	Digital Millennium Copyright Act
DNC	Democratic National Committee
DNS	Domain Name System
DNSSEC	Domain Name System Security Extensions
DTLS	Datagram Transport Layer Security
DVR	Digital Video Recorder
ECMA	European Computer Manufacturers Association
EFF	Electronic Frontier Foundation
ENISA	European Union Agency for Network and Information Security
EPC	Electronic Product Code
EPIC	Electronic Privacy Information Center
ETSI	European Telecommunications Standards Institute
EU	European Union
FBI	Federal Bureau of Investigation (U.S.)
FCC	Federal Communications Commission (U.S)
FDA	Food and Drug Administration (U.S.)
FIPPs	Fair Information Practice Principles
FTC	Federal Trade Commission (U.S.)
GAFAM	Google, Apple, Facebook, Amazon and Microsoft
GDP	Gross Domestic Product

GDPR	General Data Protection Regulation
GE	General Electric
GNI	Global Network Initiative
GPS	Global Positioning System
GSM	Global System for Mobile Communication
GSMA	GSM Association
HTML	Hypertext Markup Language
HTTP	Hypertext Transfer Protocol
HTTPS	Hypertext Transfer Protocol Secure
IAB	Internet Architecture Board
IANA	Internet Assigned Numbers Authority
IBM	International Business Machines
ICANN	Internet Corporation for Assigned Names and Numbers
ICS	Industrial Control Systems
ICS-CERT	Industrial Control Systems Computer Emergency Response Team
ICT	Information and Communication Technology
IEC	International Electrotechnical Commission
IEEE	Institute of Electrical and Electronics Engineers
IESG	Internet Engineering Steering Group
IETF	Internet Engineering Task Force
IGF	Internet Governance Forum
IIC	Industrial Internet Consortium
IIoT	Industrial Internet of Things
IoT	Internet of Things
IoTDB	IoT Database
IP	Internet Protocol
IPR	Intellectual Property Rights
IPSO	Internet Protocol for Smart Objects
IPv4	Internet Protocol Version 4
IPv6	Internet Protocol Version 6
ISO	International Organization for Standardization
ISP	Internet Service Provider
IT	Information Technology
ITU	International Telecommunication Union
IXP	Internet Exchange Point

JPEG	Joint Photographic Experts Group
LAN	Local Area Network
LLAP	Live Long and Process
LoRaWAN	Low Power Wide Area Network
LoWPAN	Low Power Wireless Personal Area Network
LsDL	Lemonbeat Smart Device Language
LTE-A	Long Term Evolution – Advanced
LTE-M	Long Term Evolution for Machines
LWM2M	Lightweight Machine-to-Machine
M2M	Machine-to-Machine
MAC	Media Access Control
mDNS	Multicast Domain Name System
MIT	Massachusetts Institute of Technology
MPEG	Motion Picture Experts Group
MQTT	Message Queuing Telemetry Transport
MQTT-SN	MQTT for Sensor Networks
NASA	National Aeronautics and Space Administration
NAT	Network Address Translation
NB-IoT	Narrowband IoT
NCSC	National Cyber Security Centre (UK)
NFC	Near Field Communication
NIST	National Institute of Standards and Technology
NSA	National Security Agency
NTIA	National Telecommunications and Information Administration
OECD	Organisation for Economic Co-operation and Development
OPM	Office of Personnel Management (U.S.)
OSI	Open Systems Interconnection
OTA	Online Trust Alliance
OTrP	Open Trust Protocol
P2P	Peer-to-Peer
PIPA	Preventing Real Online Threats to Economic Creativity and Theft of Intellectual Property (PROTECT IP) Act
QUIC	Quick UDP Internet Connections
RAML	RESTful API Modeling Language
RAND	Reasonable and Non-Discriminatory

REST	Representational State Transfer
RF	Radio Frequency
RFC	Request for Comments
RFID	Radio-Frequency Identification
RIR	Regional Internet Registry
ROLL	Routing over Low-Power and Lossy Networks
RPKI	Resource Public Key Infrastructure
RPL	Routing Protocol for Low-Power and Lossy Networks
RPMA	Random Phase Multiple Access
SCADA	Supervisory Control and Data Acquisition
SCMP	Simple Commerce Messaging Protocol
SENML	Sensor Markup Language
SensorML	Sensor Model Language
SMQTT	Secure Message Queue Telemetry Transport
SNA	Systems Network Architecture
SOPA	Stop Online Piracy Act
SSI	Simple Sensor Interface
SSL	Secure Sockets Layer
STOMP	Simple Text Oriented Messaging Protocol
STS	Science and Technology Studies
TCP	Transmission Control Protocol
TCP/IP	Transmission Control Protocol/Internet Protocol
TLS	Transport Layer Security
TOR	The Onion Router
TPM	Technical Protection Measures
TSMP	Time Synchronized Mesh Protocol
UDP	User Datagram Protocol
uIP	Micro IP
uPnP	Universal Plug and Play
URL	Uniform Resource Locator
USAID	United States Agency for International Development
US-CERT	United States Computer Emergency Readiness Team
VoIP	Voice over Internet Protocol
VPN	Virtual Private Network
VR	Virtual Reality
W3C	World Wide Web Consortium

WEF	World Economic Forum
Wi-Fi	Wireless Fidelity
WIPO	World Intellectual Property Organization
WSIS	World Summit on the Information Society
XML	Extensible Markup Language
XMPP	Extensible Messaging and Presence Protocol

PART ONE

FROM COMMUNICATION TO CONTROL

After the Internet

IF HUMANS SUDDENLY VANISHED FROM EARTH, the digital world would still vibrantly hum. Surveillance cameras scanning streets from Beijing to Washington would stream video. Self-driving trucks would haul material around an Australian mine. Russian social media bots would circulate political propaganda. Internet-connected thermostats would regulate home climates. Robots would move merchandise around massive warehouses. Environmental sensors would gauge air pollution levels. A giraffe wandering through a game reserve would trigger a motion detector that opens a gate. Bank accounts would make automatic mortgage payments. Servers would mine Bitcoin. Until electricity stops flowing, cyberspace lives.

This sounds like the prologue of a science fiction story but is just a pragmatic acknowledgment of how far digital systems have leapt from human-facing display screens into the physical world of material objects and artificial intelligence. The Internet is no longer merely a communication system connecting people and information. It is a control system connecting vehicles, wearable devices, home appliances, drones, medical equipment, currency, and every conceivable industry sector. Cyberspace now completely and often imperceptibly permeates offline spaces, blurring boundaries between material and virtual worlds.

This transformation of the Internet from a communication network between people to a control network embedded directly into the physical world may be even more consequential than the shift from an industrial society to a digital information society. The potential for human advancement and economic growth is as staggering as the accompanying society-wide dilemmas. How will work be transformed as autonomous systems and networked objects embedded with sensors and actuators subsume entire labor sectors, from transportation to food service? Will there be any domain of human existence that remains private, or is individual privacy no longer conceivable? What does the Internet embedding into the physical world mean for consumer safety and national security?

The stakes of cybersecurity rise as Internet outages are no longer about losing access to communication and content but about losing day-to-day functioning in the real world, from the ability to drive a car to accessing medical care. The Internet of things (IoT) bleeds into the real world in ways that enhance life but also can compromise personal safety and security. The nature of war and conflict transforms as the cyber-embedded physical world can be surveilled and disrupted from anywhere on Earth. The expansion of the Internet into everyday objects is a new threat matrix for national security. Dependencies on the stability and security of cyberspace, already necessary for the digital economy and the public sphere, extend deeper into human safety and the basic functioning of material infrastructures of water, energy, and transportation systems.

Internet-connected objects bring privacy concerns into intimate spheres of human existence far beyond the already invasive data-gathering practices of Facebook, Google, and other content intermediaries. Ambient data gathering of routine activities within homes and around medical and health practices can be much more privacy invasive even than surveillance of emails, texts, websites visited, and other digital content through the clear portal of a screen. Devices collect personal information about everything humans do in daily life. It is not preordained that individual privacy will ever meaningfully be possible. Even gaining personal consent for data collection is sometimes impossible because affected individuals may not be the owners of these devices or even aware of their presence. Unprecedented privacy questions arise around what personal data is gathered and shared from everyday objects and the types of government surveillance now possible in life spheres that were previously shielded from any external scrutiny.

Three cybersecurity stories highlight the rising political stakes of this embedding of digital technologies into the material world. The first involves connected medical devices and rising concern about human safety. Former U.S. vice president Dick Cheney and his cardiologist disclosed in a television interview that the doctor had, in 2007, ordered the disabling of a wireless feature on the vice president's implanted defibrillator in an abundance of caution around fears that a terrorist could carry out an assassination by wirelessly hacking into the pacemaker.[1] This seemed like a remote possibility until, ten years later, the U.S. Food and Drug Administration (FDA) issued a safety warning about cybersecurity vulnerabilities in radio-frequency-enabled implantable cardiac devices, including pacemakers and defibrillators.[2] The affected devices transmit data to a home monitor, which can, in turn, connect to a physician over the Internet. The FDA warning suggested that "someone other than the patient's physician" could "remotely access a patient's RF-enabled [radio-frequency-enabled] implanted cardiac device."[3] Cyber technologies are not only embedded in objects; they are embedded in objects that are embedded in the body.

The Stuxnet worm detected in 2010 similarly exemplifies political entanglements between digital and material infrastructure. Stuxnet was highly sophisticated code designed to infiltrate and sabotage the control systems operating Iranian nuclear centrifuges.[4] Stuxnet is typically described as a coordinated U.S.-Israeli initiative crafted to sabotage Iran's nuclear weapon aspirations, although neither the U.S. nor Israeli government officially acknowledges these claims.[5] Since Stuxnet, there have been countless politically motivated attacks on critical infrastructure including disruptions to the Ukrainian power distribution systems, which officials have attributed to Russian security services. These attacks demonstrate how control of cyber-physical infrastructure is now a proxy for state power.

The Mirai botnet is a similarly revealing example. This largest cyberattack in history was carried out by hijacked Internet-connected home appliances. More than eighty popular sites, including Amazon and Reddit, became inaccessible in parts of the United States in the fall of 2016. The cause of the outages was a massive distributed denial of service (DDoS) attack. The assault hijacked millions of unwitting devices, exploiting security vulnerabilities to implant malicious code and using these hijacked devices to flood the targeted sites with so many requests as to render the targets inaccessible to legitimate traffic. A real-world analogy would be millions of people simultaneously calling a 911 dispatcher. The dispatch system itself is not infiltrated, but the sheer volume of spurious calls makes the service unavailable to legitimate calls. As such, a DDoS attack has a similar effect as a complete outage of a besieged system. Tools for launching these attacks are readily and freely available online or as services available for hire.

This outage received considerable media attention because the sites affected, including Netflix and Twitter, were some of the most popular Internet services at the time.[6] There were much more alarming characteristics that offer insights about the nature of distributed control points in virtual-material spaces. First, the attack was carried out not directly against the affected sites but by attacking an intermediary technology necessary to keep the sites operational: the Domain Name System (DNS). The DNS is a massive, globally distributed database management system whose main function is to translate human-readable domain names (e.g., Netflix.com) into unique numbers (binary Internet Protocol, or IP addresses) used to locate virtual resources online. Because the DNS is used nearly every time someone queries a name online, it is a choke point where the flow of information can be disrupted. The attack even more specifically targeted Dyn, a company that provides managed DNS services responsible for resolving queries for the domain names of some of the sites affected. Dyn's chief strategy officer described the outage as "a sophisticated, highly distributed attack involving 10s of millions of IP addresses . . . across multiple attack vectors and Internet locations."[7]

The Mirai botnet is a specific example of a general condition that control can be exerted by co-opting or disrupting intermediary infrastructures (rather than targeted systems) to achieve some objective.[8] It is not necessary to infiltrate or attack the intended site directly but only indirectly by turning to a supporting system, such as the DNS, systems of routing and addressing, cloud computing platforms, and points of network interconnection. Indeed, the DNS has long been used for information control, from political censorship to blocking access to pirated movies, and has even longer been a target of DDoS attacks.[9] These technical infrastructures have a concealed complexity and a distributed architecture that keeps them out of public view. Attacks bring visibility to this behind-the-scenes infrastructure and also highlight the crucial role of private companies as points of digital concentration and administration on which the stable exchange of information depends.

Much more consequentially, this massive attack was carried out primarily by home appliances such as security cameras and digital video recorders.[10] The botnet, short for "(ro)bot net(work)," was a collection of interconnected devices infected with malicious software (malware), without the device owners' knowledge. Consumer IoT devices are susceptible to malware because they may contain security vulnerabilities or use weak (or no) default passwords. In this instance, the Mirai botnet scanned networks for vulnerable devices and surreptitiously infected them with malicious code used to coordinate the attack. An analysis of the attack suggested that the Mirai botnet used "a short list of 62 common default usernames and passwords to scan for vulnerable devices" and was able to access and infect mass numbers of appliances because so many people had never changed the default username and password or else used very weak passwords, like "password."[11]

The incident is also indicative of how security exploits, once developed and regardless of initial motive, can take on a life of their own. Three college-age defendants pleaded guilty to conspiring to violate the U.S. Computer Fraud and Abuse Act (CFAA) for creating and using the Mirai botnet to target connected home appliances and exploit these to execute DDoS attacks. The Department of Justice disclosed that one of the defendants "posted the source code for Mirai on a criminal forum," which others then accessed and used later to carry out attacks such as the one that disrupted major Internet content sites in the fall of 2016.[12] Media reports claimed that the motive for developing the Mirai botnet was to gain competitive advantage in the wildly popular computer game Minecraft.[13]

Connected objects are not only a potential target but also a potential threat vector from which to launch attacks. The security of popular websites and content platforms is only as strong as the security of cyber-physical systems far removed from these platforms. Their fate is intertwined. Some connected home devices are not upgradable or come with inherently weak security. In other cases, owners ignore security patches as devices become part of the taken-for-granted background edifice of daily life. Consumer objects can be weaponized when they are vulnerable to exploits, and they are increasingly within the crosshairs of those who seek to exert control across borders.

As these three examples emphasize, the design and control of connected physical objects is an emerging and high-stakes terrain of global Internet policy. Cybersecurity has now become one of the most consequential issues of the modern era, necessary for human safety, privacy, critical infrastructure, and national security, as much as for economic security, democracy, speech rights, and access to knowledge. Yet connected physical objects are notoriously insecure. There is a huge chasm between the need for security and the state of security. Realizing the improvements to human life and the economic growth possible from cyber-physical innovations is predicated upon the inherent security and stability of these systems. Technology policy must, in the contemporary context, anticipate and address future questions of accountability, risk, and who is responsible for outages, security updates, and reliability. Public policy has not yet caught up to this technological transformation and its consequences. Meanwhile, the pace of cyber-physical innovation is accelerating.

The Dissolution of Boundaries between Virtual and Physical Worlds

The Internet has already reached a tipping point. More *objects* are now digitally connected than *people*. This phenomenon is sometimes called the "Internet of things" or "cyber-physical systems," although these dispassionate phrases dampen the remarkable reality that the real world connected by digital systems subsumes biological processes, currency, and transportation systems, not just mundane material artifacts like connected coffee machines. Already measured in billions, there will soon be on the order of 20 billion or more material objects online.[14] Anyone with multiple tablets, computers, and smartphones intuitively understands the disproportionate ratio of devices to people online, but this is only a very partial accounting. Online artifacts include everything from kitchen appliances, door locks, home alarm systems, networked weather sensors, automobiles, energy system sensors, and industrial control systems (ICS).

As with other major technological changes, expectations about this material diffusion range from efficiency promises about "smart cities" and "smart homes" to Orwellian warnings that this will be the death knell of human autonomy. To be sure, increases in object connectivity will result in new industries creating interconnected products embedded with chips, sensors, actuators, and radio-frequency identification (RFID) capability. Whether one views this as a new trend or the continuation of the Internet's meteoric growth is of no consequence. What matters is that this phenomenon will have significant implications for economic growth, individual rights, business models, and governance and that there is a moment of opportunity to shape the constitution of this future.

In the vernacular of cyber-physical systems, connected things are real-world objects that directly embed cyber elements. They simultaneously interact with the real world and the virtual world. Their primary purpose is not communication among people or individual access to information such as news, knowledge, business data, and entertainment. They are geared more toward keeping systems functional by sensing and analyzing data and autonomously controlling devices. Like other communication devices, these objects interconnect via either wireless or wired networks. Industry sectors have used terms such as "smart grids" or "sensor networks." Policymakers have adopted language such as "smart health" and "smart cities." Consumer electronics manufacturers call this the "Internet of things." In practice, these systems often involve sensor networks detecting contextual changes such as in the environment (weather sensors) or a physical occurrence (a door opening, the delivery of a spare part in a manufacturing system, or a movement). Already millions of sensors monitor environmental conditions, industrial systems, security points, and the movement of objects. These systems also directly actuate devices, such as moving a mechanical system or activating a light switch.

Tropes related to the Internet of things are often consumer-centric, including home appliances and other domestic systems or an individual's car or other personal object. Beyond these everyday consumer objects, industry and local governments are an important constituency operating cyber-physical environments. For example, cities operate traffic control systems, utilities, street lights, transportation apps, and other systems connected directly to the public Internet or indirectly via proprietary networks with a gateway to the public Internet. Cyber-physical systems, of course, exist in the vast infrastructures underlying industrial sectors. Digitally connected sensors provide energy companies with intelligence about natural resources. Manufacturing companies use digital networks to manage the handling of materials, optimization of inventories, and control of robotic systems. Shipping companies use embedded RFID chips to track packages and vehicles and optimize delivery routes.

Digital systems are now control systems for the real world of things but also bodies. Biological systems are part of the digital object space. The Internet of things is also the Internet of self. The "thing" in the Internet of things encompasses a person's biological systems via wearable technologies, biometric identification devices, and digital medical monitoring systems for checking temperature, heart rate, or blood glucose level. Medical diagnostic and treatment systems similarly rely on Internet-connected devices.

Physical and nonphysical boundaries collapse.[15] Values are in tension. For example, strong cybersecurity is necessary to protect national security and individual privacy but increasingly intersects with the physical world and human body in a way that creates a host of new rights concerns. Strong cybersecurity is necessary for consumer protection and privacy, especially around connected medical devices. But cybersecurity also creates challenges for individual privacy because it can require the collection of biometric identification. Human authentication and identification take place through voice, facial, or movement recognition, retinal scans, fingerprints, and other globally unique human identi-fiers. China and other countries with authoritarian information technology (IT) approaches are using these biometric systems as part of social control programs.

The Internet transforms from being in a user's field of cognition to being an invisible background context of everyday life. Connected objects are con-tinuously sensing and engaged in constant interactivity. Humans no longer di-rectly experience connectivity through a screen but through everyday objects. This diffusion of the Internet into the material world speaks to the phenomeno-logical sense in which the Internet is receding from human view even while expanding.

A "screen" is no longer the arbiter of whether one is online or offline. This distinction has always been imprecise because one can be swept online via screens belonging to others, such as tagged in an image or recorded in the back-ground of a YouTube video. Nevertheless, in the era in which most access was screen mediated—a computer, phone, or tablet—it was obvious when someone was "on the Internet." There was some self-awareness and some choice. The shift away from screens and into material objects further blurs this online-offline distinction. It complicates individual awareness of personal data collec-tion because it is more behind the scenes. Human online exposure shifts from sometimes on, when interacting with a screen, to always on, via ambient ob-jects. Active engagement with digital networks moves to passive engagement.

Those who believe they "do not have a large digital footprint" because of personal social media choices neglect to consider the reality that modern cars capture minutiae about how they drive, phones record their every movement, and grocery store affinity cards capture consumer data. Neighborhood surveil-lance cameras record them walking their dog. These ambient technologies bring about enormous social benefits around convenience and safety. But choice becomes complicated. At one point, picking up a device with a screen—such as a laptop or phone—was a concerted choice about how and when to be online, even if that choice involved hidden power structures that affected individual rights. Now the choice is no longer present in the same way.

Offline-online hybridized spheres penetrate into the body, the mind, and the objects and systems that collectively make up the material world. The Internet is no longer just about communication but is also no longer simply a virtual space. Conceptions of the Internet as, a priori, a communication system be-tween people have to be dispelled.

The upsurge of systems that simultaneously embed digital and real-world components creates conditions that challenge traditional notions of Internet governance in profound ways. It no longer makes sense to view online and offline spaces as distinct spheres, either technically or politically, with the virtual world somehow separate from the real world. They are entangled.

All Firms Are Now Technology Companies

What counts as an "Internet company" or a "tech company" transforms in the context of systems that embed both digital and material components. All firms are now technology companies, not only traditional tech firms like Google but any company (e.g., Caterpillar, Ford, GE) that manufacturers cyber-embedded products or collects massive stores of digital data.

In most industry sectors—from financial services to consumer goods—firms historically have not viewed themselves as technology companies. They had a separate information technology department serving as a support structure for developing and delivering products and services to customers. This function was parallel to other types of enabling functions, such as human resources or finance. IT departments managed communication networks, email, data storage, and industry-specific information systems such as point-of-sale in retail or production and distribution systems in manufacturing. Computer networks and the public Internet were vitally integral to operations, but end products—whether a jacket or a refrigerator—did not embed computer networking as part of the product. They existed in the real world.

Conversely, "tech companies" have historically been viewed as born digital. These include information intermediaries, like Google and Baidu, which facilitate the exchange of content; network intermediaries like AT&T or Vodafone; or software and hardware companies like Microsoft and Cisco, whose core business is selling technology for use in other industries. Tech companies have also included born-digital retail companies like Amazon, which have no physical consumer retail presence but rather transactionally exist entirely online, albeit with massive back-end warehouses.

There is no longer a logical demarcation between born-digital tech companies and nontech companies. Companies that were once entirely digital are now producing material, real-world products that expeditiously leverage their massive data-processing capabilities and experience with cybersecurity. Apple,

Google, and Microsoft have all entered markets for self-driving cars. Google has been working on autonomous vehicles since 2009, for example, through its Waymo subsidiary.[16]

The shift of real-world product and service companies into the digital realm is just as significant, if not more significant, of a factor blurring this distinction between tech and nontech companies. GE now has a significant product investment in the "industrial Internet of things" geared toward transforming industries with sensors and vast data collection and analysis, as well as augmenting its traditional product line of home appliances with digital interconnection. Financial services have moved almost entirely online. Under Armour has produced digitally connected shoes. Levi's partnered with Google to offer an interactive jacket, embedding a tag in the sleeve to enable wireless connectivity to a mobile device. Automobile companies from Ford to Tesla have sought to develop autonomous vehicles embedding communications technology and massive data processing to such a degree that these are high-tech networking products as much as cars. Ford will compete with Google as much as with Toyota.

In other cases, it is impossible to assess whether a company began digitally or began in the physical world. Is Uber a tech company or a transportation company? Is Airbnb a tech company or a hotel service? These are examples of a new generation of firms that digitally facilitate real-world interactions but do not actually operate themselves in the physical world. Digital media companies bleed into the material world. Traditionally nontech companies are digitally integrated, and there is a rising breed of new companies that are neither fully offline nor fully online. It is clear that the boundary around digital media company or tech company is blurred.

The twenty-first-century phenomenon of all firms metamorphosing into technology companies has implications for technology policy. The most immediate concern involves the question of human rights in this hybridized context. The same types of civil liberties questions arising online in traditional digital media platforms—especially the privacy parameters around personal data collection and conditions of equality, discrimination, and access—now also apply, and even more so, to these contexts blending the virtual and the material. Another complication is cybersecurity. Many of the firms that are now suddenly also digital technology firms have historically less experience with cybersecurity. There are also not necessarily market inducements for strong cybersecurity or even upgradeability in quickly emerging product lines in which being first to market is paramount. Another of many complications is that integrating cyber interconnections in material objects makes systems traverse national boundaries in ways that can complicate jurisdiction. A physical-world product, when digitally embedded, is suddenly reachable across borders by foreign intelligence and hackers.

"Internet Users" Are Not People

This entanglement of real-world objects and the cyber world complicates even the simple category "Internet user." This once clearly measurable category is rapidly changing in the context of bots and connected objects with no human display screens. The history of the Internet's success is often told through the lens of growth in users, the number of people connected via a computer, laptop, tablet, or smartphone. The International Telecommunication Union (ITU) has consistently provided global and country-specific usage statistics about human-centric categories such as percentage of individuals using the Internet and households with Internet access.[17] By this user-centric metric, Internet growth is staggering. Half the world's population came online by 2017. In the mid-1990s, when Amazon and eBay were founded, less than 1 percent of the world's population was online, with most users in the United States. Policymakers, advocacy groups, and scholars alike gauge Internet success by such usage statistics and direct policy efforts, particularly in emerging markets, accordingly. Examples include interventions to bridge the digital divide, improve broadband penetration in the developing world, and address net neutrality, an issue typically concerned entirely with last-mile Internet access to homes.

The growth in the number of individuals online and broadband penetration rates to homes have always had limitations as success metrics. Consumer-centric views of Internet growth have often not matched Internet use in practice, for example, focusing on individual social media usage more than Internet access by major industrial sectors. Even with a content-centric view of Internet usage, the bulk of Internet traffic is not communications between two people but entertainment programming, with video streaming services like Netflix, Amazon Prime Video, Hulu, and their competitors constituting more than half of Internet traffic during prime viewing hours. Furthermore, a single person might simultaneously use multiple screen-mediated devices: a phone, laptop, tablet, work computer, home computer. Does that count as one user or five?

User-centric Internet policy interventions also miss major swaths of public-interest issues that exist outside direct consumer interfaces and in deeper layers of Internet infrastructure.

Another complication is that some "people" online are actually bots. "Bot" is a term for software code that simulates human activity or automates some repetitive task. One of the dictionary definitions that *Merriam-Webster* provides is "a computer program or character (as in a game) designed to mimic the actions of a person."[18] The 1860 *Webster's Dictionary* defines bots as "a species of small worms, found in the intestines of horses."[19] Thankfully, in the digital age, it connects more to "(ro)bot." But bots actually are sometimes autonomous worms that self-propagate. DDoS attacks make use of armies of malicious bots.

Bots have had a central role in Internet tasks for decades, such as web crawlers that autonomously scour pages to index content for search engines. They provide customized music streaming and personalized weather forecasts. Botnets are key enablers of spam, whether collecting massive stores of email addresses or distributing unsolicited marketing messages. Regrettably, botnets are also a staple of cyberattacks and cybercrime. Sometimes indistinguishable from people, they generate automated emails appearing to be legitimate but designed to carry out identity theft. Sophisticated chatbots engage in conversations with people. Intelligence communities in the United States indicated that Russians used bots, as well as troll farms of actual people, to disseminate propaganda microtargeting American voters in an attempt to influence the 2016 presidential election.

Software code masked as human social media accounts produces a nontrivial percentage of social media content. They have a variety of purposes—marketing, political propaganda, influence campaigns, news dissemination, spam, hate speech, activism. But they are not individual users. One group of researchers estimated that "between 9% and 15% of active twitter accounts are bots."[20] One can simply observe the immediate aftermath of a Twitter posting by a prominent person. Within less than a second, tens of thousands of "users" retweet the message. Much of this instantaneous content generation does not originate with actual human followers but via social media message-amplification techniques. Counting "users" can include counting nonhumans. Twitter has disclosed the scale of what the company faces in dealing with automated (nonhuman) accounts: "On average, our automated systems catch more than 3.2 million suspicious accounts globally per week—more than double the amount we detected this time last year. As our detection of automated accounts and content has improved, we're better able to catch malicious accounts when they log into Twitter or first start to create spam."[21]

The massive scale and sophistication of bot accounts make the problem impossible to address via direct human detection and intervention. Only machine learning and automated pattern-detection capabilities can address the bot tsunami flooding the digital public sphere. Scholars who study the surface of content have sometimes compounded the problem. Studying discourses in social media platform intermediaries can help propagate disinformation because it adds a veneer of quantitative legitimacy to what is actually gaming of systems.

While "Internet user" has always been an imperfect category, it is further complicated in the context of the cyber-embedded physical world. Connected objects outnumber connected people. What counts as an Internet user? Connected lighting systems and doorbells exchange data just like humans exchange data. A lightbulb is not an Internet user by traditional definition, but it might be technically more accurate to measure the number of devices online rather than the number of users online.

Many connected objects, particularly in environmental, agricultural, energy, and other industrial settings, have no formal relationship to human users and no display screen or formal user interface. Machine-to-machine, or M2M, is a significant usage category, encompassing devices in industrial settings, such as supervisory control and data acquisition (SCADA) systems or other sensing and control transactions at digital-physical borders. These devices exchange information, consume resources such as bandwidth and IP addresses, and raise all manner of cyber governance questions but are not counted as "users."

Even people who have never been online are directly affected by what happens online. Everything is connected, so everyone is affected. Phrases such as "being on the Internet" or "being off the Internet" no longer have distinct meanings. Data breaches affect non-Internet users. During a hectic 2013 holiday shopping season, the U.S. retail giant Target acknowledged that hackers gained unauthorized access to its customers' credit card numbers and other personal information. The data breach originated via an infiltration of a third-party heating, ventilation, and air conditioning system company connected to Target's network.[22] Target acknowledged that the stolen information included a customer's name, credit card number, expiration date, and card verification value (CVV) number (the three or four-digit number on a credit card), as well as home address, email address, and phone number.[23] Identity theft is a trivial matter given this combination of personally identifiable data. The retailer suggested that the massive data breach affected as many as seventy million customers and, as companies often do in such case, offered a complementary year subscription to a credit-monitoring service for any customers who shopped in their stores.[24] A non-Internet user who shopped at Target would have been swept up in this data breach. The Office of Personnel Management (OPM) data breach in which China-based hackers gained access to the personal information of more than twenty-one million U.S. federal employees could have affected any non-Internet user who ever worked for the federal government.

Someone who buys a home alarm system but is not "online" via a traditional screen may actually be online. An elderly person simply showing up for a medical appointment can be directly affected when a ransomware attack on the health-care provider prevents the person from receiving medical care. One does not have to personally be "on the Internet" to have one's life dependent on the Internet. The category of "user" continues to evolve.

The changing user context and the expansion of what counts as a technology firm, as well as the evolution of cyber-physical technical architecture, is an important starting context for discussions about the state of Internet governance.

The Cyber-Physical Challenge to Internet Governance

What are the public-interest issues arising from the Internet's expansion from a communication network to a control network whose infrastructure is enmeshed in the material world, increasingly politicized, and involving new types of firms far beyond traditional tech companies? The pace of innovation and the opportunities for human flourishing are significant but are clearly accompanied by critical economic and social concerns.

What are the rising implications for privacy, discrimination, human security, interoperability, economic stability, and innovation? Do existing models of Internet governance still apply? Who are the new stakeholders in so-called multistakeholder governance? As the technologies become more diffuse and less visible because they are embedded in material systems, the implications of these technologies become more concealed, and choice and consent become upended. Yet the digital economy, social life, and political systems are completely dependent on the stability and security of this infrastructure.

This embedding of network sensors and actuators into the physical world has transformed the design and governance of cyber infrastructure into one of the most consequential geopolitical issues of the twenty-first century. It challenges notions of freedom and power structures in Internet governance and further blurs the role of nation-states in addressing the politics of technical structures that inherently cross borders.

For much of its history, the Internet has created connections between people or between people and information. Hence, policy formulation around the Internet, as well as theory and research, has concentrated on the network as a public sphere for communication and expression or as an information system for commercial transactions.[25] Content-centric topics have included intellectual property rights enforcement, social media influence campaigns, cyberbullying, freedom of expression, and data protection. Intellectual thought has focused primarily on this visible layer of content, communication, and transactions rather than underlying material control infrastructures.

This book seeks to make visible the power structures embedded in emerging digital-physical infrastructure landscapes, explain the social and economic stakes of how these infrastructures are designed and governed, and recommend a technology policy framework that accounts for the critical public-interest concerns arising in hybrid virtual-physical systems. The most consequential global policy concerns of the present era are arising in debates over the architecture and governance of cyber-physical systems. Technology policy has to be reconceptualized to account for the expansion of digital technologies from communication and information exchange to material sensing and control. How technical, legal, and institutional structures evolve will have sweeping implications for civil liberties and innovation for a generation.

The book is written from the standpoint of both engineering and science and technology studies (STS), and the conceptual starting point is that arrangements of technical architecture are also arrangements of power. On the contrary from implying any technological determinism, this theme suggests that those who control the design and administration of technologies shape these power structures. Technologies are culturally shaped, contextual, and historically contingent. Infrastructure and technical objects are relational concepts in that cultural and economic interests shape their composition. The philosopher of technology Andrew Feenberg has suggested that "technology is power in modern societies, a greater power in many domains than the political system itself."[26] Interventions based on law or international agreements are not alone sufficient. Public policy is inscribed and concealed inside architecture.

Technical points of control are not neutral—they are sites of struggle over values and power arenas for mediating competing interests. At the same time, the natural and physical world, of course, exists. The scientific process and innovation incorporate facts about the physical world derived from lived material experience. From an engineering perspective, it is not possible to construct a solid rocket booster out of lawn clippings, no matter what powerful values will it so. Understanding the politics of technology requires acknowledging both material engineering realities and also the social construction of the same.

In 1980, Langdon Winner influenced a generation of scholars with his provocative essay "Do Artifacts Have Politics?" Winner suggested two ways in which artifacts could have political qualities, including how "specific features in the design or arrangement of a device or system could provide a convenient means of establishing patterns of power and authority in a given setting" and also "ways in which the intractable properties of certain kinds of technology are strongly, perhaps unavoidably, linked to particular institutionalized patterns of power and authority."[27] He was writing prior to the globalization and commercialization of the Internet or the development of the World Wide Web, but his themes would later resonate in scholarship addressing the politics of cyber technologies.

The late Susan Leigh Star described her 1999 STS publication "The Ethnography of Infrastructure" as "a call to study boring things" and suggested, "it takes some digging to unearth the dramas inherent in system design," in part because much of this work is "buried in inaccessible electronic code."[28] Star's theoretical and methodological work on infrastructure, including her work with Geoff Bowker, has helped influence a large body of scholarship in infrastructure studies, collectively "inverting" infrastructure from a background framework to the foreground to reveal underlying politics.[29] Part of the purpose of the present book is to make visible the behind-the-scenes architectural components of cyber-physical systems.

The starting point for examining the governance issues in cyber-physical infrastructure is conceptually identical to the framework from *The Global War for Internet Governance* (2014). Levers of control in Internet governance are not at all relegated to the actions of traditional governments but also include (1) the politics inscribed in the design of technical architecture; (2) the privatization of governance, such as public policy enactment via content moderation, privacy terms of service, business models, and technological affordances; (3) the role of new multistakeholder global institutions in coordinating cross-border critical Internet resources; and sometimes (4) collective citizen action. For example, the design of technical standards is political. These are the blue-prints, or specifications, that enable interoperability between products made by different companies. From the Internet Protocol to BitTorrent, technical stand-ards are not merely technical specifications. They establish public policy in their design features that connect to national security (e.g., encryption strength), human rights (e.g., privacy-enhancing features, web accessibility standards for the disabled), and democracy (e.g., security of election support infrastructures, an interoperable public sphere, access to knowledge). Another central theme in Internet governance is the reciprocal relationship between local decisions and global networks, which can be thought of as part of control by extraterritorial-ity. Local regulations such as the European Union's General Data Protection Regulation (GDPR) on private company policies on the other side of the world are an example of this type of cross-border influence.

The Internet of things seems like a local concern, on its surface. Cyber-embedded objects have a hard, material presence in the real world. A piece of equipment in a factory or a medical monitoring device in a home are clearly tangible objects, not just information or human communication understood vir-tually through screens. Yet they are not merely local policy concerns, any more than a social media application that someone accesses in a home is a local pol-icy concern. These local objects and the systems that connect them are a global policy frontier entangled with international security, geopolitical conflict, and human rights.[30] Because they connect to the Internet, there is always the possi-bility of someone reaching across borders to access a cyber-physical device. In some cases, the intermediating networks and technologies are different from, although they build on, the technologies supporting content-centric systems. But they also rely on the same core networks, interconnection points, and sys-tems of routing.

If distributed infrastructure points of control shape, constrain, and enable the flow of communications (email, social media, messaging) and content (e.g., Twitter, Netflix, Reddit), infrastructure connected to the physical world (bod-ies, objects, medical devices, industrial control systems) to a much greater ex-tent is able to exert economic and political effects. Global control struggles materialize at boundary points of "transduction" via sensors and actuators. Direct connections between the digital world and the physical world now proliferate. Door locks are digitally connected and can be operated without being touched by a human hand. Medical devices inside the body can convert biological measurements into digital signals transmitted over a network.

For these systems, the essence of control capability is transduction, the conversion of signals and energy forms from the physical world into the digital world, and the inverse. Examples of this conversion include electrical signals converted into pressure, or temperature in the real world converted to an electrical signal. Digital networks monitor and control real-world, material objects. Sensors capture a reading (e.g., temperature, pressure, movement, sound waves) in the real world and convert them to digital signals for transmission over a network. Actuators take the instructions from a digital signal and convert this form of energy and act on the physical world, such as causing rotary motion or a chemical reaction.

A recalibration of technology policy debates is necessary to account for the rising potential and implications of transduction. One distinction theorists have made between cyber war and "real-world war" is that cyber conflict does not result in human death. This distinction collapses as an increasing number of critical real-world systems become cyber embedded. For example, while autonomous vehicles will save lives because so many accidents arise from human error, digital networks control these vehicles, and hackers anywhere in the world can potentially sabotage or disrupt them, potentially resulting in human death.

This direct, connective manipulation of the physical world from anywhere in the world via a digital network is a powerful form of control, enhancing human life and industrial efficiency but also creating terrifying possibilities for disruption, manipulation, surveillance, and conflict—as close as within a body and as far away as industrial control systems located on the other side of the world.

The expansion of cyber into real-world, everyday objects, logistical networks, and industrial systems expands the national security threat base, the types of foreign intelligence possible, and what counts as cyber offense. Cyber is already viewed as the fifth domain of warfare. Catastrophic cyber war is not yet inevitable, but politically motivated cyber conflict is an everyday occurrence ranging from cybersecurity attacks on dissident groups to the Chinese hack of millions of records of U.S. federal government workers. Politically motivated cyber-physical attacks have already moved into critical infrastructure such as the energy sector.

A critical and novel point of control, and therefore policy concern, is how interventions and attacks in the physical world can then translate into digital manipulation, as opposed to how digital interventions can influence the physical world. The possibility of transductive attacks involving manipulation of physical readings to attack or mislead digital systems completely transforms the object of analysis of cybersecurity, which now has to leave digital networks and data stores and extend into protection from manipulation originating in the physical world.

Policy issues around intermediaries also become more complicated. What counts as intermediation in cyber-physical systems and the institutional and socioeconomic forces that shape this intermediation are more concealed and heterogeneous than traditional communication intermediation. The philosopher Bruno Latour asked in 1994, "Why is it so difficult to measure, with any precision, the mediating role" of technology or what he called "techniques"? "Because the action that we are trying to measure is subject to 'blackboxing'—a process that makes the joint production of actors and artifacts entirely opaque. Daedalus' maze is shrouded in secrecy."[31] As Latour explains, the black box itself also changes the meaning of its context, such as a speed bump shifting from an objective of not striking a neighborhood child to not damaging the suspension of one's own car. A translation occurs. Cyber-physical system intermediation may be a modern recapitulation of the Labyrinth in Greek mythology.

The cyber-physical upheaval is heterogeneous and pervasive. There are many emerging areas of technological innovation in which digital technologies are becoming embedded into the physical world. Chapter 2 examines four of these. The digitization of everyday objects includes consumer Internet of things and connected objects in smart cities. The Internet of self encompasses cyber-physical systems entangled with the body, such as wearable technologies, implantable chips, biometric identification devices, and digital medical monitoring and delivery systems. The industrial Internet of things, sometimes called the "fourth industrial revolution," involves restructurings of industries and labor around cyber-physical systems. Finally, emergent embedded systems include those embedded objects that are born digital, such as robotics, 3D printing, and arguably augmented reality systems. Understanding these heterogeneous technical architectures, and the technological affordances and characteristics they all share, is necessary for understanding emerging governance debates.

The policy issues that arise in cyber-physical systems create new problems and challenges that are more complicated and arguably more critical than even in traditional communication systems. Part 2 of the book, "The Global Politics of Cyber-Physical Systems," breaks these emerging governance issues into three arenas: privacy, security, and interoperability.

Cyber-physical system privacy concerns encroach into intimate spaces in and around the body and in material spaces of industry, the home and society that were once distinctly bounded from the digital sphere. Chapter 3 addresses this critical area. Privacy problems are also concerns about discrimination, such as using collected data for employment, insurance, and law enforcement decisions. Privacy problems in digital-physical spaces also raise a host of national security concerns. The chapter explains some of the constraints that complicate privacy and recommends a baseline privacy-protection framework to address this extraordinary policy challenge.

Cybersecurity increasingly connects to consumer safety and critical industrial infrastructure, as well as the digital economy and systems of democracy. Chapter 4 explains how the stakes of cyber-physical security have never been higher. From attacks on the energy sector to the attacks on the consumer IoT and democracy, cybersecurity governance is an existential concern in society. Regrettably, security is woefully inadequate. Market incentives privilege rapid product introduction rather than strong security. This chapter suggests baseline recommendations, across all stakeholders, necessary for improving the cyber-physical ecosystem. It also explains how cyber-physical systems complicate and increasingly shape already-difficult global cybersecurity governance questions such as when governments choose to stockpile knowledge of software vulnerabilities for cyber offense, rather than disclose them to secure critical infrastructure.

Chapter 5 examines how technical standardization faces unique challenges. Embedded objects require high security but are also constrained architectures that demand lower energy consumption and restricted processing power. The current state of interoperability is fragmented, heterogeneous, complex, and involving multiple competing standards and an expanding base of standards-setting organizations. Unlike traditional communication systems that require universality, fragmentation by sector might actually have beneficial effects, such as serving as a de facto security boundary. The chapter explains the evolution of fragmented standards in the IoT space but suggests that open standards and interoperability in the underlying common infrastructure are still vital for accountability, innovation, and stability.

The complicated concerns arising in cyber-physical systems necessitate a reconceptualization of long-held beliefs about Internet freedom. They also call into question dominant approaches, ideologies, and power structures in global Internet governance regimes. Part 3, "Rethinking Internet Freedom and Governance," addresses the cognitive dissonance between how technology is rapidly moving into the physical world and the conceptions of freedom and global governance that remain in the communication governance world.

Decades of cultural and political thought have sought to understand human autonomy and digital rights in the context of the Internet as an online public sphere for communication and access to knowledge. The goal in democratic societies has been to preserve "a free and open Internet," an uncritical concept that has become somewhat of a fetishized ideal. Chapter 6 suggests that all of the various conceptions of Internet freedom have to be challenged in light of technological change. Internet freedom has a long history, but all incarnations center on the transmission and free flow of content, from John Perry Barlow's "A Declaration of the Independence of Cyberspace" and calls for freedom from regulation to the United States Department of State's Internet freedom foreign-policy campaign. Normative frameworks should adjust both to the realities of information control from private ordering and authoritarian power and the rising human rights challenges of cyber-physical systems.

Structural transformations also challenge prevailing Internet governance power structures, imaginaries, and approaches. Provocations for the future of Internet governance are taken up in chapter 7. Policy entanglements with previously distinct spheres—consumer safety, systems of democracy, cryptocurrency, and environmental protection—expand the scope of global Internet governance. Power relations in the multistakeholder governance regime shift as new companies, new standards regimes, and new tensions arise between bordered government regulatory responses and a global cyber-physical architecture. The rising stakes of digital security, such as to consumer safety and national security, challenge some venerable norms of Internet governance. Notions of a free and open Internet, still vitally important, move toward notions of security, stability, and reliability.

Privacy and security have to take primacy as aspirational values as networks shift from digital only to directly embedded in the physical world. Chapter 8 concludes the book with a call for various stakeholders to urgently take serious cyber-physical policy choices and collectively elevate cybersecurity as a generational imperative necessary for human security, economic security, and national security. For example, a long-standing Internet policy tradition, while varying by region, is immunity from liability for information intermediaries. What counts as an intermediary in cyber-physical architectures and how should risk, accountability, and liability be reconceptualized in the high-risk era?

The technological diffusion of the Internet into the material world requires new approaches to technical architecture and governance that not only consider the content-centric protection of the digital economy and the free flow of information but also view infrastructure stability and cybersecurity as a critical human rights issue. The Internet, as a communication network, transformed how people communicate with each other and interact with information. The Internet, as a cyber-physical control system, is transforming how humans interact with the material world. This book is a provocation both to "see" digital infrastructure as it is and to understand and reimagine the politics embedded in this infrastructure. More importantly, it is the hope that this book will be of interest to any citizen concerned about the future of human rights in our digital future, in which offline and online spheres become completely indistinguishable.

2

The Cyber-Physical Disruption

"THERE IS NO REASON ANYONE WOULD WANT a computer in their home," the digital pioneer Ken Olson famously said in 1977. The modern-day equivalent would ask why anyone would want a computer *embedded in all the objects* in a home. That question is already outdated. Almost every imaginable physical object—in homes, in society, in industry—can be embedded with digital processing and communication capability, and the market for these technologies is intensifying. Finding a class of objects without embedded cyber connectivity is more difficult than finding one with this capability. Digitally embedded material devices are not a future construct.

Cyber-physical systems—arrangements of digital architecture embedded in and interacting with the material world—are everywhere. Understanding this architecture is a necessary precursor for examining the emerging technology policy questions and the stakes for society.

Cyber-physical systems cannot be viewed as a narrow class of technology (e.g., consumer Internet of things). As Gilles Deleuze suggested about social control, "the different control mechanisms are inseparable variations, forming a system of variable geometry."[1] They have to be taken as part of an assemblage of interrelated technologies, often conjoined and shared at the back end with third-party networks, with governments, or in private corporate monocultures.

In a single day, individuals in advanced economies encounter hundreds, if not thousands, of network-connected physical objects containing sensors and/or actuators. People wear connected fitness bracelets and rely on connected glucose monitors; homes contain connected coffee makers and door locks; stores house RFID-embedded retail items; vehicles contain networked sensors that detect collisions or monitor traffic conditions; work environments use networked energy systems, manufacturing robots, and security systems; municipal cyber-physical systems manage energy and transportation structures.

Policymakers rightly believe these technologies can improve public health, increase economic productivity, and create more efficient and environmentally sustainable cities. Connected objects improve the lives of people with disabilities. The cyber-embedded physical world, sometimes appropriately called the "Internet of Everything," is linked to societal improvement and economic growth. Congressional hearings have certainly stressed economic opportunity, exemplified by the chair's opening remarks in a U.S. House of Representatives hearing on the subject: "The Internet of Things marks a crucial juncture for the U.S. economy and for American consumers as our country looks for new economic engines and new sources for jobs. It promises a world in which digital and physical elements connect, gather information real-time, predict circumstances, prevent problems, and create opportunities."[2] It will take years before understanding which way the balance tips between new jobs in new IoT industries and job categories lost from cyber-physical automation. Either way, the transformation from an Internet society to a cyber-physical society will deeply disrupt structures of economic production and labor.

Cyber-physical systems, while heterogeneous and undergoing rapid technological change, are a major evolutionary chapter in the Internet's history. Similar to how the inception of the World Wide Web transformed access to knowledge and spurred entirely new industries, cyber-physical systems are now similarly transformational. Life before the web and hyperlinked information is difficult to remember. Cyber-physical systems are a similar pivot point. Instead of transforming how humans interact with and communicate with each other and content in the digital world, they are transforming the physical world and how humans and industries interact with this physical world. Acknowledging this transformation is not arguing that the disruption is occurring instantaneously. Transformation is accretionary. As Intel's head of IoT strategy summarized, "At Intel, we like to say IoT is an overnight transformation thirty years in the making."[3]

Applying the word "transformative" in this context is controversial. Actors with a stake in maintaining the prevalent structure of Internet architecture and governance and preserving dominant business models have an interest in characterizing the Internet of things as just another application on the Internet. This reference frame regards the diffusion of the Internet into the physical world as a continuation of the Internet as it has always been. Dominant institutions of Internet governance and industry-leading tech companies have some interest in viewing these changes within current economic and architectural models. Similar to Kuhnian changes in scientific knowledge that involve paradigmatic shifts in belief systems and modes of analysis,[4] changes in technical architecture, entirely new business models, and novel and even intractable policy concerns are all features of technological systems evolution that place pressure on dominant actors and provoke assertions that "there is nothing new here."

The cyber-physical transformation is not a solitary development following a sequential and orderly development path. It is entering society via different domains and originating from different actors and design communities. The Internet was never one thing but rather a heterogeneous system owned by different private actors and experienced differently by different cultures and user communities. Neither is the cyber-physical disruption one thing.

Understanding policy complications requires acknowledging this diversity. Even the category "Internet of things" has no single meaning or brand. As a Boston Consulting Group report explained, "there is no such thing as 'the' Internet of Things: today's market is heavily driven by specific use case scenarios."[5] If anything, this contextual heterogeneity, with embedded systems arising simultaneously in multiple environments, industries, and social spheres, helps to emphasize the pervasiveness of this transformation.

The category "cyber-physical systems," meant to be capacious and representative of contextual diversity, refers to arrangements of technologies that seamlessly integrate and interact with both the material world and the digital world. Although there is no precise universal definition of cyber-physical systems or even connected "IoT devices," descriptions from information science are instructive: "A cyber-physical system consists of a collection of computing devices communicating with one another and interacting with the physical world via sensors and actuators in a feedback loop."[6] The National Institute of Standards and Technology (NIST) defines cyber-physical systems as "smart systems that include engineered interacting networks of physical and computational components."[7]

The term "cyber-physical systems," while imperfect, is more accurately descriptive than "IoT" to explain this phenomenon of blurring physical and digital domains, simply because IoT, over time, has in popular discourse become synonymous with consumer markets, thereby obfuscating the larger phenomenon of embedded devices in critical sectors including agriculture, defense, transportation, and manufacturing.[8]

In formal technical-expert communities such as the Internet Society, the nomenclature "Internet of things" is not relegated to consumer products but rightly much more technically and contextually voluminous, to include industrial environments and critical infrastructure: "The term Internet of Things refers to scenarios where network connectivity and computing capability extends to objects, sensors and everyday items not normally considered computers, allowing these devices to generate, exchange and consume data with minimal human intervention. IoT includes consumer products, durable goods, cars and trucks, industrial and utility components, sensors, and more."[9]

Whether one uses the term "Internet of Everything" or "Internet of things" or "embedded systems" or "cyber-physical systems" or "network of everything" is not as important as acknowledging the very real underlying technological transformation—the fundamental integration of material-world systems and digital systems. Digitally connected computing devices have long permeated every sector that uses information and communication technologies. But these devices have traditionally exchanged information—knowledge, data, multimedia, transactions, communication content—between humans via devices with screens. A defining feature of cyber-physical systems is their integration or direct interaction with the physical world and the communication among objects or between material, real-world objects or natural environments and humans.

The following cyber-physical taxonomy helps reflect the contextual heterogeneity of these systems while also uncovering shared technological characteristics and control points: (1) the digitization of everyday objects, including consumer IoT devices and objects connected in municipalities; (2) the Internet of self, which includes objects in close proximity to the body, such as wearable technologies and digitally connected medical devices; (3) the industrial Internet of things or "fourth industrial revolution," a term that captures the cyber-embeddedness of objects in industrial sectors; and (4) emergent cyber-physical systems, which include material objects that are born digital, such as additive manufacturing (also called 3D printing), robotics, and augmented reality, a special case that does not involve cyber-embeddedness in objects but rather the human perception of this embeddedness. After a discussion of the elements of this taxonomy, the chapter offers a description and analysis of shared technological architecture and affordances of these systems and how they, in turn, shape new policy concerns.

The Digitization of Everyday Objects

The number of everyday consumer objects connected to the Internet already exceeds the number of people who use the Internet.[10] The oft-repeated but appropriate prediction suggests that "everything that can be connected will be connected." Measured in billions and experiencing rapid annual growth, the number of connected things is projected to grow (based on the most conservative projection) to twenty billion in the very near future, far higher than the entire human population on Earth.[11] What are these objects, how and why are they "connected," and who is making them?

Connected consumer devices are sometimes called "smart devices"—such as a smart water bottle connected to a mobile phone app to track hydration. Other terms are "intelligent devices" or "Internet of things" devices. All of these terms generally denote that the device can be connected to the public Internet via access such as Wi-Fi, Bluetooth, cellular, or GPS and controlled by a consumer either by accessing a website through a browser or, more often, via a specialized mobile phone app. Figure 1 provides a nonexhaustive snapshot of the types of consumer objects that have digitally connected consumer offerings, any of these easily found even via a cursory search on Amazon for Internet-connected appliances and objects.

Consumers can purchase nearly any kind of object with embedded network connectivity and sensors. The Adidas smart soccer ball contains an integrated sensor, battery, and Bluetooth network connection. The sensor can detect and record the ball's strike point, speed, trajectory, and spin when kicked from a stationary position. The ball collects and transmits data over Bluetooth to a mobile phone app. General Electric sells a line of home appliances that connect directly to a home's Wi-Fi network and then over the public Internet to a back-end system and ultimately to the owner's smartphone, whether for remote monitoring and alerts such as the refrigerator door left open and filter requiring change or for controls such as initiating water heating for afternoon coffee or turning on the ice maker.

Other devices connect via RFID chips embedded in objects. For example, Audi cars introduced integrated toll transponders into rearview mirrors. These transponders use RFID chips (similar to the separate transponders connected to windshields with Velcro) to communicate with readers at toll collection points, sharing a unique identification number tied to the vehicle owner's account, which the owner can access via the public Internet.

Home Access and Security
Door locks
Doorbell cameras
Garage door openers
Home security systems
Video/audio surveillance systems
Motion detectors
Window locks and blinds
Smoke detectors

Home Systems
Thermostats
Heating and air conditioning
Lightbulbs and light switches
Air purifiers and monitors
Washers, dryers, water heaters
Sinks, showerheads, faucets
Space heaters
Vacuum cleaners

Health and Fitness
Scales
Sleep tracking devices
Blood-pressure monitors
Oxygen sensors
Cardiac monitors
Medication bottles
Fitness trackers
Water bottles

Sports and Recreation
Sonar fish finders
Tennis rackets
Soccer balls
Footballs
Hockey sticks
Golf clubs
Treadmills
Ellipticals and other equipment

Entertainment
Music speaker systems
Televisions
Digital video recorders
Cameras
Virtual-reality headset
Augmented-reality lenses
Gaming systems

Clothing and Accessories
Glasses
Watches
Athletic shoes
Jackets
Jewelry
Sports apparel
Hats

Transportation
Automobiles
Trucks
Bikes
Traffic cameras
Traffic control systems
Train systems
Taxis

Kitchen Appliances and Supplies
Groceries
Grills
Refrigerators
Ovens
Coffee makers
Slow cookers
Dishwashers

Figure 1. Examples of connected home and consumer objects

Beyond consumer and home objects, everyday public infrastructure systems incorporate cyber-embedded physical components. Municipalities embed these in transportation and utility systems, especially cities facing challenges related to resource constraints and population growth. The United Nations estimates that roughly 50 percent of the world's population resides in cities, projected to grow to 60 percent by 2030.[12] The exact definition and boundaries constituting a city is subjective, but population growth is a real phenomenon straining infrastructure systems such as water, sanitation, transportation, and electricity. This is especially the case in megacities with ten million or more people. The need to monitor, track, distribute, and optimize such systems has prompted public and private entities alike to integrate cyber-physical systems within municipal systems. Traffic congestion alone is a critical problem in the most crowded or sprawling cities, and it is a problem that cyber-physical systems can somewhat ameliorate by using sensors to detect traffic conditions and congestion, performing optimizations to recommend routes, and deploying this information to adjust public transportation routes and traffic-light timing. Consumer-facing cyber devices that interact directly with the physical world—vehicles, traffic sensors, traffic lights—are part of what can make this type of optimization possible.

All of these private and public-facing cyber-embedded objects share technological requirements: they have to be addressable/identifiable, embedded with sensors, connected over networks, and controlled by back-end systems that process massive quantities of data. They also foreshadow emerging cyber-policy problems, with the stakes of cybersecurity affecting human safety and basic public infrastructure, as well as the possibilities for invasive surveillance and collection of personal information in previously private domains.

The Internet of Self

The body is part of the digital object space. The body is therefore now also part of the global cyber-policy landscape. The embedding of digital technologies in the most intimate spaces of individualized medical devices, fabric, and even inside the body perhaps best exemplifies the pervasiveness and biophysical control features of cyber-physical technologies.

Far closer to the body than everyday objects in kitchens and workplaces, networked devices have become intimate, personal, and in some cases embedded in or at least directly touching the body. Examples include network-connected

sexual devices, biometric sensors, and all manner of medical monitoring and delivery systems. The very personal nature of the data that mobile phones collect
(e.g., thoughts, associations, emotional health, location) might pale in comparison to the sensitive data collected by devices directly touching the human body.

Wearable technologies are perhaps the most publicly visible example of this
intense corporealization of digital devices. "Wearables" are network-connected
devices worn on (or in) the human body to perform any number of functions involving the delivery or collection of individualized data. Most do not immediately look like computing devices. They appear as everyday items worn on the
body, such as glasses, clothing and other textiles, bracelets, watches, and medical
devices. Many have sensors that pick up somatic cues such as temperature, location, biometric variables, and haptic (touch) and kinesthetic (movement) measurements. Nearly all are wirelessly connected and therefore mobile. The wireless
alternatives are as diverse as for other digital devices. Some are connected short
range via RFID. Some use personal area network wireless standards like Bluetooth. Others have embedded GPS capability connecting directly via satellite for
location triangulation. Many are connected to cellular networks, and many tie directly to apps on cell phones for users to control and view collected information.

The 2013 product introduction of Google Glass helped usher in "wearables"
as a household and industry term and foreshadowed the force of associated
public policy dilemmas. Google Glass, essentially head-mounted display and
camera technology in the shape of standard prescription glasses, provided
hands-free communication capability controlled by voice command and a small
side touch pad. One could immediately imagine the innovative and socially
beneficial applications possible, such as assisting the hearing impaired or enhancing performance in everything from surgery to military activities. But the
product also created a flashpoint for society to contemplate everything from the
etiquette of wearing the device in public and private settings and the ethics
(and, in some regions, legality) of clandestine video recording and potential implications of pairing the device with facial recognition software to identify
those who are in the device's field of view. As with all innovations, an initial
dissonant reaction accompanies the excitement around new product releases.

The earliest applications of wearables primarily involved fitness, health, and
activity tracking. Other products connected people to public services, such as
safety devices that link an individual in distress to first responders. Health, fitness, and safety wearables are completely mainstream. The subcategory of

wearable device trackers is already an enormous market, with the number of devices sold annually measured in the hundreds of millions.[13] For elderly people living alone or for people with disabilities, these trackers help maintain independent living. Many of these products embed built-in microphones and speakers so seniors can call for assistance, as well as motion sensors that detect movement indicative of a fall. Some devices also have embedded GPS capability so loved ones or authorities can easily locate a missing person with Alzheimer's disease or other cognitive disorder.

Internet of self devices also embed much deeper into the body. Already, the FDA has approved a drug with a "digital ingestion tracking system."[14] The pill, a medicine treating a variety of psychotic disorders, contains a sensor that the patient ingests. When swallowed, the sensor provides a signal verifying the ingestion that a patch on the patient's skin detects and in turn transmits to a mobile phone application. A web-based portal operated by the pharmaceutical company mediates the application on the back end. The objective of digitally connected pills is patient compliance tracking, confirming that patients have taken medicine as prescribed, whether the tracking is done by the patient or, especially for patients with serious psychological disorders, by a caregiver or doctor. Ingestible digital medical monitoring, as well as associated data accessed by physicians, has obvious applications in personalized treatment, assessment measurement, and highly tailored therapies. The technology is already developed, available, and approved.

Ingestible sensors push the bounds of what is possible in medicine, but they also are an incursion crossing a red line into inviolable personal spaces. Digitally embedded consumer devices remove the threshold of one's home as a demarcation between public and private spaces. Ingested pharmaceutical products monitor personal spaces in a way that was previously unimaginable. Pairing the inside of the stomach with a mobile phone is no longer science fiction. The technology-policy issues are profound. What constitutes notice and consent for a patient with a psychiatric disorder? Who may access the data on the smartphone or web portal, and do security measures adequately protect sensitive information about what prescription drugs someone takes? How and with whom is the data shared (insurance companies, employers, family members)? Furthermore, the same sensor technology embedded in pills can as easily be embedded in food. The social trajectory of this innovation is an open question.

The Internet of self raises privacy concerns because it inherently exists in such personal spaces. But because much of this data speaks to an individual's

Any industry with materials handling similarly employs digital object embedding. Tracking devices embed into production materials themselves for tracking products as they are developed in a manufacturing facility and into distribution and consumption. Sensors and actuators monitor and address the conditions of production, such as the temperature, pressure, and quality of a soft drink during its formulation. These processors embed into the production equipment itself, such as measuring equipment performance and predicting maintenance needs. Predictive maintenance anticipates when something will fail via sensor-driven data analytics. Similar technologies, such as GPS tracking systems on trains connected to back-end control systems, provide collision avoidance.

None of these functions—from collision detection to predictive maintenance—require human involvement. The systems communicate in a continuous feedback loop to track products, determine inventory levels, perform quality control, and many other functions. This embedding of digital capability directly into mechanical systems—especially integration beyond mere tracking—constitutes a major operational transformation of conditions of production and distribution designed to improve both output and profitability, as well as quality. An economic study of twenty countries by Accenture calculated the "likely gross domestic product (GDP) benefit to their economies if today's investment and policy trends continue on their current path . . . $10.6 trillion by 2030 for the 20 nations."[17]

The agriculture and farming sector is undergoing this same cyber-physical overlay, via digital embedding of equipment and robotics. Automatic voluntary milking systems in dairy farms are an interesting example. Dairy farming is one of the most schedule-intensive professions because of the requirement of milking cows twice daily, twelve hours apart. For family farmers, this makes vacations nearly impossible and ties them to their enterprise for the milking schedule (and early wakeup). The process is undergoing automation, in which a stanchion cow (itself embedded with a tracking chip) elects to enter the milking system for the reward of feeding and milking. A robotic system in the milking unit rises to the cow for the milking process. Automatic feeding and cleaning systems similarly pervade modern farming. Smartphone-based management systems accessed over the public Internet provide farmers with a direct interface into their entire business, providing the ability to "control lights, fans, curtains, cooling equipment, flush valves, doors . . . feeding systems, chemical levels, even the temperature of the refrigerator that monitors important vaccines and medicines."[18] Some of this automation is primarily for monitoring. But increasingly, it provides the ability to activate and control objects.

The term "fourth industrial revolution" sometimes applies to these sector-specific cyber-automation environments. The term, dating back at least to the 1980s, conveys the general diffusion of technology into all industries but especially the use of IoT capability.[19] More recently, thinkers at the World Economic Forum (WEF) have adopted this term, exemplified by the WEF founder and executive chairman Klaus Schwab's book *The Fourth Industrial Revolution* (2016).[20] The basic trajectory that Schwab and others suggest is that the first industrial revolution brought about great efficiencies in transportation and production through the use of water and steam power; the second industrial revolution involved increases in mechanical production from electrical systems; the hallmark of the third was the advent of pervasive information technology and digital systems to automate industrial systems.

The term "fourth industrial revolution" "is characterized by a fusion of technologies that is blurring lines between the physical, digital, and biological sphere."[21] Similar to other perspectives influenced by neoclassical economics, the World Economic Forum's periodization of industrial production stages assumes that the driving force of technological change is the quest for efficiency, whether reducing costs, gaining economies of scale, or improving productivity.[22] As the water-conservation system example suggests, and as concerns about privacy, human safety, and security arise around these changes, this transformation has to be viewed contextually and in light of both cultural forces and the relationship between the economic power of businesses and political influence, as well as how these systems interact with and affect the natural world. Nevertheless, the economic focus of the term "fourth industrial revolution" succeeds in conveying the material embeddedness of digital technologies in all industry sectors.

Industrial IoT systems are not merely enhancements to how industries already operate. They are disruptive to these very industries. As cyber-physical technologies pervade traditional, real-world industries, digital native companies (or completely new entrants) suddenly enter and compete in these industries because of digital expertise rather than sectoral experience. The classic example is the race for dominance in autonomous-vehicle markets and the question of whether traditional tech companies (Intel, Google, Cisco, Baidu), brand-new companies, or incumbent manufacturers such as Toyota and General Motors will dominate.

While the industrial purpose of cyber-physical integration is to improve productivity and operational efficiency or to solve an infrastructure problem such as improving water or other critical systems, the embedding of sensors in vehicles, critical infrastructure, and products complicates national security, consumer safety, and privacy. It also creates additional points of tension between law enforcement's needs for access to this data and the protection of privacy in everyday life. The escalation of cyber-physical system automation in various industrial sectors also has acute implications for the workforce. As autonomous vehicles inevitably continue to displace trucking, for example, this will challenge an entire labor sector. Jobs related to operating manufacturing equipment will similarly continue to contract.

The proliferation of industrial IoT environments especially highlights the connection between cyber-embedded material systems and national security. Greater physical dependency on digital networks heightens the stakes of keeping these real-world infrastructures operational and secure. Unauthorized access can result in the implantation of malicious code, intentional manipulation of end-point data, changes to hardware configurations, or system sabotage, as well as intelligence-gathering practices. The security of critical infrastructure depends on the security of these cyber-embedded physical systems, which gives adversaries the ability to reach across borders not only to access data and information but also to manipulate physical objects. Cybersecurity no longer protects content and data only. It also protects food security and consumer safety.

Emergent Cyber-Physical Systems

The three previous sections addressed broad categories of cyber-physical systems—everyday connected objects, the Internet of self, and the industrial IoT—that do not primarily involve technologies that are "born digital." Rather, they are extensions of existing structures around human activities and industrial processes. Cyber-embedded home-security systems are still security systems. Water-distribution systems imbued with sensors still carry water. A Wi-Fi-connected cardiac device is still a cardiac device. Cows are still milked, just autonomously.

Some emerging cyber-physical systems, however, are not enhancements to existing material structures but entirely new innovations arising directly at the physical-cyber nexus. Three examples are 3D printing, augmented reality, and some types of advanced robotics, all of which help to elucidate common technical features of cyber-material hybrids and emerging policy issues around technological spaces that integrate cyber components with the physical world.

The Jetsons, on the eponymous 1960s animated television show set in a futuristic 2060s space age, used a form of 3D printing. The family pushed a button on the "Food-a-Rac-a-Cycle" to instantaneously churn out their meals. Half a century later, 3D printers are able to use raw materials, minuscule layer by layer, to manufacture everything from customized prosthetics to novelty toys to manufacturing parts and chocolate. 3D printing, or additive manufacturing, is an emerging policy terrain existing simultaneously in cyberspace and the material world. In this case, however, the Internet is not connecting into the material world; it is constructing the material world.

The term "additive" manufacturing makes sense when the process is compared with traditional manufacturing processes that are subtractive. In subtractive manufacturing, raw materials are taken away via cutting, drilling, milling, or lathing. Additive manufacturing constructs an object via a computer-controlled laser generating one precisely specified, ultrathin layer of material at a time to cumulatively create an object. Additive technology has the advantage of precision, saving materials (generating little material waste relative to subtractive manufacturing), and saving time-consuming and laborious processes.

3D printing has particular application in environments that require high-level customization, such as fabricating individualized medical devices. An excellent example is 3D printable, customized prosthetic devices in which the prosthetic can be precisely tailored to the recipient.

Arrangements of binary digits (bits) can represent almost anything and, of course, already can be transmitted over a network and converted into anything viewed on a screen, such as a video, image, audio files, or text. The innovation and usefulness of 3D printing is that binary code represents real three-dimensional objects and then converts these into a real-world object. It takes binary representation from two dimensions into three. Digital-network-mediated additive manufacturing changes both the production and distribution of material goods. But it also raises a host of new social issues.

The policy implications of additive manufacturing in industrial settings are comparable to those in traditional industrial manufacturing, which is also often controlled by exacting computer programs. Cybersecurity and human safety are critical concerns in both environments. 3D printing, depending on its trajectory, may also disrupt distribution-dependent retail and industrial models such as the

Amazon consumer delivery model or traditional "just in time" manufacturing processes. Some goods will not arrive on a UPS truck. They will arrive over a network as zeros and ones, and a 3D printer in a home, manufacturing plant, or medical facility will fabricate them in real time.

Security, safety, and liability become more complicated. Even a simple manual for a popular 3D-printing product hints at the liability ambiguity and complexity in this space, stating that the company is not liable for any damages, even if the company has been notified of the possibility of damages, and further, the company "assumes no responsibility, nor will be liable, for any damages to, or any viruses or malware that may infect, your computer, telecommunication equipment, or other property caused by or arising from your downloading of any information or materials related to this Manual."[23] When cyber components embed in real-world products, what is the appropriate liability for the manufacturer of the 3D-printing device, versus the network connected to the device or the individual(s) who developed the specifications available online to manufacture objects?

Hackers do not need to infiltrate the printer itself but can sabotage a file specifying the instructions for fabricating the three-dimensional object. Subtle changes in the specifications can weaken material quality or build in points of fatigue and failure. The safety complications are even more consequential in industrial applications in which manufacturers, such as leading companies in the aerospace industry, routinely use additive manufacturing techniques in the production of airline parts.[24]

Three-dimensional binary representation of objects is producing three-dimensional intellectual property rights complications. The ease and low cost of capturing, replicating, storing, and disseminating digital information has complicated intellectual property battles for a generation. Theft of intellectual property—such as trade secrets and industry patents—is a significant economic policy concern. The ease of digitally sharing music, movies, and video games has transformed the way people consume media, introduced new entertainment-industry giants, and placed piracy at the center of many debates over the future of business models, cultural consumption, law, and the ever-evolving role of the Internet as a site of mediation. The same types of intellectual property complications over digital media exist with greater complexity in 3D printing. Yet systems for enforcing copyright around 3D printing are not yet in place. To ask an incongruous question, how does notice (of copyright violation) and takedown (of copyright-infringing material) occur in 3D printing, who are the intermediaries responsible for this takedown, and under what conditions should or must this occur?

Augmented reality applications raise similar policy complications and more. Nowhere is the blurring of material and virtual realms more apparent than in immersive technologies that seek to do exactly that—blend the virtual and the real. Augmented reality, or AR, systems involve the visual or other sensory superimposition of digital images and data onto human perceptions of the physical world. AR has a long history dating back at least to the early 1990s, contemporaneous to the introduction of the World Wide Web.[25] Many of the earliest applications were geared toward industrial settings. By 2002, the magazine *Popular Science* ran a story on augmented reality acknowledging that the accompanying headset technology was still too large and cumbersome to wear but would eventually amount to glasses and a small accompanying device.[26] Augmented reality applications have indeed become less cumbersome and have entered the general public domain, primarily through smartphone-mediated games and wearable devices.

AR is a physical-world extension of virtual reality (VR) or, reciprocally, a digital extension of material reality. So-called virtual reality applications do not necessarily touch the physical world in the same way by creating a visual overlay on the real world, although they can, but are usually more digitally immersive, mediated by a headset that completely covers the eyes and often an audio headset. These completely virtual systems provide incredible fictional or nonfictional experiences such as immersive journalism that brings the real world to life, multiplayer video games, flight training, and, of course, pornography. The demarcation between AR and VR is not at all a neat one because they are evolving so quickly. AR is a real-time hybrid between the virtual and material world and is therefore one of the cases that helps explain policy challenges arising as the digital world merges into the physical world.

The appropriately named concept of "mixed reality" is also now in the common tech-development vernacular, reflecting a trend in which the virtual overlay onto the material world is designed to appear as if it is part of the material world—akin to a holographic overlay—rather than a superimposition of data that is clearly a digital overlay.

Many communities first experienced AR as a cultural tsunami, via the Poké-mon Go smartphone-game craze in the summer of 2016. The game used

GPS-enabled features to overlay an animated environment over real-world surroundings and allowed players to find and capture digital Pokémon characters overlaying actual surroundings. Illustrating some of the real-world concerns about the phenomenon, Arlington National Cemetery had to publish a request for the public to refrain from playing augmented reality games on its grounds out of respect for the deceased.[27] The United States Holocaust Museum, as well as Poland's Auschwitz Memorial at the site of the former Nazi concentration and death camp, issued similar policies imploring the public to refrain from using Pokémon Go on-site and requesting that the game creator, Niantic Lab, remove its game from such places because it disrespected the sanctity of the locations. Kuwait's Ministry of Interior warned that authorities would prosecute smartphone users of the Pokémon Go app for taking legally prohibited pictures of sites such as mosques, military locations, oil installations, or other restricted sites.[28] A Duvall, Washington, police officer posting noted, "When I started in this profession never in my wildest dreams did I imagine that there would come a day when I would have to ask the public not to chase imaginary creatures behind the station at night."[29]

Mixed-reality technologies are moving beyond visual sensory perception to include physical touch. As the terminology—to "augment"—suggests, digital content is added to the real world. If one thinks about the target of augmentation as perception by the five human senses, increasingly, these innovations will include the sense of touch, called "haptic" technologies, and eventually taste and smell. Haptic technologies are those involving tactile perceptions such as exerting pressure or vibration on a wearable technology, for example, a glove simulating for users the experience of touching or moving an object in their field of view.

Many augmented reality applications are a subset of gaming, a multibillion-dollar industry, but they have important applications in areas as diverse as national defense, manufacturing, and transportation. Indicators of industry's focus on AR are clear from product-development investments and also from the prominence of products at the major consumer electronics shows.[30] AR cannot be dismissed as an entertainment-only technology any more than the World Wide Web could be dismissed as an entertainment-only technology in the 1990s. AR already enhances the lives of people with sight impairments, hearing loss, or other disabilities. Navigational and informational apps allow people to point a smartphone camera at a city location to superimpose routes, view useful information or historical pictures of an architectural site, or see an overlay of restaurants in the immediate vicinity. More critically, doctors performing surgery, fighter pilots, and people repairing complicated machinery could benefit from a visual overlay of data and schema that aids them in performing intricate tasks, as well as bringing in remote participation of others networked into the system.

These technologies involve real-world interactions and can involve real-world harms to property, the environment, and humans. As the legal scholars Mark Lemley and Eugene Volokh suggest, "People will kill and die using AR and VR—some already have. They will injure themselves and others. Some will use the technology to threaten or defraud others. Sorting out who is responsible will require courts to understand the technology and how it differs from the world that came before."[31] The pervasive surveillance conducted by AR headsets, often embedded in accessories, like glasses, that are not obviously digitally embedded, complicates privacy concerns and what counts as a private sphere.

Because mixed-reality technologies usually involve perceptions of the material world and information overlaid from the digital world, they have all the policy problems of both digital-only environments and cyber-physical systems. For example, the information overlaid digitally via AR can involve speech rights, defamation, intellectual property rights, threats, and any other policy question arising in digital content.

The area of robotics is perhaps the most emergent and disruptive technology that is born both digital and material. Not every robotic technology embeds network connectivity, but at a minimum, they contain embedded sensors collecting data from which to determine appropriate responses based on intrinsic instructions and algorithms and often machine learning. Furthermore, the term "robot" itself is intractably general and difficult to define, meaning everything from an autonomous weapon system to a sex robot.

As the scholar Michael Froomkin explains, "A measure of how early a stage we are in is that there is not yet a consensus regarding what should count as a 'robot.'"[32] However, he and his colleagues, in *Robot Law,* provide a useful definition: "A robot is a constructed system that displays both physical and mental agency but is not alive in the biological sense."[33]

A further complication is that a robot is not always a cyber-physical system because it does not exist in the physical world. Some (ro)bots are digital only, such as a social media bot designed to spread propaganda, promulgate hate speech, harass a targeted account, spread spam, or create automated discourse as part of a public-relations campaign. DDoS attacks use bots; there are diagnostic bots, chatbots, and search bots, the web crawlers that scour the web to index webpages and other content. Some are news bots for automated journalism, news amplification, or fake news dissemination. They call into question truth and raise epistemological issues in the same way that physical robots raise ontological issues. They, as Froomkin's definition states, have agency, but they also embed parameters and boundaries that are programmed into their design.

Robots as portrayed in popular culture and that have more popular intrigue are physical, rather than digital only, and are anthropomorphized in some way. Wall-E, the robot in *Lost in Space, Terminator,* and the *West World* humanoid robots have autonomous and unique personas. Other than sex robots and robots designed for social purposes such as caring for the elderly and medical patients, cyber-physical robots in everyday use are much more utilitarian and esoteric, such as manufacturing-production-line devices or autonomous warehouse devices that are robotic replacements of workers. In this regard, robotic cyber-physical systems are part of the industrial Internet of things. The nomenclature is divergent. The objects and technological structures converge. As such, autonomous robots—whatever their ultimate purpose—raise similar policy issues around human safety, workforce automation, security, intellectual property rights, and critical infrastructure protection.

Common Technological Features of Cyber-Physical Systems

In the same way that laptops, personal computers, and smartphones constitute only the 1 percent surface of the vast 99 percent behind-the-scenes infrastructure of information and communication technologies, so too are embedded physical objects only the surface of a vastly larger system of services, technologies, institutions, and infrastructure making up cyber-physical systems. Understanding policy challenges requires understanding technological points of control and architectural characteristics, even while acknowledging the heterogeneity of these systems. Much of the infrastructure supporting connections between people and connections between material objects is shared, albeit different in scale. Some features are unique to cyber-physical systems.

Several technological advancements have converged to create the conditions enabling this integration of digital communication systems with the physical world. Microprocessors have become increasingly more powerful and miniaturized, even while the cost of these processors has decreased. Intel's founder,

Gordon Moore, as far back as 1965, made a sanguine prediction forecasting exponential increases in the processing power of chips over time. He suggested that the number of transistors able to be integrated on a circuit would double every two years. This "Moore's Law" prediction has held true over time, and increases in processing power and associated miniaturization have become critical enablers of embedded systems. Miniature semiconductors are in everything from automobile brake systems to sneakers.

The massive quantity of data collected by cyber-embedded objects would not be useful without advancements in data science, as well as high-capacity cloud computing architectures necessary to store and process this data. Apart from these obvious enabling technologies that make cyber-physical systems (as well as traditional information systems) possible, the following describes some common distinguishing characteristics of cyber-physical systems. What distinguishes the technical architecture also distinguishes the political architecture.

Direct Physical-Virtual Interaction

The crucial common feature of all cyber-physical systems is the combination of interaction/existence in the physical world with embedded networked computational elements. Information systems and cyber-physical systems have distinct engineering concerns, most pertinently in that the latter require engineering practices to design and optimize for *both* digital computational systems *and* physical processes. *Fluid dynamics, thermodynamics, and mechanical engineering are just as integral as electrical and information technology engineering.*

Material and computational features are seamlessly integrated in consumer IoT products, wearables, or Wi-Fi-connected medical monitoring systems. In industry sectors of all varieties, production and distribution operations and the products themselves are part of systems that are virtual but involve tangible material equipment and objects. Newer and emergent virtual-physical-blended environments such as augmented reality, 3D printing, and robotics share this inherent integration. These devices embed both material and cyber elements and simultaneously interact with the physical world and the connected digital world.

This direct interaction with the material world is the primary characteristic that extends cyber-physical systems out from information systems that exist entirely in the digital realm—such as social media, content search engines, traditional industry information systems, and financial systems. Information-only systems, of course, also have a massive material support infrastructure of servers, switches, antennas, fiber-optic cable, and so on.

This feature of real-world interaction changes the nature of policy questions and associated solutions because the real-world stakes of outages, attacks, surveillance, and dependencies by default involve consumer safety and critical tangible information systems rather than merely digital systems. It also *expands the expertise necessary to design, manage, study, or govern systems, such as requiring understanding of hydraulics and pneumatics as much as information technology.*

Transduction

The interaction of embedded objects between the physical world and the digital world involves transduction, the conversion of one form of energy to another. Sensors detect ("sense") and capture a signal from the real world (such as motion, sound, pressure, temperature), convert the signal to electrical form, and digitize and transmit this signal over a digital network. In this regard, a sensor acts as a transducer (Latin: "to lead across") that converts signals in the physical world into electrical signals. In contrast, an actuator is a device that "acts" on the physical world, converting an electrical form into tangible manipulation of the physical world. The sensors gather and transmit information from something in the physical world. The actuators receive information that instructs something to happen in the physical world. In other words, it takes electrical energy and converts it into a mechanical or other energy mode.

Not long ago, networks were called "computer" networks, reflecting the assumption that end devices on the network were personal computers or other screen-mediated devices. Now these end devices are real-world objects such as trucks and lightbulbs, that incorporate networked sensors and actuators. Figure 2 provides a logical mapping of the transductive conversion that takes place in a device that is both an actuator and a sensor.

As shown in the sample list of inputs, sensors in embedded objects can pick up stimuli such as pressure, temperature, and motion in the real world. Some inputs are similar to information system inputs, indicative of the overlap between information systems and cyber-physical systems. Some of the transductive technologies at end points are the same, such as embedded microphones that convert physical sound waves into electrical signals. The digital encoding of sound waves can serve as an example of how any type of continuous (analog) physical

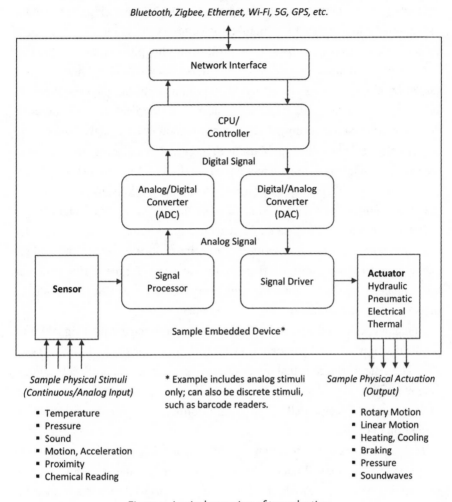

Figure 2. Logical mapping of transduction

input can be sampled, encoded, and represented in binary code for transmission over a network. The audio input is an analog, real-world signal, a continuous physical waveform resulting from the compression of air molecules and measured by a number of properties including frequency (cycles of the wave per second) and amplitude (the magnitude of the wave at a fixed point in time).

A microphone captures the waveform and converts it into an analogous electrical signal that also varies continuously. Converting the continuous waveform into discrete binary representation (zeros and ones) involves a three-step process: (1) sampling the magnitude of the signal at fixed, infinitesimally small, intervals (e.g., thousands of samples per second); (2) quantizing, or rounding the samples into one of a finite number of voltage values; and (3) assigning a binary code to each quantized value. Following this process, a continuously varying physical waveform is converted into digital—discrete values represented by binary code. Because the analog input from the physical world is sampled and rounded (quantized) to the nearest discrete number, it is a crucial design reality that the ensuing digital representation never exactly captures the original physical phenomenon. Margins of representational error are inherent to the system, commensurate with any analog-to-digital conversion. The material world is analog and continuously varies. The digital world is discrete.

Other examples of specialized sensors in embedded objects include range detectors for calculating distance, gyroscopes for measuring angular velocity (i.e., rotation), sensors for determining locational position, chemical readers, anemometers for measuring wind speed, thermometers for measuring temperature, and pressure sensors for measuring everything from weather conditions to blood pressure to the flow of liquid in a pipeline.

Actuators perform the converse function, transforming a digital signal into a physical action, whether pneumatic, electric, or hydraulic or other physical system. The salient feature is that cyber-physical systems do not only exist simultaneously in the digital and physical world; they can perform the core function of transduction—reciprocally converting information from one world into information in the other world.

Technical levers of transduction, as a feature of cyber-physical systems, help shape policy questions. What are the policy concerns arising at the transductive intersection between the material and the physical, as well as in the support infrastructures that enable this interface? *These transductive spaces are new spaces for social improvement and economic efficiency but are also points of vulnerability for manipulation, surveillance, and attack.* The evolving point of vulnerability is that, rather than attacking or infiltrating a digital technology directly, it is only necessary to intentionally manipulate the physical environment that a sensor then reads, trusts, converts, and transmits.

Autonomy and Machine Learning

Another defining feature of cyber-physical systems is autonomy. Humans can sometimes be entirely excised from systems, once operational. As an Internet Society definition of the IoT suggests, this quality of autonomy is the ability of materially embedded digital devices "to generate, exchange and consume data with minimal human intervention."[34]

Autonomous elements are already part of many information technology systems, even those not connected to physical artifacts or the natural world. Much happens without direct human intervention. Autonomous cybersecurity systems detect and address malware and identify network anomalies. Autonomous weapon systems are already in use.[35] Web crawlers fuel search engine data.

User engagement with content and screen-mediated applications can convey the false impression of control when, in reality, content is only the surface of a malleable and evolving technical architecture. This architecture becomes broader and deeper in the realm of cyber-physical systems, involving human relinquishment of some real-world functions to machines, with digital systems increasingly assuming tasks once performed by humans, whether driving a car or administering medical treatment. Digital systems—code, protocols, algorithms, and hardware—are themselves created by human designers and shaped by their values and interests. But the concealed complexity, material embeddedness, and data-driven machine learning of these systems ascribe a power that, at a minimum, diminishes the autonomy of the humans that use them, even while reciprocally empowering humans.

A memorable pronouncement in the chilling Cold War movie *Dr. Strangelove* suggested, "The only thing everyone can agree on is no one is responsible." The quote, in the age of cyber-physical systems, raises the question of whether humans have the ability to control technological systems or whether technologies acquire an autonomous agency apart from human volition. For decades, thinkers from or influencing science and technology studies have examined how artifacts take on agency (Martin Heidegger, Jacque Ellul, Albert Borgmann, Lewis Mumford), alternatively warning about the alienating and destructive consequences of autonomous technology or promoting agency as a prospect for liberation. Methodologically, the actor-network theory research program (especially as espoused by Bruno Latour) ascribes agency to nonliving actors as well as humans and living organisms as a way to reject either social or technological reductionism within other methodologies. In 1977, Langdon Winner published *Autonomous Technology: Technics-out-of-Control as a Theme in Political Thought*. Winner was addressing the belief that technology, once developed, tends to "follow its own course, independent of human direction."[36]

This acquired agency and autonomy, leading to technology becoming out of control, has long been a concern of philosophers and has shaped science fiction depictions from *Terminator* to *Matrix* to *Ex Machina*. It is true that sensing and actuating occurs without human intervention. Once a transduction system is in place, it can have autonomy and agency. Individuals within proximity of the device might not even be aware of its embedded cyber-physical features.

Rather than autonomous technology remaining a fear about something that *could* happen, this feature of *autonomy is specifically designed into cyber-physical systems*. Some are designed ex ante to require no human intervention. As such, these systems are sometimes described as machine-to-machine implementations.[37] Humans have an interface through which to view and analyze data but are not required to be present to operate the system. Others are semiautonomous, sometimes requiring human intervention and sometimes acting with no need for human control. Anyone driving a car with advanced automatic braking inherently understands this idea of semiautonomous systems.

The continuous and pervasive feedback loops enabled by autonomous technologies have never before been possible. This feedback loop involves real-time sensing of continuously changing material conditions, instantaneous processing and analysis of this information, and immediate delivery of responses that can result in an actuator manipulating something physically. Continuous readings from medical devices, for example, are transmitted in real time to a back-end information system that performs data analysis, communicates with other systems, and directs adjustments in treatment.

A crucial characteristic that will shape possible policy responses is that autonomy is not only about a system performing a task with no human intervention, such as being programmed to take a temperature reading every minute. Autonomy also involves the ability for cyber-embedded objects to learn, adapt, change, and improve, based on a continuous feedback of collected data. Indeed, advancements in machine learning are enabling ever-greater autonomous systems, for both traditional information systems and cyber-physical systems. Programming is no longer relegated to static coding of fixed algorithms into systems to specify exactly how they perform a task. Programming is about dynamically enabling the code to use statistical inference and large quantities of data to itself learn, adapt, and predict. This is certainly the case for facial recognition, speech recognition, and, more to the point for embedded objects, the ability to predict failures and maintenance needs on the basis of massive stores of historical data.

This feature of autonomy means that the object of intervention for policy questions is directed toward not only people, content, or even institutions but, to a greater extent than ever, technology with its own dynamic and evolutionary agency. This feature complicates accountability and responsibility. Autonomous features of technology, and especially how technology can evolve autonomously via machine learning drawing from many data sources, critically complicate norms of accountability, risk calculations, and liability.

Constrained Architectures

Design parsimony is another feature of a large class of (but not all) embedded systems. They have, by design, architectural limitations relative to more broad-purpose end devices for information-only systems. Instead of serving as a blank slate for multiple applications, they are engineered for ad hoc, specific purposes (and physical space constraints) that are highly context specific and narrow, such as sensing motion, activating a light, or moving a door lock. Relative to traditional end nodes (laptops, servers, smartphones, personal computers) connected to the Internet, embedded cyber-physical objects often do not require the same microprocessing resources or memory capacity to perform their appointed tasks. Back-end data-analysis systems certainly have enormous processing and storage requirements, but end devices do not always. They are also sometimes not in an environment that enables direct AC power or a direct wire-line connection to a network but rather are often small, wirelessly connected, and battery powered. In short, a constrained system involves devices "with restricted memory, energy, and processing power."[38] The Internet Engineering Task Force's definition of a constrained network node is helpful: "A node where some of the characteristics that are otherwise pretty much taken for granted for Internet nodes at the time of writing are not attainable, often due to cost constraints and/or physical constraints on characteristics such as size, weight, and available power and energy. The tight limits on power, memory, and processing resources lead to hard upper bounds on state, code space, and processing cycles, making optimization of energy and network bandwidth usage a dominating consideration in all design requirements."[39]

The design rationales for limiting processing power, memory, and electrical power are context dependent but often include the economic need to constrain the costs of routine sensor devices, limiting size and weight to fit into small objects or spaces, or limiting power in dangerous or combustible environments. Characteristics that are taken for granted in some traditional communication networks, such as high throughput, reliability, and the capacity to use large packet sizes, are not necessarily characteristics of networks connecting embedded objects.

Architectural constraints create political constraints. For example, legislating certain requirements into devices—such as privacy enhancements or security—may not be possible without redesigning systems to include greater memory and processing power and allow for enhanced code complexity. These general restrictions of power, computational resources, memory, and packet size also create limitations on the ability to implement network connectivity features (and protocol stacks like Transmission Control Protocol/Internet Protocol, or TCP/IP) that have become de facto standards in most other environments and have prompted adaptations and initiatives to develop protocols specifically designed for low-power and low-computational-resources environments.

Network Architecture Heterogeneity

What is the "cyber" in "cyber-physical"? One common characteristic of all cyber-physical objects is that they are able to connect to a network to communicate with each other, with back-end applications that perform analysis and serve as command and control systems, with human-facing apps, with cloud computing and many other infrastructural elements. Similar to screen-based information devices, embedded objects connect to these networks in numerous ways. Some connect directly to broadband networks via a cable (e.g., twisted pair, coaxial, or fiber optic). Many embedded objects connect wirelessly. Wireless connectivity is not a single technological category in itself but a constellation of different approaches using different standards and different electromagnetic frequency spectrum range. Local, short-range wireless connectivity options include Wi-Fi, Zigbee, Bluetooth, RFID, and other near-field alternatives that do not require device pairing but use magnetic induction in a passive reader activated by an active transmitter. There are also many completely closed and proprietary specifications that are manufacturer specific. Longer-range options include GPS and cellular telephony.

Indeed, features of cyber-physical systems include the rise of proprietary protocol architectures, increasing use of gateways, and technology heterogeneity. Even the classic definition suggesting that if a device is reachable via IP, it is on the Internet, and if it cannot be reached, it is not on the Internet has ambiguity around the definition of "reachable." Engineers in the IETF often use IP in definitions of the Internet of things. On the other hand, groups outside the Internet's historically dominant technical community sometimes omit use of the Internet Protocol as part of defining the Internet of things. For example, the ITU definition of the IoT does not specifically list IP as a requirement. "The IoT network infrastructure may be realized via existing networks, such as conventional TCP/IP-based networks, and/or evolving networks, such as next generation networks."[40]

Some cyber-embedded devices connect directly to the public Internet. Others, whether industrial or consumer IoT objects, do not directly connect to the public Internet but through a gateway. Regardless of direct or indirect assemblage, embedded systems transmit data over the same core networks that support content-based communications like email, social media, and commercial and financial transactions. When they are connected to a proprietary network operated by a manufacturer, they can still be connected to networks that are, in turn, connected to the public Internet.

In the opening decades of cyber-physical system deployments, even in the narrower area of consumer IoT, there has been nothing close to a universal and consistent set of technical standards. Instead, numerous standards bodies compete; specifications conflict and overlay; and proprietary and monopolistic specifications have proliferated. But a foundational policy question arises. *The goal of preserving a "universal" Internet with shared, open standards has always been present in Internet policy and design communities. Does the massive proliferation of embedded devices challenge this value?* These openly available and generally royalty-free standards, such as TCP/IP, have promoted interoperability and universality and, because they enable multiple, competing implementations, have contributed to rapid innovation. These advantages would similarly convey to embedded systems. However, it is also reasonable to argue that fragmentation in the cyber-physical system space can serve as a check on security vulnerabilities arising from exposure to global networks.

Most importantly from a policy perspective, it is not helpful to dismiss these systems as "separate from the rest of the Internet" or too heterogeneous to address. The collectivity of connected networks—both cyber-physical and information systems—have to be brought squarely together in policy and research discourses. The Mirai botnet, among other incidents, demonstrated how local, cyber-physical conditions can directly affect the integrity and security of the broader global system.

Embedded Identification—Only on a Massive Scale

Each device that forms part of a cyber-physical system, commensurate with end nodes on any communication system, requires unique identification and therefore addressability. *Because the number of embedded objects is growing so rapidly and already measures in multiple billions, the ability to scale address space accordingly is a crucial design concern.* Some of these devices, but not all, require globally unique IP addresses, either natively or connected through a gateway. One of the great Internet policy challenges of the past decades has been the question of how to provide incentives for the implementation and use of Internet Protocol version 6 (IPv6), the relatively newer Internet address standard that expands the number of available addresses from roughly 4.3 billion to an incomprehensibly large number. The proliferation of IP-connected embedded objects, which already far outnumber the world's population of humans, will be another complicating variable. The need for massive pools of globally unique identifiers for embedded systems should provide an incentive for IPv6, yet many manufacturers are not natively designing it into products, which are brought quickly to market and without concern about universal standards.

There are also many identification approaches specific to cyber-physical systems. In general, the problem of identification standards, identity management, and identity authentication in the IoT is in flux. There are many distinct and sometimes noninteroperable forms of identification, some completely proprietary. Other approaches have become de facto norms in specific contexts, such as the use of RFID microchips/tags in certain environments.

RFID microchips/tags provide a unique identification number, often a permanent physical number on a tag that can be read over radio waves over a short (contactless) distance. The chip contains a transponder that transmits a radio signal when it comes into proximity with and senses/receives a predetermined signal from a reader, also sometimes called an "interrogator" or "transceiver." An RFID system also includes some type of back-end data-management system that looks up and processes information on the basis of the unique object identification number. Tags are active (conventional radio devices with an embedded power source) or passive, containing no internal power source but rather drawing power from an RFID reader in its vicinity (through inductive, electromagnetic field coupling, for example, where the tag antenna receives the electromagnetic power from the reader and charges an on-tag capacitor). To some extent, these radio identification chips are functionally similar to optical barcode readers, but they use radio waves rather than light. RFID technologies are used here as only one example of physical identification system, but they are in wide use in applications such as toll collection, retail theft detection, and supply-chain management.

The same types of policy questions that have arisen around the Internet address space arise in this space of cyber-physical identification systems. What are the privacy considerations of uniquely identifying devices—whether physical or virtual identification—and how does this data, especially in combination with other data, create new sites of conflict between law enforcement, individual privacy, and national regulations such as privacy statutes in the European Union? What cybersecurity mechanisms, such as cryptographic authentication, are necessary to prevent tampering with and spoofing of identification systems? Given the rapid growth in connected objects, the ability to scale unique identities into the billions and billions range is a crucial policy concern.

Arrangements of technology are also social, political, and economic structures. Technology is not separate from being human. Each of the technical characteristics just described also has accompanying policy characteristics. The deployment of cyber-physical systems is not only a technological phenomenon but a social phenomenon. With this backdrop of a taxonomy of types of cyber-physical systems and a description of their shared technical characteristics, the next chapters examine three co-constructed policy concerns around privacy, security, and interoperability.

PART TWO

THE GLOBAL POLITICS OF CYBER-PHYSICAL SYSTEMS

3

Privacy Gets Physical

THE FEDERAL BUREAU OF INVESTIGATION (FBI) issued a haunting public service announcement admonishing parents about the privacy and safety concerns that Internet-connected toys posed to children: "The FBI encourages consumers to consider cybersecurity prior to introducing smart, interactive, internet-connected toys into their homes or trusted environments. Smart toys and entertainment devices for children are increasingly incorporating technologies that learn and tailor their behaviors based on user interactions. These toys typically contain sensors, microphones, cameras, data storage components, and other multimedia capabilities—including speech recognition and GPS options. *These features could put the privacy and safety of children at risk due to the large amount of personal information that may be unwittingly disclosed.*"[1] This one caveat about one category of cyber-embedded object exposes the many dimensions of privacy risks and complications now concealed in the mundane physical objects inhabiting the most intimate spheres of human existence. As toys become cyber embedded, they embody all of the characteristics of cyber-physical systems that complicate policy concerns. They connect to the global public Internet, usually through a Wi-Fi connection or Bluetooth or other short-range network pairing it to an Internet-connected smartphone, potentially exposing a child to exploitation, identity fraud, or government surveillance from anywhere in the world. These systems are not multipurpose devices like smartphones but rather constrained devices designed for a specific application context. Yet invasive corporate data-collection practices around these objects can capture, aggregate, and share personal information about children—including name, home address, IP address, interests, facial recognition and other images, voice-recognition patterns—even if these practices violate laws such as, in the United States, the Children's Online Privacy Protection Act (COPPA).[2] These toys often include machine-learning elements that tailor the toys' interaction with a child on the basis of interaction history, and they embed sensors designed to interact with the physical world, whether touch, movement, or sound.

Privacy complications emerging in embedded toys underscore how all companies are now tech companies that gather and process digital data, not just content intermediaries such as Google but toy companies such as Mattel. The protection of personal data is not only from hackers and digital-content intermediaries but from the corporations that sell these embedded objects. Some disclose their data-gathering practices, but if the majority of users do not read terms of service for content intermediaries, very few parents would read through the entirety of "terms and conditions" (if any) while assembling a toy in the ebullient moments after a child unwraps it.

A baby's room in a home should be, more than any other private or public space, a completely safe environment. These rooms now routinely house video-surveillance cameras to allow parents to remotely monitor children from a smartphone app. In 2013, parents using the Chinese-made Foscam camera were horrified to find that a miscreant gained access to the streaming video and image of their sleeping baby, could control the camera, and was able to shout at the baby over the system.[3]

Inexpensive indoor security cameras lay bare the privacy complications arising in consumer IoT systems. These devices connect to the public Internet to allow home or business owners to receive phone alerts. They are wildly popular precisely because they provide such a valuable societal function, the ability to monitor the security of one's home or business from anywhere in the world. At the same time, vulnerabilities or weak security sometimes allow foreign intelligence agents or criminal hackers to peer into someone's living room from anywhere in the world. Cameras are capable of twenty-four-hour surveillance and recording and often upload and store this private video in cloud services. These systems sometimes embed biometric identification features, especially facial recognition, and, via machine-learning advancements, are even capable of learning to recognize and authenticate the family dog. Such biometric recognition creates a meticulous record of when individuals come and go, who they interact with, and what they are doing. The policy issues are immense. Do these systems have privacy policies? How is consent sought and by whom? Are products upgradeable to patch security vulnerabilities? Who owns the rights to personal video, how is it shared with third parties, and are companies legally obligated to notify customers of data breaches? Answers to these questions are inconsistent.

Transparency and notice to consumers about data gathering and sharing practices should represent absolute minimal standards of practice. But even this minimal standard is difficult to attain. With no awareness and no consent, people can be swept up in ambient data collection carried out by municipalities or via embedded objects owned by other citizens. Even when device ownership is clear, personal data collection via embedded objects is not always appropriately disclosed. The smart-television manufacturer Vizio agreed to a privacy-related settlement of $2.2 million to the U.S. Federal Trade Commission (FTC) and the Office of the New Jersey Attorney General on charges that the company had "installed software on its TVs to collect viewing data on 11 million consumer TVs without consumers' knowledge or consent."[4]

The complaint alleged that Vizio TVs continuously tracked everything the consumer viewed through the television on a "second-by-second basis," collecting nearly one hundred billion data points a day in total, stored this data indefinitely, captured personally identifying information like IP address and MAC (Media Access Control, i.e., Ethernet) address, and sold this data to third parties.[5] Worse, the complaint alleged that third parties could use this information to assess users' behavior across devices, such as whether viewing an advertisement on a television prompted the person to access a website from another device. The FTC, in this case and more generally, advised companies to disclose data-gathering practices ab initio, to gain consent related to both data collection and sharing, to provide user choice, and to adopt consumer protection principles related to security and disclosure.

In the digital realm generally, it is an understatement to say that privacy is not going well. This assessment is independent of the newer, more personally invasive privacy challenges arising in cyber-physical systems. It pertains to digital intermediaries generally. The business model of information intermediaries— social media platforms, rating systems, content-aggregation sites—primarily involves giving away free services in exchange for data-collection-driven targeted advertising. This business model has helped fuel the growth of the

Internet and incentivize the development of innovative products and services, but it has relied on the practice of massive, privacy-invasive data collection. This data-collection-driven business model has induced a cultural shift in what counts as the private sphere, collecting innermost thoughts manifested in online searches, likes, locational movement, and behavior online. This private surveillance is also what has enabled massive government surveillance of citizens. In the context of broader geopolitical concern over terrorism and national security risks, governments have heightened incentives to carry out pervasive government surveillance. In authoritarian contexts, surveillance is a form of control over citizens.

Consumer data breaches are another factor diminishing individual privacy. Massive consumer data breaches have hit, among other institutions, the retail behemoths Target and Home Depot, the insurance giant Primera Blue Cross, Equifax, Yahoo!, and the U.S. Office of Personnel Management. Incursions into such personal spheres compromise expectations of privacy, and especially when they are highly publicized, such as in the Equifax case, they affect conceptions of trust in the digital systems that now underpin most economic and social transactions. At the same time, many of these privacy-compromising practices are hidden from direct human view: data collection to fuel twenty-first-century business models, government online surveillance practices, and massive data breaches.

As the Internet moves from a communication system to the pervasive control structure that fuses together the material world and the digital world, to what extent do these practices of surveillance-based business models, invasive government surveillance activities, and data breaches extend into the cyber-physical realm and further escalate already-extant privacy concerns? The escalation and stakes are already clear. The Hong Kong–based toy maker VTech Electronics agreed to pay a $650,000 settlement for collecting, without consent and without disclosure, personal information about children and for failing to reasonably secure this data, via controls and encryption, resulting in a data breach of personal information about children.[6] Benign-sounding "smart city" initiatives such as "smart" energy meters collect data on usage that is tied directly to name, address, billing information, and other personally identifiable information. Breaches or unauthorized data sharing can result in identity theft and the identification of sensitive personal information and behavior, such as when people are home and their associated energy consumption.[7]

Cyber-physical systems radically escalate privacy concerns well beyond the world of content into the most private spheres in and around the body and in material spaces within work, industry, and everyday societal systems. The surface of surveillance is ubiquitous and pervasive, online and offline, in public and in previously isolated or private spheres. These privacy concerns are also no longer merely privacy concerns. They are simultaneously concerns about safety, autonomy, national security, and sometimes discrimination. Data-collection practices around how someone eats, drives, sleeps, and exercises create an exhaustive backdrop for determinations about employment, law enforcement responses, and insurance. Indeed, embedded systems connect directly to these other spheres, through employee fitness programs, license-plate readers, and autonomously collected driving data that determine insurance rates. Data collection around industrial systems creates a sprawling attack service for foreign intelligence gathering.

Realizing the economic and social benefits of IoT innovations ultimately requires trust in these systems. Privacy concerns clearly escalate in cyber-physical systems. A privacy-protection framework has to anticipate and address the technological disruption of cyber-physical systems as arguably the most challenging privacy problem ever to confront humanity.

The Background Context: Surveillance as Business Model

The least accurately predictive meme of the Internet era is now widely understood to be the web-surfing dog in the *New Yorker* cartoon, accompanied by the caption, "On the Internet, nobody knows you're a dog." This exemplified the 1990s aspiration that the Internet would enable anonymity. It also reflected the lived sensory perception that "surfing the web" in the privacy of one's home was something actually done in private. The World Wide Web (as well as browsers) was brand new, moving the world from proprietary and closed online systems to the open Internet. The arc of history has revealed this phenomenologically private act of surfing the web as, realistically, the least private thing one can do.

The nexus of online revenue models and widespread government surveillance has powerfully shaped the evolution of individual privacy. Prospects for default privacy faded as the consumer Internet evolved from a subscription model to a biome of free services across the spectrum of email, social media, information-aggregation sites, messaging, and search, all monetized by interactive digital advertising. These models transformed consumers from paying customers to valuable stores of data and recipients of microtargeted ads based on context, content, behavior, location, and association online.

Instead of money changing hands between customers and providers, money changes hands between providers and advertisers. Facebook's market capitalization long hovered around $500 billion, even though it has never charged a subscription fee from its hundreds of millions of social media users. Like Google and other large content intermediaries, Facebook primarily generates revenue through the monetization of consumer data. This model has opened Internet access to billions of people. It has also changed the norms of what counts as privacy.

Technological limits in processing power, storage capacity, and data analytics once served as a natural constraint on personal data collection and analysis. Increasing processing power and storage, computational data science, and artificial intelligence have brought volume, precision, and predictive ability to information collection about individuals. Advancements in locational precision—via mobile phone GPS, for example—have further refined precision data collection. This revenue model based on online advertising is only sustainable via the constant collection and accrual of personal information. Google, Facebook, Twitter, and other social media companies have access not only to the content individuals choose to disclose on their sites but also to considerable metadata, the information surrounding content that reveals highly personal information: location, phone number, unique software imprint, IP address, device information, cookies, activity data, and network connections.[8]

Depending on the company and, increasingly, region, intermediaries routinely share collected data—content and metadata—with third parties with which the subscriber has no formal relationship, contractual association, or even knowledge. For decades, privacy advocates have expressed concern about third-party data sharing, a norm since at least the rise of social media platforms.

These data collection and sharing practices came to greater public attention with the disclosure that the British political consultancy Cambridge Analytica harvested data from millions of Facebook users to aid the presidential election campaign of then-candidate Donald Trump and the campaign advocating for the UK Brexit vote to leave the European Union. Third-party data sharing was not an unusual practice, but it attracted widespread attention and controversy because of the political context and some of the specifics of how personal data was shared. By May 2018, Cambridge Analytica ceased operating and filed for insolvency in the United Kingdom, albeit arguing that the company has been "vilified for activities that are not only legal, but also widely accepted as a standard component of online advertising in both the political and commercial arenas."[9]

Facebook's president, Mark Zuckerberg, responded to public concern about Cambridge Analytica's access to personal information by explaining the circumstances and outlining steps to prevent a similar incident. Alarmingly, because Facebook was designed to encourage subscribers to share their contacts and information about friends, a Cambridge University researcher was able to access data about friends of individuals who voluntarily took a personality quiz that the researcher had developed. According to Facebook, the researcher "was able to access tens of millions of their friends' data" and also shared his data with Cambridge Analytica.[10] Facebook announced a number of measures purportedly designed to better protect subscriber data, including restrictions on data given to a third-party developer app and greater requirements for data-access approval. This is just one example of many privacy-eroding incidents.

The critical privacy questions inherent in the business models of content intermediaries extend to cyber-physical systems:

- Will targeted online advertising also become a dominant revenue model for cyber-physical systems, such as health wearables and consumer IoT devices?
- To what extent will personal information gathered from intimate physical spheres be combined with massive data stores already consolidated and handled by third-party data aggregators?
- Do voluntary corporate measures suffice for protecting privacy, or is sweeping regulatory action necessary to protect citizens from potential harms of corporate data-gathering practices?
- Do traditional approaches such as notice, disclosure, and consumer choice even apply in cyber-physical systems?

Another background context is that a global patchwork of regulatory approaches address privacy in various ways. Governments have an interest in preserving the ability to access personal data from information intermediaries.

Because information flows almost entirely over infrastructure and platforms owned and operated by the private sector, government surveillance primarily occurs via government requests to the private sector to disclose data. Documents leaked in 2013 by the intelligence analyst Edward Snowden drew attention to both the extent of government surveillance (not just in the United States but in many other countries) and the direct connection of this surveillance to leading technology companies. As shown on one leaked slide on the National Security Agency (NSA) PRISM program, major companies including Microsoft, Yahoo!, Facebook, Google, and Apple were portrayed as sources of user information such as emails, chats, photos, and Voice over IP (VoIP).

Disclosures about the sweeping extent of government surveillance, facilitated by private digital intermediaries, have drawn attention to the role of the private sector in determining many dimensions of privacy: whether someone's real name is required to have an online account; the extent of personal data collected and how it is shared with third parties; and the gatekeeping function of determining when to turn over user data to governments around the world under various laws, circumstances, and norms.

As the political scientist Ron Deibert graphically portrayed private-industry data capture years ago, "Like a giant python that has consumed a rat, Facebook captures, swallows, and slowly digests its users."[11] How much more will the personal data collected by cyber-physical intermediaries swallow society unless there are adequate privacy measures that protect individuals and create the trust necessary for the expansion of the digital economy? The logic of advertising-driven data-collection models, and associated problems, already extends (and escalates) in cyber-physical systems. But cyber-physical systems also create a real-world, intimate plane on which unique privacy concerns materialize.

The Radical Escalation of Privacy Concerns

The digitization of material objects complicates privacy in ways that eclipse concerns about social media disclosures. Cyber-embedded material systems—consumer objects, industrial structures, medical devices, augmented reality, and emerging hybrid systems—are bringing about great efficiencies and life improvements. To do so, these systems operate via continuous sensing and processing. This constant data collection reaches much further into daily economic and social life than ever imaginable in screen-mediated contexts alone and intensifies the scope of surveillance. The ability for the private sector and governments to track human activity, thoughts, and intimate life now permeates the material world.

A laptop or personal computer screen is no longer a protective portal demarcating whether or not one is observed. Privacy is affected by ambient data collection from systems with which people have no ownership or contractual relationship—such as traffic-management systems, tracking devices in retail stores, or devices in other people's homes. This data collection extends beyond devices that companies and individuals purchase into systems with which these entities have no commercial or usage agreements. Without screens, terms of agreement, or ownership, how do companies secure human consent? How do they reveal privacy policies or data gathering and sharing practices? One of the most consequential questions about the pervasiveness of cyber-physical systems is the extent to which data gathered from every domain of human existence is merged together in back-end fusion centers that already aggregate data from diverse sources, public and private.

The nature of cyber-physical data represents actual behavior and physical state in the real world. Collection becomes highly personal. But it also becomes wholly global in that observation can cross borders and involve foreign surveillance or other cross-border scrutiny. The intimate and precise nature of this information raises concerns about inferential discrimination against people in employment, political freedom, financial credit, and insurance.

Digital Privacy Becomes Intimate

One misconception, and sometimes a justification for opposition to even modest regulatory constraints around privacy practices, is that data collected from things does not involve individuals. The following argument exemplifies this view: "a smart refrigerator does not need any personal information to know that it is running low on milk."[12] This argument is certainly true for a subset of industrial implementations, such as sensors in energy pipelines or materials handling tracking during manufacturing and production. It is also accurate that the refrigerator does not *need* any personal information to detect and communicate an inventory shortage. But smart refrigerators contain microphones, creating a potential point of ambient surveillance in one's home. They are also connected to the public Internet and thus can combine with personal information via unique identifiers and devices tied directly to individuals. A hacked refrigerator can reveal information to thieves about whether a family is away on vacation.

Samsung introduced an innovative, voice-activated refrigerator with the ability to access the Internet, stream music, order groceries, and dictate memos. This refrigerator offers parental controls to restrict children's access in the same way one might on a traditional desktop computer. A smart appliance is only useful if it is network connected to an individual's smartphone app and calendar and possibly to an interactive grocery delivery service. In other words, the device is almost always connected to something that links it to a personal identifier, whether an IP address or a unique software imprint and personal information associated with a phone. Even if not directly linked to an individual's personal information, the IP address that the refrigerator uses (if permanently or recurrently) or unique software configurations can reveal a great deal to data-aggregation sites and combine with more personal information. The metrics that a refrigerator or other appliance collects reveal highly personal information such as the amount of beer consumed or the nature of one's diet, creating sensitive portrayals of health that could potentially lead to discrimination in employment and insurance.

Of direct relevance to privacy, cyber-physical devices in homes contain microphones, cameras, and video recorders and therefore bring the potential for total surveillance into the previously most inviolable of personal spaces. These devices are, of course, useful and socially desirable. In many ways, they are inevitable as it becomes increasingly difficult even to find products without cyber-embedded capability. But these devices also create a voluntary system of surveillance of audio, images, and video.

Smart televisions that connect directly to the Internet are an example of how connected consumer devices involve trade-offs between convenience and privacy risk. The need for this device arises from legacy cable-television subscription models that lock out access to popular Internet-born programming platforms like Netflix, Hulu, Amazon Prime, and YouTube. Smart televisions are just traditional televisions with the addition of integrated Internet connectivity, such as an Ethernet port or Wi-Fi access to a home's broadband connection. The majority of new televisions have this capability, allowing for natively streaming online programming, as well as browsing the web and using apps and multiplayer games.

Privacy concerns around Internet-connected TVs entered policy discourses in 2013, when security researchers at iSEC Partners claimed to have gained unauthorized access to features embedded in the 2012 Samsung smart TV, including the camera and all the features controlled by the browser.[13] A hacker or government intelligence agent would presumably be able to redirect the viewer to a rogue browser and, more pertinent to privacy, be able to take control of the television's camera and remotely and surreptitiously spy on people in proximity to the device. Samsung responded by issuing a software upgrade, accentuating the importance of upgradeability in consumer IoT devices.

Cyber-physical systems entangle much more personally with issues of sexual privacy, coercion, and harassment, an amplification of problems in information systems. As the law professor Danielle Citron explains, "The law needs updating again to combat destructive invasions of sexual privacy facilitated by networked technologies."[14] Citron is referring to a host of digitally enabled online information problems ranging from revenge porn to online sexual harassment.

The online sphere already amplifies opportunities for harassment and control. Attacks—whether cyberbullying, hate speech, revenge porn (posting sexually explicit images or videos of a former partner without the person's consent), sexual harassment, or defamation—are effective because they create a permanent searchable record of online abuse and because they reach a potentially large audience. Phone-tracking features and other locational apps also provide avenues for abusive spouses to track and locate their partners. Content intermediaries have a mixed track record of dealing with these ever-evolving abuse mechanisms, in part because of the large volume of incidents but also because of inconsistent adherence to terms of service and the challenge of dealing with the laws and norms of different regions in which they operate. But those who are subjected to online harassment could at least turn off the screens and retreat into the safety of their homes. The cyber-physical context is more integrated into material surroundings, so screens are not a natural protective boundary from harassment.

Domestic violence and abuse cases also now have consumer IoT dimensions. Law enforcement personnel already understand well the connection between the IoT and domestic violence.[15] Embedded devices create an entirely new terrain for harassment. Ghost-like incursions into home environments—changing the temperature or unlocking doors—are an unfortunate new threat in domestic abuse situations. A partner who formerly resided in a home often retains control of systems from his or her smartphone.[16] Some abusive interventions are active, including intimidation or harassment via remote tampering with connected home devices or turning off or blocking access to systems. Some are passive, such as coercive control via tapping into video-surveillance cameras. The abusive partner is sometimes the legal owner of the device and services, so this harassment does not involve "hacking." The same innovations, especially con-nected surveillance cameras and home alarm systems, that protect individuals from harm can facilitate harassment by estranged partners. Exploitation of technology has long been a tool for domestic abuse.[17] Now the surface for digital exploitation has expanded to the physical world.

Cyber-embedded objects that are on or in the body create even greater per-sonal privacy concerns. Wearable technologies are intimate objects, but new product manufacturers do not have the same dialectic relationship with privacy concerns as traditional technology companies. The digital-only sphere, even with its privacy problems, has had an evolution of terms of service and a rising public awareness of data collection. Cyber-physical systems, often brought quickly to market for competitive advantage, have not yet confronted privacy issues in the same way.

As an extreme example of privacy issues arising in this cyber-physical ter-rain, customers sued a sexual products company over its collection and trans-mission of personal and sexual information via its Bluetooth-connected vibrator and smartphone remote-control app. The company had introduced an app-mediated feature in which customers (or their partners) could remotely control the product from a smartphone. The lawsuit alleged that the company failed to inform the customer about data collection, thereby violating an Illinois statute on consumer fraud and deceptive business practices. Specifically, the class-action lawsuit alleged, "Unbeknownst to its customers, however, Defendant de-signed We-Connect to (i) Collect and record highly intimate and sensitive data regarding consumers' personal We-Vibe use, including the date and time of each use and the selected vibration settings, and (ii) transmit such usage data— along with the user's personal email address—to its servers in Canada. . . . Defendant's conduct demonstrates a wholesale disregard for consumer privacy rights and violated numerous state and federal laws."[18] The company, Standard Innovation, settled the class-action lawsuit for $3.75 million. Sex-tech wearables are already a sizable industry and one that is quickly moving beyond accessories to sex robots. The artificial intelligence sex robots connected directly to the Internet raise every imaginable confidentiality concern about data collection and sharing.

Human-implantable chips that break the barrier between human flesh and cyber technologies are even more of an incursion into what counts as a private human domain. In 2004, the FDA approved a subdermal RFID chip, VeriChip, designed to enable health-care providers to instantly access patients' medical records.[19] Medical professionals and entrepreneurs have long expressed interest in human-implantable computer chips designed to store a person's medical records. An emergency-room doctor could scan a patient for the presence of the chip and instantaneously learn information about blood type, allergies, insurance, medical history, and other personal details.

Human-implantable chips already have a long history. In 1998, a professor at the University of Reading in the United Kingdom voluntarily inserted a silicon microchip into his arm. Professor Kevin Warwick specialized in intelligent buildings and was studying the implantable chip as a security monitoring and authentication method for gaining access to certain areas of the building.[20]

Modern-day RFID medical-implant technology is nearly identical to the "Home Again" microchips injected into pets and livestock to identify them using a unique identification number that can be cross-referenced with information on file for that number. The microchips are the size of a grain of rice and implanted directly into flesh. These medical and informational microchips are not tracking devices in the same way that GPS-connected smartphones are. They do not contain their own internal power source but rather derive power from a close-proximity scanner to transmit the information contained on the microchip.

Even while some regions, such as Scandinavia, see voluntary adoption of human chip implantation, it is an open question whether people will submit to widespread chip implantation in their own bodies, either in the interest of convenience or under the pressure of coercion. Drawing public attention to this question, a Wisconsin company issued a press release announcing an optional program for employees to be voluntarily implanted with an RFID chip to manage their access to resources at work.[21] The company, Three Square Market, expected fifty employees to volunteer for the chip, which would be implanted between the thumb and first finger and, via near-field communications and data stored on the chip, allow workers to make food purchases, use copy machines, log in to computers, and gain entry to rooms.

Contemporary products on the market include the Danish company BiChip's human microchip implant that allows for RFID-read payment in popular crypto-currencies (e.g., Bitcoin, Ripple), as well as storage of medical information, driver's license, and passport data. The company envisions the human implant, injected into the hand, as an "alternative Payment System integratable with cryptocurrency wallets."[22]

Science fiction movies have imagined a future in which human beings were voluntarily or involuntarily implanted with microprocessors that tracked their location or contained personally identifiable information. This once-inconceivable idea has manifested itself in contemporary society. It is no longer science fiction.

Human emotion is another cyber-physical privacy sphere. The 2018 report of the Internet of Things Privacy Forum flags human emotions as a space in which IoT technologies are certainly addressing: "The proximity of IoT technologies will allow third parties to collect our emotional states over long periods of time. Our emotional and inner life will become more transparent to data collecting organizations."[23] This concern is understandable, considering that the biometric sensors embedded in fitness and health monitors can detect human biological data closely associated with emotional status—such as temperature, heart rate, and blood pressure. These measurements, coupled with speech picked up on microphones, especially capture emotional state. One's inner life is already monitored via contextual analysis of social media postings, what one reads, and especially search queries. For example, searches for "suicide" or "depression" or "infatuation" or "anger problem" speak volumes about human emotions relative to biometric measurements. The inner life of the mind may be one area in which content platforms encroach on privacy as much as or more than cyber-physical infrastructure.

Carrying around a smartphone already creates privacy issues because it enables locational, intellectual, and behavioral tracking. The convenience and communication innovations of smartphones often supersede these concerns. The same trade-offs exist in cyber-embedded material systems. They enhance human life. They also raise unprecedented privacy concerns in intensely personal areas. The cyber-embeddedness of objects that directly communicate with or within the human body are more directly invasive because they are part of the physical world as much as the digital world.

Privacy evolves again.

Cyber-Physical Privacy and National Security

A barrage of media articles in early 2018 drew public attention to a once-im-plausible connection between personal fitness privacy and national security. An online heat map designed to depict collective and anonymized patterns of where runners and cyclists traversed was interpreted to reveal the locations of U.S. military personnel.[24] The exercise mobile app and web platform, Strava, sup-ported tens of millions of fitness enthusiasts. The product was designed to work with a diverse array of devices including iPhones and Fitbit fitness bracelets and serve as a resource helping athletes to track their performance metrics, con-nect with other athletes, access ideas for routes, and compete with themselves and others. It also allowed runners to opt for useful safety features such as shar-ing their position with loved ones in real time and connecting into health de-vices like heart-rate monitors.

Such health and fitness applications provide beneficial intelligence and safety features for individual users and enable them to connect to like-minded fitness enthusiasts. Collectively, the millions upon millions of data points collected from tens of millions of users of the fitness platform, when aggregated together, depict concentrations of fitness activity. Unless an individual user activates a privacy setting that marks the data private, the company collects, anonymizes, and aggregates the data with information that the company gathers about other subscribers. Strava's so-called heat map was essentially a data visualization de-picting the movements of its users. In other words, this collective data revealed clusters of activity where subscribers exercised and, as such, inadvertently de-picted concentrations of possible military troops (or potentially intelligence op-eratives or international aid workers) located in dangerous areas.

Members of the U.S. House of Representatives Committee on Energy and Commerce responded to the controversy with a request for a briefing from the company's chief executive officer on its data and security practices and for a re-sponse to national security concerns that they phrased as follows: "security an-alysts have raised the possibility that this information may expose the identities and locations of personnel at military sites and other sensitive areas."[25] One concern addressed the tracking of military supply routes and movements, presumably because of the ambient continuous data collection that can occur outside of intended app usage. The committee members also expressed concern about the possibility of deanonymizing data to identify specific individuals and also the extent of data sharing with third parties.

This one incident is illustrative of the connection between privacy regarding wearable digital devices and broader concerns about national defense. Even Internet of self wearable devices raise cross-border, global policy concerns and sometimes even national security concerns. What immediately jumps to mind is the old adage "loose lips sink ships," only now the danger is not what military personnel might say but what their technologies might reveal without their knowledge. How can military policies stay ahead of quickly evolving technologies? What default settings should companies establish for location data? It is not generally in the interest of companies to set the default to keeping data private because of business models that rely on the monetization of data or because of product dependencies on maximizing aggregate data (e.g., a heat map of user activity).

Cyber-physical system privacy connects with national security in many other ways, including terrorist surveillance and foreign intelligence access to these systems or any defense infrastructure that integrates cyber-physical components. This issue is also an extension of already routine (and already politically complicated) practices of government access to information and communication-technology data stored by private intermediaries.

Then U.S. director of national intelligence James Clapper, in his statement on the intelligence community's worldwide threat assessment before the Senate Armed Services Committee, said, "In the future, intelligence services might use the IoT for identification, surveillance, monitoring, location tracking, and targeting for recruitment, or to gain access to networks or user credentials."[26] Clapper's statement includes the recognition that, beyond traditional consumer IoT devices, augmented reality and virtual reality systems are one of the technology areas that both challenges cyber defense and also provides a new playing field for intelligence gathering. It is no longer necessary to access phone conversations or information on an encrypted smartphone when law enforcement can gain similar information from a microphone on a television or the data collected via a Bluetooth connection in a car.

Cyber-physical systems represent an entire new domain of private surveillance and therefore government surveillance—both foreign intelligence gathering and domestic surveillance, whether to identify and target political dissidents, to track terrorists, or to carry out foreign surveillance of critical cyber-physical infrastructure. Intelligence gathering, government surveillance of citizens, and law enforcement are no longer relegated to communications but now extend to the digital control systems that run transportation, energy, and other sectors.

Public policy, while traditionally in areas of uncertainty while technology evolves, will have to evolve to address the bounds of government access to encrypted (or even unencrypted) information on consumer and industrial cyber-physical systems. The capacity for foreign intelligence gathering from Internet of things technologies also helps emphasize the criticality of securing these devices, not just for privacy but for national security.

Cyber-Physical Surveillance as Social Control

The privacy-advocacy community often focuses concerns on businesses: private data collection and the privacy harms arising from how this information is monetized to deliver customized services and highly targeted online advertising. A larger problem is authoritarian government surveillance. This condition is a global political problem rather than a business-model issue, but it relies on the exact same technologies and depends on the privatization of data collection and the fusion of public and private resources.

Society has become accustomed to passive surveillance cameras designed to provide private businesses and law enforcement with information about incidents such as a theft from a store. Contemporary technologies based on artificial intelligence, machine learning, facial recognition, and other interactive real-time capabilities are completely upending the role of these cameras.

Surveillance cameras have transformed into completely different technological artifacts and arrangements of social control. They are capable of much more than passive video recording. Nowhere is the potential and reality of total government surveillance starker than in China's extensive network of surveillance cameras, many of which include facial recognition software that instantaneously connects a face to a person's identity. This pervasive control system both identifies and behaviorally nudges citizens.

Facial recognition is a powerful form of biometric identification. Media attention to China's system has been significant due to the Orwellian nature of applications and the revolutionary capability of the technology. The BBC reported on Chinese police use of facial recognition to identify and arrest a suspect who blended into a crowd of sixty thousand at a concert.[27] The Beijing Subway system announced the installation of facial scanners to identify passengers who failed to pay (as well as biometric palm scanners in lieu of tickets).[28] Similar facial recognition is also used as identification in banks, apartments, and various businesses. In Shenzen, China, enormous digital display screens shame-display the identity of those who have jaywalked, on the basis of facial recognition.[29] Perhaps the most surreal example of the privacy-compromising use of this technology is facial-recognition-controlled toilet-paper dispensers in public bathrooms in Beijing and elsewhere, designed to ration paper and solve a problem of overconsumption and so-called theft of paper. Police in Beijing also tested augmented reality glasses that perform the same functions as public cameras, including facial recognition and access to citizens' information.

Systems of distributed cameras with facial recognition and artificial intelligence capability can track location, association, and sometimes emotion. One could argue that this tracking capability is already embedded within smartphones (and it is), but there is some choice exercised by citizens in carrying a smartphone and no choice whatsoever in facial recognition surveillance. These surveillance-control systems are part of China's evolving social credit system, in which various measures of "trustworthiness" and penalties for lack of trustworthiness, whether measured by jaywalking or by politically objectionable speech, shape a social score that affects human rights such as the ability to attend certain schools, travel by plane, or stay in a luxury hotel. The same technological assemblage that enacts digital surveillance serves as an apparatus controlling material access and movement in the physical world. Connected objects from cars to cameras are technologically able to provide total government surveillance, especially in public places. Information collected about one person, in combination with information on others, creates a record of association and proximity. Systems of using facial recognition to enact widespread surveillance of citizens and collect behavioral data that feeds into its social scoring system are powerful control.

Such concerns about digital surveillance often invoke the French philosopher Michel Foucault's theorizing about the power and social control of the philosopher Jeremy Bentham's Panopticon prison design, in which a central tower enacts social control because it creates a visible, permanent, unverifiable potential surveillance in which a prisoner might be watched at any time and therefore must behave as if watched.[30] This model has utility in describing digital content systems, but cyber-physical systems subvert this model entirely. There is no central tower serving as an entry point for surveillance (the role that the display screen plays in content mediation). The surveillance is everywhere, over everyone, and increasingly in everything from cars to wearables to bodies. Where Foucault's work does apply is in suggesting that the machine of surveillance is a "machine to carry out experiments, to alter behavior, to train or correct individuals."[31] The practice of shaming jaywalkers in China on the basis of facial recognition and public display on large digital screens reverts disciplinary approaches away from private law enforcement mechanisms back to the public spectacle of the gallows.

Authentication has become more socially complicated, taking away prospects for anonymity. At one point in the Internet's history, design and governance decisions fashioned possibilities for anonymous speech and behavior online. Making unique Internet identifiers logical (software defined) rather than physical (linked to specific hardware) was one such decision. This ideal was reflected in conceptions of democratic freedom online, such as the so-called Arab Spring. What has actually happened, and to some extent needed to happen, is the establishment of systems of authentication and identity, such as the use of public-key encryption to certify that commercial and financial websites are legitimate. In the broader digital realm, it has also bled into the use of biometric identification in which systems capture, digitize, transmit, and analyze unique biological characteristics to authenticate human identity, to authorize behavior, or to enact powerful authoritarian governmental or commercial surveillance.

Biometric identification is part of the larger class of transductive inference systems in which the physical world is converted into digital systems for some control intervention. Authentication once involved a thing one knows, such as a password, or a thing one possesses in real time, such as token-based authentication or so-called two-factor authentication, in which a temporary code transmits to a smartphone. A much more powerful form of human identification is biometric: unique finger prints, voice recognition, facial recognition, retinal or iris eye scan, palm vein scan, DNA, and increasingly movement, such as typing pattern or gait analysis. Biometric transduction, in certain contexts, is an important cybersecurity or physical access technique.

Policing and law enforcement, across societies, increasingly rely on networked, continuous feedback connections to the physical world and tied to back-end public databases. These systems carry out routine activities such as catching speeders with sensors and cameras, using license-plate readers to identify stolen vehicles, and flying drones for surveillance of civil unrest.[32] Cyber-physical systems profoundly affect the capability of law enforcement and other first responders in ways that, among other goals, facilitate efficacy and minimize response time. Connected vehicle technologies can trigger traffic lights to speed the flow of an emergency vehicle. License-plate readers connected to national databases alert police to stolen vehicles or people with outstanding warrants for arrests or on terrorist watch lists. Body-worn cameras record interactions between police and citizens. Closed-circuit television cameras are ubiquitous in Beijing, Washington, DC, New York, and other major cities. Data collected in cars (as well as, of course, smartphone position data collected and sold by Internet service providers, or ISPs, to third parties) provide law enforcement with detailed location at nearly all times. These are all current technologies that are already present and routinized.

As always, the same technologies that serve democratic societies (e.g., legitimate and accountable law enforcement access to automobile data as part of an investigation) serve as modes of authoritarian control (e.g., blocking access to transportation systems as part of social control). The rapid advancement of digital identification applications in the private sector complicates these possibilities, whether the use of biometric identification to access a theme park or continuous data collection in a privately owned automobile.

The technology of facial recognition works extremely well. Facebook, Apple, Google, and other born-digital companies have already demonstrated this capability to translate real-world human biological features into digital identification. Technological change in this area trends well ahead of policy responses. There is no longer a physical boundary or technological constraint against the ubiquity and efficacy of surveillance. There are also diminishing opportunities for citizens to exercise reasonable choice to opt out of this surveillance.

Inferential Discrimination

The continuous, ubiquitous information collected via cyber-physical systems constructs new possibilities for discrimination. Cyber-utopian imaginings have envisioned the Internet as a sphere in which differences in race, sex, ethnicity, and religion vanish. Particularly in the text-dominated world of the early public Internet, one could not "see" who else was participating in discussion boards, so all were equal. This notion of equality was not necessarily promulgated by cyber libertarians but rather the businesses that inherently profited from the growth of the Internet. The 1997 "Anthem" television ad, placed by the prominent Internet service provider MCI, exemplifies this market philosophy. The now-often-analyzed ad, placed during the height of the 1990s dot-com boom, promised, "There is no race. There are no genders. There is no age. There are no infirmities. Only minds."[33]

Race, sex, sexual orientation, religion, ability, and other categories have not disappeared online but have become more complicated. For example, online harassment of women, or of people with female names, is a problem in all online spaces, from Wikipedia editing to video games.[34] As the media scholar Lisa Nakamura explains, "racism and sexism have continued to flourish on the Internet, and indeed to some extent have even come to define it, despite our supposedly 'post-racial' historical moment."[35]

Taking human communicants out of a technological system does not remove bias or discrimination. In the same way that humans have, to varying degrees, biases around race, culture, gender, class, and so on, technology is not neutral. Among the most notorious and concerning examples of racial and ethnic problems instantiated in software, facial recognition programs tagged images of African Americans as "gorillas" and images of Native American dancers with the culturally inappropriate word "costume." More generally, researchers have found that the machine-learning algorithms behind facial recognition have accuracy disparities based on skin color and male and female attributes.[36]

Autonomous or semiautonomous technologies mediate much of information exchange: bots, algorithms, artificial intelligence, and, at a minimum, technologies that reflect the values and biases of designers. Discrimination is not only a factor in design and in algorithms and machine-learning software implementations that operationalize algorithms but also in the decisions about what data to include, how it is prioritized, and assumptions about what it represents. For example, geographical/locational data can serve as an approximate indicator of race and ethnicity. Prioritization of certain classes of data over others are value judgments.

Different types of inferential and inductive discrimination are possible depending on the data collected and how it is shared. Privacy advocates and scholars have historically expressed concern about the discriminatory possibilities of private companies' digital data collection, especially massive commercial data brokers that aggregate data from multiple private-sector sources and then share this data with law enforcement and other public-sector actors.[37] In the article "The Scored Society: Due Process for Automated Predictions," Danielle Citron and Frank Pasquale examine how big-data mining is predictively used to rate individuals' suitability as citizens and consumers in areas as diverse as credit risk, employability, rental-housing reliability, and worth as a customer.[38] Data aggregation can result in real harm and stigmatization in critical life spheres—employment, housing, financial services—with very little transparency and due process.

Concerns about algorithmic scoring and data discrimination escalate in the cyber-physical space and make data privacy practices and regulations much more consequential. The type of data collection possible via cyber-physical systems has implications in authoritarian countries and democratic countries alike. Physical data collection feeds directly into authoritarian surveillance practices and citizen ranking systems. China's national social credit system already factors in variables such as speeding tickets, speech, payment histories, and many other areas of people's lives to rank trustworthiness and to determine whom the government views as good citizens. People with high scores receive favorable treatment, for example, on loans, and those with lower scores can be subjected to restrictions on travel.

In countries with less authoritarian approaches to information technology, the effects of data-gathering practices could, in effect, mirror authoritarian environments. The ultrapersonal data collection inherent in wearable and close-proximity technologies shifts the concern from the biases that enter technology design ex ante to the discriminatory practices that arise from this data collection ex post. FTC analysts acknowledge that privacy concerns are also concerns about direct harms that can arise from how the constellation of gathered data can provide a consumer profile that companies can use to determine whether to hire, insure, or provide credit to individuals.[39] Examples of consumer services directly affected by cyber-physical system data collection include the following:

- Insurance eligibility or rates
- Employment decisions
- Credit rating
- Predictive worth to businesses
- Law enforcement evidence gathering and predictive metrics
- Political communication targeting

Fitness bracelets help individuals monitor fitness level and health status. But this same data provided to insurers as a decision factor for coverage or to an employer as a precursor to employment or as part of an employee wellness program ties this information to the potential for bias against individuals because of a medical condition or lifestyle circumstance, such as being overweight or not regularly exercising. While individual personal fitness and health data anonymized and aggregated into a population health dashboard has great potential to alert public-health officials to possible disease outbreaks, this same nonanonymized information about individuals provides a quantitative input to discrimination.

Modern automobiles exemplify how connected objects, and the extent of data privacy practices around these connected objects, complicate individual experience around everything from insurance to law enforcement. The cost of car insurance increasingly relies on a customer's day-to-day driving habits, as indicated by the sensor data accumulated from connected cars. In this usage-based insurance model, insurance companies partner with car manufacturers to gain access to real-time information about location, miles driven, routes taken, speed, brake wear and tear, tire pressure, oil temperature, and other ambient data that collectively reveals drivers' safety and performance. Map data in cars includes speed limits, so this information, in combination with continuous data collection of speed, immediately indicates the extent to which a driver exceeds posted speed limits. This is a disruption to insurance-industry models, as continuous, real-time streaming transmitted directly from automobiles supplants premium calculations based on claim history.

These plans offer lower insurance premiums for drivers with safe or infrequent driving patterns, so they have tangible benefits to safe drivers. The norm is for drivers to opt in to these services, but given that simply signing up provides a discount, this creates a two-tier system for those who are willing to turn over data and those who are not. The choice to opt in or not is part of the differential framework of discrimination. Exogenous creep of data collection means that this data also enables targeted ads to customers in a highly segmented and esoteric approach based on demographic and performance information.

In the same way, law enforcement no longer requires access to phones but only access to automobile systems and intermediary networks, which can store call logs, as well as highly specific information about location and driving habits. Cars were once only mechanical devices. Now they integrate both mechanical and digital elements and are connected to networks for navigation, entertainment, roadside assistance, and specialized apps.

The considerable amount of data collected also creates a target for data thieves and identity theft and also a target for direct harm to particular individuals. Creating misleading transductive data can ruin an attack victim's credit or insurance ratings. In this regard, the possibility for discrimination is complicated not only by the privacy of collected data but also by the associated security features. Privacy depends on cybersecurity.

Rethinking Privacy for the Cyber-Physical Era

Samuel Warren and Louis Brandeis, in their celebrated 1890 *Harvard Law Review* essay "The Right to Privacy," argued that "political, social, and economic changes entail the recognition of new rights, and the common law, in its eternal youth, grows to meet the new demands of society."[40] Responding to the technological context of the rise of photography and the intrusion of newspaper society pages into personal lives, these legal thinkers envisioned privacy as the right to be left alone. They also envisioned the concept of privacy as evolutionary with societal changes.

What no one in the nineteenth century could have envisioned was that incursions into the right to be left alone would extend to people's internal life—their most intimate thoughts and private communication practices, as well as their day-to-day activities within traditionally private spheres of home life, health and medical condition, and sexual activity. Admittedly, the routine surveillance of what people are thinking (e.g., online searches, news sharing), doing (e.g., online purchases, location), and saying (e.g., social media posts, comments, messages) has already raised privacy questions that were once unimaginable.

The cyber-physical disruption pushes the bounds of privacy concerns much further, bringing digital networks into physical domains of privacy that were previously sacrosanct. One starting point for addressing cyber-physical system privacy dates back to the 1970s, when mainframe computers enabled the widespread collection and storage of personal information. In this context, a U.S. governmental advisory committee introduced the concept of fair information principles around personal electronic privacy. In the contemporary context, these ideas have evolved into a broad set of principles, the Fair Information Practice Principles (FIPPs), which have often served as a framework for privacy in policy discussions in the United States, Canada, and parts of Asia and in frameworks suggested at the Organisation for Economic Co-operation and Development (OECD).

Approaches that draw from the FIPPs framework vary by version, such as the FTC and the U.S. Department of Homeland Security (DHS) in the United States, as well as the European Union and OECD. To use one example, DHS issued the following eight principles in 2008 as a guide for its privacy program:

- Transparency. Providing notice of personal information collection, use, and dissemination
- Individual participation. Including principles of consent, access, and redress
- Purpose specification. Explaining the purpose of data collection and relevant authority
- Data minimization. Ensuring that collection is directly relevant to a specified purpose and retained only as long as necessary for this specified purpose
- Use limitation. Imposing constraints on usage and sharing for the specified purpose in the notice
- Data quality and integrity. Ensuring accuracy and relevance
- Security. Safeguarding information from unauthorized access, modification, or disclosure
- Accountability and auditing. Demonstrating compliance with principles[41]

Some of these are difficult to apply in the contemporary cyber-physical context. Setting aside the question of the extent to which these principles (and sets of similar principles) are adhered to in practice in various contexts, either by governments or the private sector, the preliminary question relevant to this study is whether they are realistically *applicable* at all to cyber-physical systems. There are some underlying themes that, while possibly ideal for the IoT, are completely unrealistic. For example, human engagement is not always possible. It is not always feasible to notify the individuals who are directly affected by data collection, nor is there always a mechanism to gain consent or allow redress. Nevertheless, the basic principles have remained influential in policy discussions and documents and are a good starting point for moving from principles to praxis.

The question of what can and should be done faces inherent challenges. As is always the case in cyber-policy debates, values come into conflict. In the realm of content control, one person's privacy is another person's censorship. In the realm of cyber-physical system control, privacy to some extent conflicts with performance and innovation. Innovation and performance of sensor and actuator systems necessitate massive data analysis. Unlike content intermediaries, for which a primary impetus for data collection is the generation of advertising revenue (as well as customized services), the data collection in cyber-physical systems is fundamental to system performance, such as vehicle navigation. Law enforcement and intelligence-gathering goals also contradict with privacy protections, such as strong encryption.

Privacy frameworks for cyber-physical systems have to start from the assumption that massive data collection is fundamental and endogenously necessary for systems to operate. Solutions also have to be system centered rather than human centered because of the implausibility of relevant individual participation and consent. These structural features escalate the importance of issues such as data minimization across systems, radical transparency, ex post accountability, and moving to a conceptualization of privacy as a broad social and economic good rather than only an individual human right.

Innovation and Performance Depend on Mass Data Collection

One complication in addressing contemporary digital privacy issues is structural. Mass data collection in cyber-physical systems is endemic to the very operation of the systems. The collection of data via a constant feedback loop of sensors and actuators is part of the service itself. In the information intermediary space, a structural part of massive data collection is for the monetization of free services via targeted online advertising. Data restrictions in the content intermediation space can erode business models. Data restrictions in the cyber-physical intermediation space are restrictions on the operation of these systems.

Public policy has to realistically acknowledge that much social and economic good emanates from this constant data collection. Embedded devices designed to aid the disabled and elderly or care for the sick require continuous data collection. Cyber-physical systems in the agriculture sector can help to reduce pesticides, maximize food output, and reduce water consumption. Continuous feedback sensors in oil pipelines can quickly flag a leak that would, if undetected, result in environmental damage. Intelligent traffic systems can minimize delays and associated pollution. License-plate readers help police identify stolen vehicles or people with warrants out for their arrest. All of these activities require continuous sensing, networking, processing, and feedback. These structural dependencies and the associated societal benefits have to be acknowledged and even facilitated in privacy approaches.

Consent Is Complicated

Cyber-physical systems disrupt privacy-protection ideologies in another fundamental way. So-called notice and choice principles no longer easily apply. A traditional privacy recommendation, especially espoused by those who call primarily for voluntary industry self-regulation, is "notice and choice," meaning that companies should transparently provide notice of privacy approaches, and consumers should then provide consent to these practices by agreeing to terms of service. The consumer agrees to the terms, called the "fine print" in an earlier age, and thereby agrees to the data-gathering practices of the device manufacturer. Notice and choice are already problematic concepts, even when it is feasible to provide notice and gain consent, but they often do not apply at all to the Internet of things.

When individuals primarily accessed the Internet from personal computers and laptops, this provided a natural boundary demarcating when one was online or offline. It also provided a clear portal through which individuals could agree to the terms of online services and platforms. The advent of smartphones and other portable devices obviously changed the parameters of this boundary, providing 24/7 access that accompanied one's every movement. But even this ubiquitous, continuous, and portable device access provided a clear gateway into the online realm and could therefore provide a screen boundary.

Screen-display technology allowed for various layers of choice: the device could be turned off or left home; applications could be selected or removed; and individuals could choose whether or not to agree to the terms of service. Apart from specific statutes around medical, financial, and children's data, this policy prescription of notice and choice dominated privacy approaches for decades.

The privacy scholar Helen Nissenbaum has coined the expression "post-consent privacy" to challenge the notion of user choice and consent around privacy issues in the online public sphere.[42] Consent-based approaches have not sufficed even for content platforms like social media, with which consumers directly interact. Research indicates that privacy policies are rarely read, insufficiently comprehensible, and completely disconnected from users' privacy expectations.[43] Notice and choice, including meaningful disclosures about privacy policies, have been necessary but not sufficient to address privacy.

To a much greater extent, consent is complicated, and sometimes not even possible, in cyber-physical systems. Transparency, notice, and choice are not always possible. Nissenbaum's concept of "post-consent privacy" is ideally suited for framing this fundamental condition of privacy in cyber-physical systems. Cyber-physical systems do not always have a one-to-one relationship to an affected person or a formal relationship to the person at all. Humans are no longer always end users; they might not even be aware of either the embedded device or the nature of data collection.

Even when one can explicitly agree to terms of service for privacy practices, consent becomes complicated. Embedded systems often change hands without the opportunity to secure consent from the new owner. A further problem is that an agreement to allow collection and sharing with third parties provides no consent or agreement for how the third party will then use or share information.

A more general problem is that the digital embeddedness of the material world is not visible to humans because of the relative concealment of sensors, networks, transponders, and back-end data-analysis systems. Miniaturized microprocessor transponders in everything from manufacturing supply chains to consumer retail products and home objects are often not obviously apparent to humans. The wireless networks and transponders that sense the tags are also not readily visible; neither are the back-end data-management systems.

The nature of privacy in the cyber-physical domain is most complicated because data collection occurs on systems that are in the control or ownership of other people and businesses. It is not always possible to opt out, to provide consent, or even to be aware of the surveillance. This circumstance involves governments and industry but also especially the constant information gathering practices of technology end users.

"Sousveillance" (from the French: "view from below") as opposed to "surveillance" (view from above) has already evolved into a term that captures the essence of this ubiquitous, distributed capture of images, video, sound, data movement, temperature, and facial expressions by everyday citizens rather than by centralized authorities or by private industry. Rather than organizations observing people, "sousveillance" usually refers to the inverse Panopticon, whereby citizens observe authorities.[44] A citizen recording police activity on a smartphone is an example of the disruption of the primarily one-way surveillance flow of authorities enacting surveillance on customers, citizens, and everyday human activities into more symmetrical observational flows that can hold governments and large corporations (and other citizens) accountable.

Attributing empowerment to the ability to surveil the surveillers via wearable technologies, as many people have, misses a key feature of technical architecture and governance. The observation possible via embedded systems does not just observe authorities but everyone. The concern is not as much being swept up in ambient surveillance as providing a fire hose of data to the private intermediaries that collect, share, and monetize the data and, by extension, to the governments—authoritarian and democratic alike—that obtain this information from private companies.

The central characteristic of augmented reality systems—the ongoing gaze and processing of the surrounding world—creates this privacy concern for those who are unknowingly caught up in this recording. Someone wearing an AR device could record conversations, capture images and video, and connect into voice or facial recognition systems, all without the knowledge or consent of the people in the vicinity of the device.

Consent becomes complicated endogenously, in objects in the most proximal and intimate spheres, and especially exogenously, in the pervasive context of measurement collection from devices and systems with which humans have no direct contractual arrangement or even awareness. Ambient, background data collection in all material terrains of life complicates consent, thereby making it difficult for any one person to have meaningful choice or to opt out.

Companies should absolutely disclose the data collected and seek consent when possible. But if individual notice and choice is infeasible for those who are swept up in digital physical systems, in one's own home, another person's home, in an industrial or retail setting, or in public, addressing privacy from a policy standpoint has to extend beyond traditional concepts of individual notice and choice.

Cyber-Physical Privacy as a Societal Good

Even while pervasive data collection is endemically necessary for real-world feedback systems involving digital sensors and actuators, and because of the intrinsic barriers to meaningful individual consent, privacy frameworks also have to be an inherently structural element of these systems. The privacy challenges already explained make clear that the word "privacy" itself is complicated, multivariable, and still difficult to define. It is culturally elastic, susceptible to co-option from forces with an interest in its definition, and highly context specific.[45]

The challenges in the cyber-physical domain connect variously to a patchwork of concerns: discrimination, government surveillance, foreign intelligence, boundary control, anonymity, confidentiality, personal information dissemination, safety and health, harassment, identify formation, and the right to simply be left alone.

One historical feature, and now limitation, of privacy advocacy is that it approaches this area as an individual problem rather than a global economic and political problem. An inherent public policy asymmetry exists. Public policy views the advantages of massive data collection as a public good while viewing the harms in this same context as an individual problem.

Especially in the cyber-physical arena, privacy has broad public purposes, in the same way as freedom of expression is not only about individual rights but also about public power and democratic stability. Freedom of expression is an individual civil liberty but also more broadly facilitates democratic self-government and fosters a marketplace of ideas.

The privacy law scholar Julie Cohen has explained why "privacy is an indispensable structure of liberal democratic political systems," with "freedom from surveillance . . . foundational to the capacity for innovation" as well as "foundational to the practice of informed and reflective citizenship."[46] Considering the stakes of cyber-physical privacy to national security, democracy, and the digital economy, as well as trust of citizens in these systems, the importance of viewing privacy as a public good with economic and political implications increases considerably; privacy is a societal problem requiring structural solutions that are not only legal but multistakeholder. No one solution alone will incentivize or require the privacy practices necessary for everything from national security to trust in the digital economy.

Cyber-physical system privacy structures will require principles of data minimization and radical transparency, as well as a multistakeholder approach of enforcement that includes legal constraints, voluntary industry measures, third-party certification, citizen education and engagement, and technical solutions.

Data Minimization

One argument that society should not be concerned about the privacy of connected material devices is that each digitized device collects data used specifically in the service of expediency and convenience surrounding that particular device. Referring back to the refrigerator example, the appliance collects data used to aid a household in determining what food to buy at the grocery store or to be delivered via a grocery delivery service.

Historically, data has extended far and wide beyond that needed to operate a device or create convenience and expediency around the device and has extended far beyond the company from which the device was purchased. The data fuels the business decisions of industries even at the furthest perimeters of the consumer interaction. In other cases, data is combined because of control monocultures that tie together devices made by the same manufacturer.

The automobile is a prime example of the exogenous creep of data beyond the point of accumulation and beyond the company with which the consumer has a direct relationship. Most modern automobiles embed built-in data-collection mechanisms. Data includes information that one might expect, such as speed, brake pressure, seat-belt usage, and acceleration. This information contributes to safety and performance improvements in future vehicle designs, generally, or makes calculations about maintenance needs of the data-generating car, specifically. But cars are capable of gathering even more personal information, such as entertainment predilections, body weight, and location. The location-gathering data in itself creates privacy concerns because it captures some of the most private actions of individuals, such as where one shops, eats, lives, and works and whom one visits. The tracking mechanism in a car can gather highly personal data that precludes privacy of movement, association, labor, and consumption. Cars also have built-in cameras (e.g., backup cameras) and so are capable of collecting images as well as other data.

What is automobile data gathered for, in addition to its contributions to vehicle safety and maintenance and possibly even future reduction in environmental emissions? Answering this question only requires an examination of the business models and product descriptions of the third-party companies involved in back-end data-integration markets for connected cars. Data-integration companies seek to provide value by combining data from car manufacturers, vehicle data from individual cars, and data from mobility-service providers.[47]

In the same way that online communication data is monetized and drives the business models of information intermediaries, car and other device data is monetized and used for targeted delivery of ads in cars, "smart city" traffic management or toll planning, insurance rating/scoring for drivers, or data suggesting where gas stations, convenience stores, and other retail sites should be optimally located.

The larger concern comes with the combining of data sets. As the U.S. National Science and Technology Council's "National Privacy Research Strategy" suggested, "The availability of disparate data sets is setting the stage for a 'mosaic effect,' where analysis across data sets can reveal private information or generate inaccurate inferences, even though in isolation the data sets may not raise privacy issues."[48]

The principle of data minimization, although it sounds like an oxymoron, has historically been associated with digital privacy in all contexts. The underlying idea is that the gathering, holding, use, and sharing of data should be relegated to the immediate purpose and context in which a specific task is occurring and only shared beyond this purpose with clear and explicit consent.

Data-minimization approaches are critically essential for cyber-embedded physical systems and serve multiple purposes. Given that information-intensive sensors and actuators and back-end or edge data-analysis systems are intrinsically necessary for a system to operate, this operational data, explicitly stated in advance, forms a natural boundary around the scope of data collection that accords with the reasonable expectations of those who are affected by this collection. Data minimization, as a principle, can serve both the intrinsic requirement for data feedback loops within cyber-physical systems and the societal advantages of providing a reasonable expectation for data not to be shared beyond the innovation and technical efficiency goals of the system. Industry-specific considerations (e.g., embedded medical devices versus industrial control systems) will affect the balance between operational efficiency and privacy. However, bounding data on the basis of operational performance (rather than aggregation and monetization of data for direct marketing) not only minimizes harm to those who are potentially affected but also limits the lure and impact of cybersecurity data breaches.

Moving from the content intermediary norm of collecting as much data as possible to store, aggregate, combine, and sell to third parties for monetization to a cyber-physical system norm of collecting the data necessary for innovation and operational efficiency would be a radical change, but it is one that is indispensable for privacy, innovation, trust, and critical infrastructure protection. Privacy advocacy often pursues a one-trick pony of national law applied to particular technologies. Considering the rapid pace of technological change in this area and considering that technological systems cross borders in ways that complicate jurisdiction, this approach alone is problematic. Data minimization and transparency, security, accountability, and other relevant principles require a multipronged approach involving technical design and standards, regional policies (e.g., the European Union's General Data Protection Regulation, or GDPR, adapts data minimization as a core tenet), court rulings and precedents, industry self-regulation, consumer education, and third-party certification.

Shifting to Multistakeholder Privacy

Cyber-physical systems present the greatest privacy complications ever to confront humanity. The success or failure to address privacy will have implications for trust in the digital economy, human rights, and innovation. Proposed solutions are too often relegated to institutional mechanisms that are readily understood or visible to policymakers and scholars, such as corporate terms of service or laws. Privacy is shaped multivariably by technical design, institutional policies, market demand, and legal constraints. Like most areas of Internet governance, it is a multistakeholder problem requiring multistakeholder solutions.

Technical solutions have to be part of a broader framework of privacy for the Internet of things. Meaningfully addressing privacy has to commence in the design stage of products and services and even prior to design, in the development of common technical specifications that can be used to address privacy. The Internet engineering community has emphasized that "IoT devices often have even greater privacy concerns due to access to the user's physical environment and personal data."[49]

Voluntary industry privacy measures and third-party rankings and certifications of these measures are also components of advancing IoT privacy. Industry transparency is critical. Even though notice and consent are complicated, transparency is not. An important part of accountability is corporate openness, from system design and implementation to usage and management. Some areas requiring open disclosure of privacy practices include: *privacy design,* transparency about privacy considerations designed into technical architecture; *privacy operation,* disclosure of company policies on the collection, use, sharing, re-purposing, and retention of data, including public-private data sharing; and *privacy crisis management,* disclosure of data breaches and security vulnerabilities. Security practices are closely tied to privacy, especially cryptographic approaches that prevent the unauthorized access of highly intimate stored or transmitted data and authentication methods that regulate access to devices and data. Because of the heterogeneity of cyber-physical systems, industry privacy principles and approaches will vary by sector. Automobile manufacturers' privacy norms will be different from medical-device manufacturers' privacy practices.

Many chapters of Internet innovation have proceeded well without heavy regulatory constraints. IoT privacy, commensurate with IoT security, does not necessarily have an inherent market incentive for privacy practices. In many ways, market incentives discourage privacy practices. Companies have an economic incentive to monetize data by third-party sharing or retaining data for unforeseen future repurposing. Companies have a disincentive to disclose when data breaches have occurred. Furthermore, as described earlier, the very operational success of data-science-driven systems requires enormous data inputs.

Because the technologies and consumer bases of transnational companies cross borders, constraints in one region have sweeping effects on constraints in others. The European Union's GDPR is probably the most comprehensive example of governmental constraint on data-collection practices and also of the way local or regional policies reverberate globally. The European Union approaches privacy of personal information as a fundamental right, even while acknowledging that it must be balanced against other fundamental rights. The regulation has strong provisions for requiring maximal transparency, the right of citizens to access data that has been collected, the right of erasure (the right to be forgotten), and strong data-minimization requirements, such as the following: "The processing of personal data for purposes other than those for which the personal data were initially collected should be allowed only where the processing is compatible with the purposes for which the personal data were initially collected."[50] The GDPR has had some harmonization effect globally because large companies have adapted privacy policies to comply with these requirements, at least to a certain extent. Law alone is insufficient, but necessary, to fulfill the Warren and Brandeis 1890 charge to meet the new demands of society.

4

Cyber-Physical Security

IN THE MIDST OF POLITICAL ACRIMONY OVER ongoing investigations into Russian interference in the 2016 U.S. presidential election, DHS and the FBI issued a technical alert warning about the Russian government cyber-targeting critical Western infrastructure sectors including "energy, nuclear, commercial facilities, water, aviation, and critical manufacturing sectors."[1] The report explained how Russian government actors had infiltrated, among other things, energy-sector networks. These Russian actors, rather than attacking the intended sites directly, began by infiltrating less secure organizations that already had a trusted relationship with the target organizations and used these trusted parties as periphery levers from which to direct malware, spear-phishing, and other techniques toward the intended targets. According to the intelligence assessment, "In multiple instances, the threat actors accessed workstations and servers on a corporate network that contained data output from control systems within energy generation facilities. The threat actors accessed files pertaining to ICS or supervisory control and data acquisition (SCADA) systems."[2]

The potential of cyberattacks to also be physical-world attacks crystallized in December 2015, when hackers disrupted Ukrainian electric-power companies, causing power outages for approximately 225,000 customers.[3] A DHS investigation described the incident, which targeted three Ukrainian power-distribution companies, as "synchronized and coordinated" and executed using "either existing remote administration tools at the operating system level or remote industrial control system client software via virtual private network connections."[4]

The Ukrainian president, a year later, acknowledged a concentrated series of thousands of cyberattacks targeting state institutions including the treasury, as well as part of the Kiev power grid, and attributed these attacks to Russian security services.[5]

It is difficult to call such activities anything short of cyber war or certainly at least cyber conflict. The technological acceleration of the cyber-physical world is matched by the acceleration and sophistication of attacks. As Gordon M. Goldstein of the Council on Foreign Relations summarized, "While some bureaucratic actors within its government are not capable of operating at Internet speed, America's adversaries—hostile sovereign powers, transnational criminal enterprises, hacker and terrorist collectives—continue to attack with all the relentless intensity and innovation afforded by a constantly evolving arsenal of modern cyberweapons, penetration technologies and tactics."[6]

"Welcome to the world of high-risk technologies," wrote the sociologist Charles Perrow about the inevitable risk of large-scale systems in his classic 1984 book *Normal Accidents: Living with High-Risk Technologies.*[7] Primarily writing in the context of nuclear-energy systems and in the aftermath of the Three-Mile Island nuclear accident, Perrow argued that, regardless of safety measures put into place, accidents are inevitable. Features such as system interdependencies and interactive complexity exacerbate this risk. The commercialization and globalization of the Internet would surely be part of Perrow's narrative if written today.

Cyber dependencies in all of society's critical systems elevate the Internet to the ranks of high-risk systems, like nuclear energy, in which the consequence of failures and outages have potentially catastrophic effects. Cybersecurity policy decisions should begin with the recognition that digital technologies will never be 100 percent secure, even while the term "secure" itself is culturally and politically malleable. History suggests caution about claims, usually from nontech communities, that, for example, "blockchain technology provides unbreakable security."

Cyber risk is inevitable, in the same way that there is always engineering risk in other complex arenas, from nuclear-energy systems to space programs. From the *Challenger* space shuttle explosion to the Fukushima Daiichi nuclear disaster, the history of technological success is the history of technological failure.

Internet history is replete with discoveries or exploitations of vulnerabilities and security holes. Beginning with the Morris worm of 1988, attacks on the Internet have exploited design or implementation weaknesses. A federal court convicted the Cornell University graduate student Robert Morris of violating the United States Computer Fraud and Abuse Act (CFAA) by releasing a self-propagating worm that exploited a known security vulnerability in the Internet.[8] Of the fewer than one hundred thousand people using the Internet at the time, primarily in universities, research institutions, and military installations, approximately 10 percent were affected by this multiday outage.[9] What has changed is that the consequences of outages have dramatically risen with growth and with socioeconomic dependency on digital systems.

The state of cybersecurity, generally, is alarming. Critical problems exist deep within infrastructure and seep into components that enter many industries. Some are product specific. Some are politically motivated attacks. Some subvert cybersecurity innovations into modes of attack, such as using cryptography for ransomware assaults that cryptographically lock systems until a ransom is paid, often in Bitcoin. Ransomware enters systems through either an unpatched (or previously unknown) software vulnerability or a phishing prompt in which a system user clicks on a link or opens an attachment through which malicious code downloads onto a device. Already, hospitals and health-care systems are targets for ransomware attacks in which patients' records and medical information systems are locked up until the health-care provider agrees to pay a ransom. Symantec's 2017 *Internet Security Threat Report* estimated that the average ransom payment demanded in such attacks rose from $294 in 2015 to $1,077 in 2016 and that the number of ransomware infections increased by 36 percent.

The infamous NotPetya ransomware was a malware exploit of Windows vulnerabilities that locked files until the victim (hospitals, individuals, financial institutions, etc.) paid a Bitcoin ransom. Even with a payment, there was no guarantee that perpetrators would unlock systems. The attack spread across North and South America, Europe, and Asia and caused billions of dollars in damage. The U.S. government has publicly attributed the ransomware attack to the Russian military. The Trump White House, in 2018 attributed the NotPetya attack to Russia. According to the White House press release, NotPetya "was part of the Kremlin's ongoing effort to destabilize Ukraine and demonstrates ever more clearly Russia's involvement in the ongoing conflict. This was also a reckless and indiscriminate cyber-attack that will be met with international consequences."[10]

Ransomware approaches are likely to target cyber-physical objects, not only online systems. Attacks that exploit vulnerabilities to shut down a transportation system or energy-delivery system or medical device not only will be dangerous but will also have chilling effects on trust in technology.

The Heartbleed bug was one of the most notorious infrastructure vulnerabilities, involving an exposure in OpenSSL (a widespread software implementation of core Internet infrastructure security protocols) allowing remote attackers to view critical data, "possibly including user authentication credentials and secret keys, through incorrect memory handling in the TLS [Transport Layer Security] heartbeat extension."[11] Vulnerabilities in software and hardware, generally, can infiltrate cyber-physical products. Vulnerability discoveries and attacks are incessant, with some of the most critical breaches scarcely entering the popular press, such as the Meltdown and Spectre attacks that can disclose sensitive information by taking advantage of "CPU [computer processing unit] hardware implementations . . . vulnerable to side-channel attacks."[12]

Many of the most high-profile security incidents are naturally massive data breaches. The 2013 Target data breach affected the credit card information of forty million customers and personal information (including home addresses) of seventy million customers.[13] Yahoo! disclosed, in 2016, that hackers had stolen the account information of more than five hundred million users in 2014. The company attributed the theft of information to a state-sponsored actor and admitted that the personally identifiable data stolen included names, email addresses, phone numbers, birth dates, passwords, and in certain cases security questions.[14] Three months after the disclosure of this theft of personal data of more than five hundred million user accounts, Yahoo! then announced that a third party informed the company of a separate previous incident involving theft of personal information from more than one billion user accounts, it believed, by the same state-sponsored actor.[15]

As a clear indicator that one does not need to be an "Internet user" to be affected by a data breach, the consumer-credit-reporting giant Equifax disclosed a data breach affecting 145 million people.[16] According to the company's account of the incident, the personal information exposed in the data breach was highly sensitive—names, Social Security numbers, birth dates, home addresses, and in some cases credit card numbers and driver's license numbers.[17]

Security is never only about technology. It is political. Infrastructure security is intertwined with political power. The cybersecurity arena has become the primary locus for global power struggles over Internet governance. More than any other area, the design and implementation of cybersecurity mediates competing societal values. Strong security protects economic activity such as online banking and commerce and also facilitates privacy and data protection. Conversely, weaker security is sometimes required to serve intelligence gathering, law enforcement, and national security. High-profile debates over cybersecurity make these tensions visible. One prime example was the Apple encryption controversy about whether law enforcement should or could force Apple to develop a mechanism to access an encrypted phone in the wake of the San Bernardino terrorist attacks. There is rising public attention to cybersecurity because of the stakes of these controversies and especially questions around election hacking.

The global digital economy, democracy, and the public sphere depend on the stability and security of cyberspace. An outage in infrastructure is not just a technical outage but a disruption to financial flows and to basic social and economic functioning in the modern era. Trust in online banking systems, digital commerce, digital health-care systems, and transportation-management systems depends on strong security, whether through end-to-end encryption, error detection and correction, access control via virtual private networks and firewalls, or authentication via public-key cryptography or certificate authorities. Cybersecurity is also a precursor for civil liberties. Privacy requires encryption and access control. Speech requires reliable infrastructure because a technical outage blocks communication flows.

Increasingly, democracy itself depends on cybersecurity. Data breaches, infiltration of networks, and hacking erode the stability of democratic systems, individual civil liberties, and trust in the economy. Trust in digital systems is a precursor for basic functioning in the world. These points of security and trust are points of control over commerce, the public sphere, and individual privacy.

Part of infrastructure-embedded control also lies in the cumulative potential energy of state cyber-offense capability, both politically engineered code and also knowledge of vulnerabilities and code that exploit these vulnerabilities, usually called zero-day vulnerability and exploit stockpiling. It used to be that the discovery of protocol or software vulnerabilities would be shared with the software or hardware manufacturer for correction. Now the hoarding and stockpiling of digital vulnerabilities is both a market phenomenon and a source of state cyber power. One clear control arena around cybersecurity pertains to vulnerability disclosure.

The political force with the greatest cybersecurity proficiency—both offensive and defensive—increasingly controls the economy, the political sphere, and the international security arena. As such, cybersecurity is the most pressing problem of the modern era. A joint U.S.-UK technical alert issued by DHS, the FBI, and the United Kingdom's National Cyber Security Centre (NCSC) in 2018 claimed "high confidence that Russian state-sponsored cyber actors are using compromised routers to conduct man-in-the-middle attacks to support espionage, extract intellectual property, maintain persistent access to victim networks, and potentially lay a foundation for future offensive operations."[18] National security now depends on routing and protocol security, as much as on the protection of data stores and the securing of end devices.

The work of Ron Deibert and his Citizen Lab at the University of Toronto has theorized and explained connections between cybersecurity and control struggles. In *Black Code: Inside the Battle for Cyberspace* (2013), Deibert explains the subterranean battles over cybersecurity at the nexus of rising state power, cyber espionage, and the central role of private intermediary power underneath it all.[19]

Many cybersecurity attacks are indeed politically motivated. In 2014, Sony Pictures experienced an incursion in which hackers obtained and publicized sensitive internal corporate data including email records and employee salaries and also prematurely released upcoming Sony films. The "Guardians of Peace" group claiming responsibility was seeking the cancellation of an upcoming Sony movie, *The Interview,* because its members objected to the story line's inclusion of a plot to assassinate North Korean leader Kim Jong-Un. Some U.S. sources, including the FBI and the Obama administration, attributed the attack to North Korean sources, although technically, the attack could have been carried out by a disgruntled employee or political operative inside Sony. In the attack's aftermath, North Korea's Internet connection to the rest of the world went down, with some North Korean sources reportedly blaming the U.S. government. Whether or not the technical particulars of this cybersecurity attack and counterattack are ever publicly released, it serves as an exemplar of the increasing politicization of the Internet.

The future of the subterranean Internet—the Dark Web—raises even greater concerns for human security and Internet stability. Many cybersecurity breaches are *visible* and public examples of both the network's vulnerability and the increasing economic and political stakes of hacking. Much political and economic conflict, however, is occurring in *less visible* clandestine areas of cyberspace. The term "Dark Web" refers to the part of cyberspace used for activities shielded from search engines and typically reliant on sophisticated anonymizing technologies. It is often used for unlawful activities such as markets for identity theft, zero-day exploits, assassins, weapons, human trafficking, and the illegal drug trade, but it is used for lawful communication as well.

How do public-interest debates around digital security transform in the realm of cyber-physical systems? The embedding of digital technologies in the material world, and the ensuing control struggles therein, transforms cybersecurity and digital-control debates into a monumental concern. Cybersecurity risks that once primarily involved compromising personal privacy or disrupting interpersonal communications and information access now include the prospects of harming human life, disrupting critical industrial sectors, serving as a more potent arena for global conflict, and potentially influencing the outcome of democratic elections.

To what extent can cyber objects be susceptible to ransomware? What is the appropriate balance between law enforcement access to data and privacy when the data in question is in the most intimate physical objects surrounding human social and economic life? Who is responsible for securing cyber-physical systems that often change ownership or reach end-of-life and are no longer upgradeable or never were upgradeable in the first instance? What cybersecurity requirement mandates should be designed into cyber objects? The political and economic dependency on cybersecurity accords with society's rising dependency on digital physical infrastructure. The security of this infrastructure is now a precursor for human security and safety, as well as the stability of the digital economy and systems of democracy.

Cyber-physical systems complicate already-controversial cybersecurity governance debates. One of these debates involves the question of when governments should notify manufacturers and the public of vulnerabilities they detect, versus stockpiling knowledge of these vulnerabilities and exploits based on these bugs for cyber offense. The significant, sometimes life-and-death, implications of cyber-physical systems complicate the public-interest calculation about whether to hoard or disclose vulnerabilities, as well as other contentious cybersecurity governance issues such as the legality of security research and the debate about government access to encryption back doors.

Material Terrains of Cybersecurity Conflict

It can no longer be argued that bullets will never be fired online. This argument had a rational basis when one viewed Internet policy only through the lens of information content. Content-centric policy issues such as free speech, morality, defamation, and intellectual property rights seldom raise issues of immediate human security. The blending of offline and online components upends this argument. Sabotaging the brakes on a car, incapacitating a medical device, and disrupting power-distribution systems can have the same dangerous effects as conventional weapons. Cybersecurity once only pertained to what happened "online." Now it pertains as much to the physical world as the virtual. The consequences of all cybersecurity problems and solutions—encryption, authentication, access, identity management, public-key cryptography—escalate. Without strong security, unauthorized interests, from criminal hackers to foreign adversaries, can gain access to the most intimate details of one's day-to-day life. Cybersecurity now has graver implications for consumer safety, the digital economy, critical industrial infrastructure, cyber conflict, and systems of democracy. All of these concerns amplify the economic consequences of cybersecurity breaches, such as loss of business functionality, reputational damage to the affected manufacturer, or theft of intellectual property such as the algorithms and other trade-secrecy-protected information that can be leaked during a security breach.

Cyber-Physical Security and International Conflict

Cyberspace is already the fifth domain of warfare, along with land, sea, air, and space. It is both a defensive sphere and a vector for offensive attacks. Cyber-physical systems raise the stakes for defensive cyber strategy against foreign adversaries and nonstate actors and are a clear terrain of cyber offense. The Stuxnet code targeting Iranian nuclear reactors is an example, as are the Russian attacks on the Ukrainian power systems. The future of espionage will target cyber-physical systems as much as communication systems. The ability to gather data about traffic patterns and energy consumption may have more utility in information warfare and espionage than audio or text-based transmissions among military personnel or political leaders do. Militaries also use IoT devices as part of operations.

Concern about critical infrastructure security has a long history, especially in the United States. In 1996, prior to the global spread of the Internet and preceding the September 11, 2001, terrorist attack on the United States, President Bill Clinton issued an executive order establishing a President's Commission on Critical Infrastructure Protection that identified cyberterrorism as a threat to physical systems: "Today, the right command set over a network to a power generating station's control computer could be just as effective as a backpack full of explosives, and the perpetrator would be harder to identify and apprehend."[20]

After September 11, 2001, concern about the cyberterrorism threat to critical infrastructure escalated. The U.S. "National Strategy to Secure Cyberspace" acknowledged the importance of cybersecurity to address the context of computer networks controlling real-world utility systems including water distribution, the electrical grid, and transportation systems, as well as financial markets and other information-dependent industries.[21] This concern primarily addressed the role of information-control systems in keeping physical systems operational.

The embedding of digital sensors and actuators into these material systems complicates security risks. Twenty years after the 1996 President's Commission on Critical Infrastructure, a new Commission on Enhancing National Cybersecurity sounded an alarm about the risks associated with digitally embedded material systems. "Although this connectivity has the potential to revolutionize most industries and many facets of life, the possible harm that malicious actors could cause by exploiting these technologies to gain access to parts of our critical infrastructure, given the current state of cybersecurity, is immense."[22]

Even while national security depends on cybersecurity, the two forces of cyber offense and defense are often in opposition. Balancing countervailing objectives of offense and defense shapes many policy debates, from export controls to encryption-strength restrictions to decisions about when to disclose known vulnerabilities in software. Weak security is sometimes in the interest of intelligence gathering and counterterrorism. Strong end-to-end encryption, for example, restricts law enforcement's access to digital information, even while that access is necessary to protect national critical infrastructure from costly and damaging attacks.

Politically motivated cyber conflict is very real. North Korean malicious cyber activity is referred to by U.S. authorities as "HIDDEN COBRA."[23] The virulent "WannaCry" ransomware locked up hundreds of thousands of computers worldwide by exploiting a critical vulnerability in Windows systems. The malware was technically a worm in that it spread quickly and autonomously by scanning for and exploiting vulnerable systems. Microsoft had issued a bulletin notifying customers about the vulnerability and issuing patches to mitigate the problem, but systems that were not yet upgraded or using older, unsupported versions of the operating system remained vulnerable.[24] Victims of the attack spanned more than one hundred countries, with Asia and the European Union hit particularly hard. The attack infiltrated numerous industry sectors including financial services, manufacturing, and telecommunications. Hospitals were affected, disrupting the ability of medical professionals to access patient records, appointment schedules, and essentially deliver health care.[25] The WannaCry perpetrators demanded payment in Bitcoin in exchange for a promised decryption key that would allegedly unlock the disabled systems.

The consensus assessment of governments in Australia, Canada, Japan, New Zealand, the United Kingdom, and the United States, as well as Microsoft Corporation, attributed the destructive attack to North Korea.[26]

The North Korea–originating attack had an even more politically charged component that speaks to the politicization of cybersecurity. The software vulnerability at the heart of the attack had been detected initially by the U.S. National Security Agency, which originally withheld rather than disclosed the vulnerability and which developed cyber-offensive code to potentially use for national security reasons. The malicious code used in the WannaCry attack was allegedly developed by the NSA and appropriated by North Korea in a cyber incursion into NSA systems.[27] Because the malicious code exploited a vulnerability in Microsoft Windows, this is an example of how governments sometimes withhold knowledge of software vulnerabilities and developing cyber weapons that exploit these vulnerabilities, rather than immediately reporting them to the product developer. The rising stakes of cyber-physical systems should factor into the balance between strong cybersecurity and approaches that leave vulnerabilities unpatched, a policy debate addressed later in this chapter.

Cyberattacks frequently target the energy sector and other physical infrastructure systems, especially in Europe and North America.[28] Intelligence sources have attributed numerous energy-sector attacks to Russian actors. To understand the vulnerability and solutions, it is helpful to understand how these attacks take place. Technical explanations from the United States Computer Emergency Readiness Team (US-CERT) provide intricate details.[29] In short, attackers often initially focus on organizations on the periphery of the intended target but with a trusted relationship with the targeted organization. The initial attack begins with well-established and easy-to-carry-out techniques such as spear-phishing attempts that ultimately gain access to a site's source code, email credentials, and virtual private network (VPN) connections. The attacker then weaponizes these compromised assets, such as implanting malicious code on a website that is trusted by individuals in the targeted organization. The attacker can then collect users' credentials, access the organization's network, download tools from a remote server, conduct reconnaissance on the internal network, and ultimately access files related to ICS or SCADA systems. These systems monitor and control many physical processes.

Considering the cyber embeddedness of these physical processes, it is self-evident how national security depends on cybersecurity of these systems. The private sector operates and therefore secures these systems, further demonstrating the privatization of essential governance functions. National security depends on cybersecurity, which depends on both public and private actors.

Consumer Safety Depends on Cyber-Physical Security

Security researchers funded by the Defense Advanced Research Projects Agency (DARPA) demonstrated (including live on *60 Minutes*) the ability to wirelessly connect to a car and disrupt braking and acceleration by remotely hacking into the car's emergency communication systems.[30] Autonomous vehicles are likely to save lives by eliminating human error, but they create a new set of risks, due to design error or vulnerability to hacking or both. Consumer safety and the protection of property now depend on cybersecurity.

Critical breaches sometimes masquerade as whimsical news items, such as the hack of a casino's fish tank. Attackers traced to Finland infiltrated a Wi-Fi-connected fish tank and, by extension, the casino's network.[31] By accessing the tank, the hackers circumvented the casino's network security measures in order to access and exfiltrate sensitive data from the casino's servers. Fish tanks, or at least their constitutive parts, are now connected to the same global network ecosystem that connects people online to their bank accounts. Inexpensive, connected fish-tank products on the market include tank power-management systems, underwater cameras, salinity-management devices, and aquarium thermometers. The purpose of these devices is primarily monitoring to ensure that the environmental conditions—temperature, water level, salinity, food delivery—are optimal for fish and to enable the owner to monitor and administer systems remotely.

Everyday cyber-embedded objects enhance human life (and, apparently, fish life). Like other technological shifts, new innovations create new risk sets. A network is only as secure as its least secure component. One insecure device, such as a connected lightbulb, can expose Wi-Fi or other network credentials to hackers or other malign actors, who can gain access to other resources on the network or implant malicious code for launching a DDoS or other attack.

Smart door locks exemplify this combination of human convenience and potential security risk. These are keyless entry systems connected with Bluetooth or Wi-Fi, or Z-Wave or another low-energy mesh-wireless approach designed specifically for smart-home automation. Network-connected locks provide home owners with great conveniences and control capabilities. Owners use voice commands or smartphone-app commands to activate the lock and remotely set access controls and schedules. Some provide geofencing features that automatically lock the door if the owner's mobile phone position moves outside a designated perimeter. Similar to home alarm systems, the devices send alerts to a home owner in the event of a forced entry or system tamper. These locks are especially convenient for vacation-rental owners who use the system to remotely manage access for customers.

The convenience of network-connected smart door locks is offset by the notorious cybersecurity risks of these devices. Policy conferences on the IoT (and security conferences like DEF CON in Las Vegas) have sometimes included a demonstration in which a presenter hacks into a smart door lock. A team of UC Berkeley engineers examining smart-lock security found that "flaws in the design, implementation, and interaction models of existing locks can be exploited by several classes of adversaries granting them capabilities that range from unauthorized home access to irrevocable control of the lock."[32]

Connected medical devices further raise the stakes of security. A DHS bulletin warning about security vulnerabilities in a brand of pacemaker described the potential impact as follows: "Successful exploitation of these vulnerabilities may allow a nearby attacker to gain unauthorized access to a pacemaker and issue commands, change settings, or otherwise interfere with the intended function of the pacemaker."[33]

Implantable networked medical devices sometimes have minimal security by design because these controls impede doctors from accessing devices in critical moments.[34] While there have not been any known cases of hackers killing or harming someone by infiltrating a medical system, many vulnerabilities have come to light in which someone could potentially do just that. The Johnson & Johnson unit Animas issued a letter to insulin-pump customers notifying them of a security vulnerability in wireless pumps and, in particular, that "a person could potentially gain unauthorized access to the pump through its unencrypted radio frequency communication system."[35] In this case, the probability of infiltration of the unencrypted connection between insulin pump and control unit is low. This is in part because the wireless connection between the two devices is local (not connected to the public Internet) and would require a hacker to be in physical proximity to the wireless connection. Nevertheless, the broader threat posed by networked access to medical devices means that there is the possibility of administering a lethal dose of insulin by hacking into the connection.

The Weaponization of Embedded Objects

The same devices that require greater protection are also themselves threats, as the Mirai botnet attack so vividly demonstrated. The security of connected objects is not only about the security of these connected objects. It is about the security of every device, service, platform, and information resource online, whether virtual or physical. Local objects, when connected, become global terrains both for launching attacks and to direct attacks.

Connected devices in homes and in the most personal of spheres appear completely localized. Phenomenologically, the device seems hyperproximate in that it has a local material presence and its usage context is usually highly circumscribed. But the very instant these objects connect to a digital network, they are opened up virtually to infiltration from actors located anywhere in the world. They are physically local but logically global. These potential actors include foreign governments (as well as local and national governments) as well as criminal hackers. These same actors can exploit these devices as an attack vector from which to disrupt anything online or offline. In the same way that other infrastructure domains have become a proxy for political and economic power, so too has IoT infrastructure.

Cyberattacks launched from seemingly anodyne connected objects are a new threat plane and concern for entities tasked with protecting networks, whether public or private. The owners of the devices may have even less incentive to address security than do manufacturers that are concerned with bringing products to market quickly. Device owners are usually not aware of DDoS attacks carried out by their IoT devices, and even if they were aware, the device exploitation might not directly affect them. As the security expert Bruce Schneier summarized in congressional testimony in the wake of a 2016 Internet outage caused by infiltrated IoT devices, "your security on the Internet depends on the security of millions of Internet-enabled devices, designed and sold by companies you've never heard of to consumers who don't care about your security."[36]

Hacking Infrastructures of Democracy

Democracy now also depends on cybersecurity. Less than a month before the election of U.S. President Donald Trump, in an announcement without U.S. historical precedent, the intelligence community issued a joint statement indicating that the Russian government directed efforts to hack into email accounts belonging to U.S. political institutions and individuals. The intelligence community claimed that "these thefts and disclosures are intended to interfere with the U.S. election process."[37] The announcement followed the release on Wiki Leaks of thousands of Democratic National Committee (DNC) emails that were potentially damaging to the presidential campaign of Hillary Clinton.

After the election, DHS and the FBI released a joint analysis report providing technical details about malicious cyberattacks by Russian sources targeting sites and networks associated with the U.S. election. The U.S. government then dubbed these election-related cyberattacks "GRIZZLY STEPPE."[38] Russian civilian and military cyber operations used, among other techniques, spear-phishing approaches in which an email falsely appeared to be from a trusted source but contained a link to a fake website intended to capture personal information such as a password or a link that installs malicious code that can infiltrate and monitor systems.

Foreign election meddling has not only been directed at the United States. European elections, including the French presidential election and the Brexit vote, were similarly targeted. Whether Russian cyber operations influenced the outcome of these elections will never be decisively known, but the development is indicative of the turn to Internet infrastructure for political influence as well as the direct connection between cybersecurity and democracy.

The security of material cyber-physical systems has direct implications for speech contexts, media systems, and democracy. Information subversion efforts exploit human knowledge about news accounts or events in the political sphere. Fake news is most effective when the deception has a whiff of truth, as the adage "all lies are wrapped in truth" suggests. The extent to which misleading information seems plausible has substantial effects on human cognition and content credibility. The incorporation of highly personalized information about the intended target of misinformation adds credibility to the message.

The acquisition of data from highly personal cyber-physical systems—health devices, home systems, and cars—will enhance the social-engineering effectiveness of information subterfuge. Personalized data collected from the Internet of things will enhance the effectiveness of spear-phishing techniques. Phishing attacks target individuals via email, whether criminals trying to steal account information or political operatives trying to obtain email credentials, as was the case in the DNC email infiltrations. These attacks are effective because they appear to originate from a trusted source, such as an employer, friend, or technology provider, or contain information that only a trusted insider would know. Cyber-physical system information from an individual's daily life would make phishing attempts more credible and effective.

It is a trivial exercise to envision how the infiltration of cyber-physical systems could disrupt democratic elections. Content-centric election interference has involved email phishing attacks, probing of voter rolls, and influence campaigns in social media. Disrupting or influencing elections using cyber-physical system infrastructure would be much more direct and immediate, such as tampering with traffic lights and transportation systems to disenfranchise voters or to create local emergencies and outages that divert time and attention from voting. To be effective, attacks would not have to be directed at actual polling places, like schools and libraries. They could just be contiguous infrastructure attacks that, in conjunction with massive stores of aggregated political data, microtarget select groups whose absence would potentially skew election results while remaining completely undetected.

Denial of service attacks are one of the most efficient ways to disrupt the political sphere. Indeed, the history of DDoS attacks is a political history. Examples include the attacks in Estonia in 2008 and Georgia in 2009, as well as attacks that targeted Iranian government sites during political upheaval around the same time. DDoS attacks are also a traditional authoritarian government approach to controlling the media by disrupting their communications infrastructures and online platforms.[39] DDoS attacks incapacitate a targeted computer by simultaneously inundating it with queries from thousands or millions of distributed devices. In previous decades, these queries originated from computers. Already, botnet attacks using IoT devices like insecure digital video recorders (DVRs) have disrupted information sites, a shot across the bow for how cyber-physical system cybersecurity not only affects the physical systems themselves but also content and information sites and any type of online presence.

A politically potent scenario for democracy would involve these exact types of easy-to-perpetrate DDoS campaigns targeting information environments (political entities, prominent media outlets, local law enforcement) around significant public-interest events like elections, geopolitical crises, or natural disasters. DDoS attacks could, of course, also target the security apparatus designed to address the attacks themselves, such as private technology companies or computer emergency response teams (CERTs). Addressing these emerging connections between the IoT and democracy is self-evidently urgent.

The Urgency of Cyber-Physical Security Action

Security is not at all sufficient, at any layer of cyber-physical systems. A vast chasm exists between the critical need for security and the state of cybersecurity. Despite the enormous societal stakes, expert communities from industry, government, and civil society agree that security is an urgent problem:

"Not enough is being done to strengthen the security and privacy of consumer IoT."
—The Internet Society[40]

"The adoption of IoT brings cybersecurity risks that pose a significant threat to the Nation."
—National Institute of Standards and Technology[41]

"Security is not keeping up with the pace of innovation."
—U.S. Department of Homeland Security[42]

"The possible harm that malicious actors could cause by exploiting these technologies to gain access to parts of our critical infrastructure, given the current state of cybersecurity, is immense."
—President's Commission on Enhancing National Cybersecurity[43]

"Attacks on IoT deployments could dramatically jeopardize people's security, privacy and safety, while additionally IoT in itself can be used as an attack vector against other critical infrastructures."
—European Union Agency for Network and Information Security (ENISA)[44]

"Many questions arise around the vulnerability of these devices, often deployed outside a traditional IT structure and lacking sufficient security built into them. Data losses, infection by malware, but also unauthorized access to personal data, intrusive use of wearable devices, or unlawful surveillance are risks."
—Article 29 Data Protection Working Party[45]

"The provision of wide area connectivity to an ever-widening variety of IoT services will increase the whole ecosystem's exposure to fraud and attack."
—GSM Association[46]

IoT devices are vulnerable, and this is a market failure, a political failure, and a technical failure. One economic determent to security is the competitive pressure on companies to rapidly introduce products and services into markets. Incentives for first-mover advantage outpace incentives for prioritizing security. Another constraint is both technical and economic. Inexpensive, miniature sensor devices do not always have the capacity to integrate security features, at least not without additional cost to manufacturers. The added cost of security can price devices out of competitive markets. Another challenge is one of experience. All real-world sector firms are now also technology firms, but relative to born-digital companies, they have less institutional experience with digital data and infrastructure security.

It is also easier and less costly to attack than to defend. An expert Commission on Enhancing National Cybersecurity, appointed by President Obama, summarized this condition, "Some threats against organizations today are from teams composed of highly skilled attackers that can spend months, if not years, planning and carrying out an intrusion. These teams may be sponsored by nation-states or criminal organizations, hacktivist groups, and others. Less skilled malicious actors can easily purchase attack toolkits, often with technical support, enabling them to readily participate in criminal activities. A security team has to protect thousands of devices while a malicious actor needs to gain access to only one."[47] The attack plane is everywhere because everything is increasingly interconnected. At the same time as interconnection rises, technological heterogeneity and complexity also rise.

Consumer behavior constitutes an important part of cybersecurity, but individuals historically have had little ability to see cyber-physical security problems. For example, individuals using a home IoT device do not necessarily know whether the embedded device is hijacked and weaponized; whether it contains a product vulnerability; whether component parts, possibly manufactured in another country, contain a back door for foreign surveillance; whether there has been a data breach affecting them; whether a hacker or intelligence actor has directly accessed systems; or whether a product is upgradeable or no longer supported. Even when privacy and security incidents are widely reported, there can be a disconnect between perception and behavior. Buying behavior continues to expand IoT markets at the same time as consumers express concern about IoT security.

If cyber-physical security is woefully deficient, what needs to happen? There is a window of opportunity for urgent action. Because of the high stakes to society and the economy, some consensus is forming around recommendations and principles for IoT security. As emphasized throughout this book, cyber-physical systems are not at all only a "thing" but a global ecosystem. Some systems are consumer facing. Others are primarily industrial systems. Still others are born-cyber-physical systems such as 3D printing. Many of the emerging recommendations for security skew toward consumer devices but are arguably applicable to these other areas.

The sources of policy proposals for securing systems are diverse and copious—the U.S. Department of Homeland Security,[48] the Global System for Mobile Communication Association (GSMA),[49] the Commerce Department's National Telecommunications and Information Administration (NTIA),[50] the Internet Society, the IoT Security Foundation,[51] the Cloud Security Alliance,[52] Internet Engineering Task Force (IETF) working groups, the National Institute of Standards and Technology, the United Nations ITU, the International Organization for Standardization (ISO), U.S. congressional bills, IoT national plans in Brazil and elsewhere, South Korea's IoT security roadmap, and many other sources.

Because cybersecurity systems are used in a variety of contexts—from health care to the energy sector to smart-grid transportation systems—security requirements and approaches sometimes have sector-specific dimensions. But many approaches apply more generally. Systems contain similar technological characteristics and components; they face the same adversaries and threats; and they require similar solutions. They are largely interconnected, so, given that weaponization of embedded devices is a threat to all, what one sector does affects all other sectors.

Some cross-cutting recommendations are merely nonbinding principles. Others are more tangible policy recommendations. Still others are recommendations for voluntary actions by developer communities or calls for third-party certification and statutory measures for holding companies accountable for se-curity. Most direct actions toward many stakeholders. For example, the DHS "Strategic Principles for Securing the Internet of Things" has recommended actions that all stakeholders, including manufacturers, service providers, and business and consumer users, should take.[53]

Security is only as strong as the weakest component of a system. A single cyber-physical system has many components: embedded physical objects, net-work infrastructure, associated applications, third-party services, back-end cloud-computing services and database systems, protocols, and management tools. Successful approaches comprehensively address the entire cyber-physical system. Security is about not only an end object but the entire ecosys-tem. The integration of mechanical, material systems with digital components and network connectivity dramatically expands the attack surface from which to infiltrate the device.

Furthermore, many components of these architectures are inherently cross-bor-der, with the possibility of network topologies, server distribution, and services located anywhere in the world and, more likely, simultaneously anywhere in the world. Component parts are made in one part of the world and assembled in a product that is technically "made in" another country. As such, this creates a pre-carious supply-chain challenge. For example, a part manufactured in China with black-boxed security enters products assembled in the United States. Security mechanisms and best practices have to apply to every component.

Security is not a monolithic practice. It is a term that encompasses many objectives, including maintaining the *availability* of services (taken away by ransomware or DDoS attacks), assuring *confidentiality* of information (com-promised by weak or no encryption, man-in-the-middle attacks, etc.), and main-taining the *integrity* of data. Security includes *authentication* of devices, sites, autonomous systems, and identities and *access controls*.

In the same way that security is not a single practice, neither do attacks follow a single script. Because sensors and actuators exist in real-world objects, attackers can physically tamper with, acquire for the unauthorized extraction of data, or otherwise materially interfere with systems. Systems can be subject to software or firmware attacks, man-in-the-middle attacks, eavesdropping, ransomware, and routing and DDoS attacks, among others. The types of attacks on cyber-physical systems are expansive and varied. The following sections present some reasonable recommendations to improve security, as well as suggestions for addressing the question of what ex ante incentives and ex post accountability mechanisms could incentivize these principles and actions.

Security by Design at Product Inception

The competitive pressure to bring products quickly to market, especially for consumer IoT products, has often diminished the potential for thoughtful long-term security design from product inception. Technical design choices are choices about values and about market competitiveness. Cyber-physical system design factors in processing-power requirements, energy power, size, and speed, all of which sometimes constrain the addition of necessary security mechanisms. The normative value of designing strong cybersecurity in these physical systems is a necessary precursor to fortifying critical societal infrastructure and national security, promoting basic human privacy, and ensuring human safety and security. As the NIST Cyber-Physical Framework recommends, "Security needs to be built into CPS [cyber-physical systems] by design in order to be sufficiently flexible to support a diverse set of applications. This security should include component security; access control; as well as timing, data and communications security."[54]

Access control is an area that has historically been deficient. Improving in this area requires designing certain features into systems. Whereas the default for most information systems is to require password authentication, this has not been the case in the IoT. Simply put, systems should have passwords. The passwords should not be hard-coded but require purchasers to update them (with strong passwords) upon installation. The issue of access and authentication applies to the back-end web systems and applications as much as, and even more than, embedded end devices themselves. For systems with substantial consumer-safety dimensions, two-factor or multifactor authentication is preferable. One-factor authentication is a password; two-factor authentication is a password and the requirement of inputting a real-time code sent to a phone; three-factor authentication could include these two inputs as well as biometric identification, such as fingerprint access.

The security design process should similarly anticipate and address the problem of brute-force attacks. A brute-force attack is exactly what it sounds like, the use of automated tools that try thousands of passwords in a matter of seconds. Designers can opt to build solutions into most systems, including an embedded mechanism to lock an account or device after a fixed number of password attempts, as well as tamper and manipulation detection.

Defaults are an essential part of security by design. Unless strong protection is activated as a default, rather than an optional setting selected later by a user, security by design may be ineffective.

Many components of cyber-physical architectures use proprietary specifications. This is sometimes not ideal for security. Industry standards that are time-tested and designed by large expert communities are generally more secure than proprietary approaches. This is especially urgent for complex protocols related to encryption and communication. As chapter 5 addresses, IoT standardization and interoperability are areas that are unsettled, a condition that is itself unsettling for cybersecurity. Some standards derive from existing, tested specifications; others are emerging to address the unique physical requirements and associated safety concerns of cyber-physical environments.[55]

Complicating "security by design" is the reality that rarely is a system designed from scratch. It subsumes components made in other countries and embedding, in some cases, numerous (even hundreds of) standards designed by different standards-setting institutions or proprietary components that are not even able to be inspected and assessed, as well as drawing from code already written, whether open source or otherwise, and in some cases built on an operating system already developed. It is complicated. Security by design is necessary but not, by itself, sufficient.

Upgradeability and Life-Cycle Management

The security expert Bruce Schneir's memorably titled 2014 *Wired* op-ed "The Internet of Things Is Wildly Insecure—And Often Unpatchable" sounded an important alarm about vulnerabilities in embedded systems: many of these objects are not patchable or upgradeable.[56]

Security holes are part of technology. Technology developers issue software upgrades in order to correct known vulnerabilities. Operating systems and software applications on a phone or laptop are routinely upgraded to patch vulnerabilities. This either happens automatically or requires an end user to agree to an upgrade installation, transmitted through either a wired or wireless connection.

The standard practice of upgrading software to correct vulnerabilities that are discovered does not easily convey to cyber-physical systems. Cyber-embedded physical systems are often not software upgradeable and not supported on an ongoing basis once sold into the marketplace. There may not be a clear user interface through which humans can consent to download an upgrade or arrange automatic upgrades.

One argument against making cyber-physical devices upgradeable, or building in strong security at all, is that product turnover is very high, so the device will be replaced anyway. This is not at all always the case. Kitchen appliances, cars, and televisions have life spans that measure in multiple years, not months. Even when products and services originate with the capability to be patched and upgraded, they can quickly reach end-of-life with regard to manufacturer support. History suggests that products continue operating long after they are no longer supported. Whether a device is upgraded or not is also complicated by ownership conditions. Devices in homes or businesses can have several concurrent owners and can change ownership over time as new occupants appear.

The significant public-interest implications of device security, including human safety and the exploitation and weaponization of insecure devices to carry out damaging and massive attacks, suggest that upgradeability, and specifically remote upgradeability, has to become as normative a practice for cyber-physical systems as it is for traditional information systems. Given that patch management is a critical deterrent for ransomware, the often unpatchable quality of everyday cyber-embedded objects creates a vulnerable and pervasive threat matrix for ransomware, as well as DDoS weaponization, malware, worms, and other exploits. Leaving physical-world objects and systems with security vulnerabilities is untenable. Updates are also necessary to add additional features, if not to patch vulnerabilities. As the Internet Society stresses in its IoT security recommendations, "Timely, verifiable, and effective patches and updates to address vulnerabilities are a critical aspect of security."[57]

Upgradeability is necessary, but it brings its own security risks and requirements. The upgrade process, such as a patch automatically downloaded over the air, unless itself secure, presents an opportunity for a malicious actor to implant malware, conduct man-in-the-middle attacks that intercept and then alter the transmission, initiate DDoS attacks, or block the download. The update process itself requires several dimensions of extra security checks. One is to authenticate the integrity of the software download to make sure it has not been modified. Another is to establish that the originating source of the download is authentic. Cryptographic signature techniques can accomplish both of these objectives. Another requirement is to maintain the confidentiality of the download by encrypting the software update prior to transmission and then decrypting it upon receipt. Software updates sent over the air on an unencrypted link would create the possibility of theft of intellectual property and expose the software to those who could exploit it for future attacks.[58]

As with everything in this evolving landscape, even something as simple as requiring upgradeability is complicated. It is a security mechanism that itself requires security to implement. Ownership of devices and associated services change hands and can interrupt patch-management arrangements. End-of-life management is another important dimension of security. At some point, products are no longer supported, and it is ideally contingent upon manufacturers to communicate this to device owners and for enterprises and individuals to stop using products when they are no longer supported with upgrades. It is difficult to envision that a sizable percentage of people would discard and replace working products because of the cessation of software upgrades. It is also not realistic to assume that users of these devices would know when a product is no longer updated, any more than knowing that a security vulnerability exists. This end-of-life problem has created an interesting new word: "abandonware."

Transparency and Disclosure

Private companies are a powerful form of governance in the digital sphere and especially in the hybrid digital-physical sphere, as already addressed extensively in this book. They enact public policy via design, administration, security and privacy practices, terms of service, and other actions. A critical question is what provides the legitimacy for this privatization of governance. One dimension of legitimacy and accountability is transparency. Yet much that is related to security is completely concealed and out of public view. It is a consensus of industry groups, the advocacy community, and security experts (and policymakers in some regions) that best practices in cyber-physical system security include greater disclosures.

Opportunities for disclosure exist at various points: when systems/products are designed, when they are purchased, during routine use, after security problems arise, and when product security is no longer supported. The following are examples of baseline disclosures, not meant to be exhaustive but rather indicative of general transparency practices necessary for legitimating the public-interest power of private companies.

Security Design Disclosures. The product design stage and the point when a product is purchased by an individual or a business both provide an opportunity for disclosure of basic security features. Is the product upgradeable and able to accept security patches? If so, are patches issued automatically, or do they require user consent (if possible)? Are passwords hard-coded? modifiable? encrypted? Are there access controls to mitigate against brute-force attacks? Do communication components use standard encryption to ensure confidentiality in transmission?

Data Collection Disclosures. The amount of data processed and transmitted between sensors/actuators and back-end cyber-physical system databases is immense. The data stored is voluminous. As many security-breach examples have already demonstrated, these back-end stores are rich targets for data theft. Many features of data collection intersect with security: What data is collected, and how is it used? With whom is it shared? How is data securely stored, and how long is it retained?

Vulnerability Disclosures. Nearly all digital products have vulnerabilities. The complexity of combining real-world material objects and cyber components, along with the rapid innovation and product development life cycle for these products, means that vulnerabilities are a given. Best practices call for immediate notification of threats and vulnerabilities, when discovered and corrected, and disclosure of actions necessary to mitigate the flaw.

Data Breach Disclosures. Disclosure of data breaches, when they occur rather than years later, is an important component of transparency. All fifty U.S. states have data-breach notification laws, although a federal law would arguably make it easier for companies than dealing with fifty different requirements. The European Union's GDPR requires that companies disclose personal data breaches within a seventy-two-hour window after becoming aware of the breach. One complication is the question of what constitutes a "personal" data breach in cyber-physical systems that are one step removed from direct human interaction. Nevertheless, the notification must include information about the nature of the breach, as well as the type and volume of data affected and a description of the measures taken to address the breach. Because so many companies do business in the European Union, the GDPR is having global effects, but this is one area where global harmonization of policies would be helpful. The requirement for companies to disclose data breaches, a requirement far short of holding them liable for breaches, should be a baseline practice voluntarily adhered to by companies and enforced by law in all regions.

Exogenous Incentive Structures: Liability, Market Pressure, Accountability

In an environment in which competitive pressures, such as being first to market with low-cost products, serve as intrinsic disincentives to strong security, what external structures are necessary to improve cyber-physical security? Considering the interlinkages between cyber-physical systems and privacy, safety, and national security, this is a crucial policy question. For IoT providers that sell ongoing services, such as those that provide cloud-computing storage or administration of multiple household devices, there is an inherent incentive to keep customer-base services operating and free from security problems. For providers that sell a one-off product to consumers, who then own the product and have no ongoing relationship with the manufacturer, there are fewer incentives, other than concern about the reputational harm or liability that arises when serious security problems occur. What can incentivize improvements to cyber-physical security? What can incentivize the types of security by design measures already described or making systems upgradeable or adhering to transparent security practices? A number of exogenous forces are positioned to incentivize stronger cybersecurity. These include the following:

- Insurance-based incentives
- Liability clarification and regulation
- Third-party certification
- Retail gatekeeping
- Government procurement influence

The same types of insurance incentive structures (e.g., lower premiums) that have prompted businesses and households to improve safety by installing security systems and fire-detection systems can serve as incentives for improving cybersecurity. The World Economic Forum, the Global Commission on Internet Governance, the Internet Society, and many other expert communities have stressed the role the insurance industry can play in incentivizing strong security. The Internet Society's "IoT Security for Policymakers" report emphasizes, "The insurance industry can prioritize better privacy and security requirements as a condition of their underwriting. By looking at the security of the IoT devices and related applications and services used by companies, insurance agencies can factor the risk they present into determining insurance premiums and prices."[59]

Cyber insurance markets are nascent but growing rapidly. Cyber-embedded material objects have consumer and industry safety implications that are different in kind from traditional content and communication systems. As such, insurance companies that underwrite companies have a direct interest in product security. The cyber-physical nexus, because it includes material products and more tangible consumer-safety issues, may be more readily adaptable to liability insurance structures than digital-only products. Liability insurance is not only about personal data breaches but also about more tangible harms such as injury (a connected car malfunction) or economic damage (an outage of an industrial IoT system). Underwriting decisions and premium structures can serve as incentives for best practices.

Liability is an area in need of regulatory clarity. In other sectors, ex post concerns about liability have helped incentivize safety and performance standards. In the Internet of things realm, there is almost no clarity about who is responsible for security problems and how they should be held accountable. As the European Union Agency for Network and Information Security explains the liability problem, "The lack of a clear assignment of liabilities might lead to ambiguities and conflicts in case of a security incident, especially considering the large and complex supply chain involved in IoT. Moreover, the question of how to manage security if one single component were shared by several parties remains unanswered. Enforcing liability is another major issue."[60]

Discussing Internet liability at all is controversial because the tradition, generally, has been immunity from liability for Internet intermediaries. Moving from content to cyber-embedded physical objects is prompting a reevaluation of norms and legal immunities. Chapter 8 discusses this shift and the inherent values in tension over this issue. Real consequences for problems are necessary to incentivize greater security performance. Regulatory clarity around liability is essential and an urgent necessity in the cyber-physical domain. In the same way that cyber-physical systems are heterogeneous in their constitution and application, a one-size-fits-all approach to liability is probably not ideal. It may be more politically feasible to address liability on an industry-specific basis, but greater accountability and liability is an important step for bringing cyber policy in step with technological changes.

External certifications and trust marks, as well as labeling, could also induce some cybersecurity improvements. Certification frameworks come from many types of institutions, from standards alliances to consumer groups. The IoT space is quickly evolving and highly fragmented, and so historically have been efforts to create external ratings and certifications for security in this space. One complication is that a trust mark can make a product seem secure even if, after the trust mark is assigned, a serious security flaw is discovered. Nevertheless, a framework for certifying best practices would provide an incentive for industry security behavior, and policymakers have proposed legislation directing the establishment of voluntary certification structures.[61]

Retail companies that sell IoT devices can serve to hold manufacturers accountable via the market power of pulling products known to have security problems. An example of this type of action involved a response to a security vulnerability in a children's stuffed animal. CloudPets smart stuffed animals allowed a family member to transmit a voice message to the toy from a mobile app and, in turn, allow children to record their own voice by pressing a paw. Researchers identified security problems in the CloudPets animals, including leaking of account credentials and more than two million children's voice recordings, prompting major online and offline retailers (e.g., Walmart, Amazon, and Target) to discontinue selling the product.[62]

Government procurement policies are always a lever of influence. As enormous purchasers of equipment, governments exert market influence via procurement policies. National IoT policies should include procurement provisions requiring that purchases comply with certain requirements. A proposed IoT security bill in the United States called for procurement practices ensuring that products are upgradeable via patch management, certifying that devices do not use hard-coded passwords or contain any known vulnerabilities, and adopt industry standards for communication and encryption protocols.[63]

Those who sell products have an incentive to bring innovative products to market swiftly. But these same companies also have an interest in adhering to internal corporate values about product security, as well as avoiding liability and public-relations consequences of breaches and security problems. In an ideal world, cyber-physical industries would voluntarily comply with security best practices and embrace self-certification of these practices or external certifications and trust marks that vouch for compliance. It is very unlikely that this will happen without market pressure, regulatory constraints, and other exogenous forces. No one pressure point will suffice. Taken together, these actions can help create an incentive structure for addressing serious inadequacies in cybersecurity overall.

Consumer Responsibility

Although many cyber-physical devices operate autonomously, once operational, humans install these systems. This is the case for everything from household devices to industrial Internet of things systems. The industry term "collaborative security" reflects the need for shared involvement and responsibility from all stakeholders.[64] This is an appropriate aspiration for the Internet of things as well. Those who purchase and install systems have a responsibility to be aware of the product's privacy and security policies, when available, including not only devices but also associated back-end systems and applications, and to take whatever precautions are available.

The Internet Society's Online Trust Alliance (OTA) has suggested recommended practices for businesses implementing consumer-grade IoT devices, although many arguably also apply to informed consumers. Some of the recommendations involve procurement decisions, such as avoiding certain products altogether, including those that are not upgradeable or that contain hard-coded passwords, or purchasing only systems that support encryption.[65] Best practices include disabling functions not being used, including cameras, microphones, and access when not needed (such as on a television).[66] Other OTA-recommended best practices include access-control mechanisms such as updating and strengthening passwords, using multifactor authentication when possible, managing permissions, restricting automatic Wi-Fi connections, and even placing IoT devices on a separate firewalled network (similar to a guest network), as well as maintenance functions such as keeping software updated and removing devices when they are no longer supported.[67]

Because individuals are not always aware of the existence of cyber-embedded devices or their inherent security properties, some of these recommendations will be difficult. As transparency, labeling, and certification practices increase, those mechanisms will help to advance consumer awareness and empowerment to participate in collective security practices.

Disrupting Traditional Cybersecurity Debates

The technical and political characteristics of the cyber-physical era completely recalibrate already-complicated cybersecurity debates. The attack surface of cyber-physical systems, meaning the points where unauthorized breaches can occur, is much wider than in information systems. All the cyberattacks possible in information and communication technologies are still possible in cyber-physical systems, but, in addition, cyber-physical systems are susceptible to real-world physical attacks that raise the stakes of vulnerabilities. Many public policy issues around cyber architecture require reformulation in light of the stakes and complexities of the Internet's material diffusion:

- *Zero-day vulnerability stockpiling.* When should governments stockpile knowledge of zero-day vulnerabilities (a software bug not yet known by the software manufacturer and therefore not fixed) for national security cyber-offensive capability versus disclose these vulnerabilities so manufacturers can correct products?
- *Encryption back doors.* To what extent should back doors be built into cyber-physical system and device encryption for law enforcement access in light of the enormous consequences of security problems?
- *Security research legality.* Under what conditions should research that probes for and discloses system vulnerabilities be legally permissible?
- *Hacking back.* When, if ever, should it be permissible for companies to hack back against attackers as an active cyber-defense mechanism?

Stakeholders have dug into their various positions on these policy debates in the context of information systems but not necessarily cyber-physical systems. All of these questions involve complicated and politically fraught choices between competing values, in some cases the urgency of national security versus the urgency of securing critical infrastructure. The values calculation shifts as cyberspace diffuses into real physical space. In the same way that boundaries are blurring in engineering arenas, boundaries are blurring in policy arenas.

Zero-Day Vulnerabilities and Exploits

"Zero-day attack" sounds like a user setting in a virtual reality war game. Regrettably, zero-day vulnerabilities and exploits are real and ground zero for cybersecurity conflicts among hackers, device manufacturers, and governments. A zero-day vulnerability is a detected flaw (i.e., bug) in software that the manufacturer of the software has not itself yet discovered or been apprised of and therefore has not yet mitigated. It is a security flaw out there in the wild. The presumption when using this terminology is that a third party, such as a hacker or government agency, has discovered this vulnerability but chosen not to disclose it to the vendor for appropriate mitigation. A zero-day exploit is code designed to perpetrate an attack or otherwise infiltrate a system by exploiting the zero-day vulnerability that the attacking party discovered but that is unknown publicly or by the manufacturer.

Zero-day vulnerabilities are now a front line of cyber conflict. Bugs are sometimes politically co-opted rather than corrected. It has become a widespread government practice to choose to stockpile knowledge of zero-day vulnerabilities and to use the knowledge to develop cyber-offense exploit code rather than to notify relevant product developers so they can patch the security problems. The U.S. government retains roughly 10 percent of the vulnerabilities it finds, on the basis of a national security calculation to do so.[68] The purpose of this nondisclosure is the potential or actual ability to exploit these weaknesses for intelligence gathering or law enforcement investigation or simply as cyber arms capability.

In the cyber realm, especially when the Internet involved smaller user communities of trusted users, discoveries of software bugs or protocol-implementation vulnerabilities were disclosed to the manufacturer of the relevant software or hardware. Rational thought suggests that a software problem discovered in a Microsoft product should be disclosed to Microsoft so that the company can release a patch that upgrades and amends the software appropriately. This is no longer de rigueur.

In the contemporary context, vulnerabilities are not necessarily disclosed to product manufacturers, even when a fee (sometimes called a bug bounty) is available. Economic motivations for withholding knowledge of system vulnerabilities from relevant companies include the intent to sell vulnerabilities for a profit. Indeed, there is a gray market for selling knowledge of vulnerabilities and exploits of these vulnerabilities. Political motivations for hoarding zero-day information are varied, but they increasingly involve nation-state decisions to develop offensive cyber code, or exploits, that can be deployed for espionage, intelligence gathering, or law enforcement or in the event of geopolitical cyber conflict.

The risk of this zero-day stockpiling is that critical infrastructure remains vulnerable to disruption or infiltration/exploitation by another government or malign actor. In the wake of the global disruptions caused by the WannaCry attack, Microsoft president and chief legal officer Brad Smith issued a forceful statement criticizing the practice of governments hoarding technical vulnerabilities for cyber-offensive capabilities: "This attack provides yet another example of why the stockpiling of vulnerabilities by governments is such a problem. . . . We have seen vulnerabilities stored by the CIA show up on WikiLeaks, and now this vulnerability stolen from the NSA has affected customers around the world. Repeatedly, exploits in the hands of governments have leaked into the public domain and caused widespread damage. An equivalent scenario with conventional weapons would be the U.S. military having some of its Tomahawk missiles stolen."[69]

The obvious problem of hoarding knowledge of flaws is that the information can fall into nefarious hands, whether criminals, terrorists, or adversarial governments. Cyber exploits, like other weapons, fall into the hands of those who use them to repress political opponents. In 2016, the Citizen Lab at the University of Toronto reported that the United Arab Emirates government targeted a zero-day iPhone operating-system exploit essentially to install spyware to monitor a human rights defender.[70] The Citizen Lab further claimed that the exploit infrastructure used was connected to an Israel-based cyber company that developed spyware products for government intelligence and cyber defense and that Mexican health interests supporting a soda tax were targeted with the same exploit. Citizen Lab notified Apple of the operating-system vulnerability exploited, and Apple confirmed and issued a patch for the vulnerability and issued a security update for its affected operating systems. To provide a sense of what a security-update notification looks like, the following is the one immediately released by Apple.

Security Update 2016-001 El Capitan and
Security Update 2016-005 Yosemite

Released September 1, 2016

Kernel
    Available for: OS X Yosemite v10.10.5 and OS X El Capitan v10.11.6
    Impact: An application may be able to disclose kernel memory
    Description: A validation issue was addressed through improved input
        sanitization.
    CVE-2016-4655: Citizen Lab and Lookout

Kernel

    Available for: OS X Yosemite v10.10.5 and OS X El Capitan v10.11.6

    Impact: An application may be able to execute arbitrary code with kernel
       privileges

    Description: A memory corruption issue was addressed through improved
       memory handling.

    CVE-2016-4656: Citizen Lab and Lookout[71]

The Israeli Justice Ministry indicted a former employee of the Israeli cyberse-curity firm NSO Group for allegedly stealing and attempting to sell smart-phone-cracking spyware software used by law enforcement.[72] The former employee was charged with trying to sell the tool on the Dark Web to a foreign adversary.

Zero-day exploit tools developed by or for governments or by or for hackers have been stolen, released, or used by governments and hackers for malicious purposes. Many of these are tools with grave security implications allowing un-authorized access, implantation of malware, or other damage to critical net-work infrastructure. As a US-CERT alert warned, "In August 2016, a group known as "Shadow Brokers" publicly released a large number of files, includ-ing exploitation tools for both old and newly exposed vulnerabilities. Cisco ASA [Adaptive Security Appliance] devices were found to be vulnerable to the released exploit code."[73]

Once vulnerability exploit tools are available, the risk is that they can leak out into the open. When vulnerabilities are not corrected, the risk is that they can be discovered and exploited.

All areas of Internet governance decisions are fraught with tensions between competing values. In the case of government decisions to hoard rather than disclose vulnerabilities, the competing values are intelligence, law enforce-ment, and potentially war capability versus the need for reliable and secure in-frastructure for economic and social stability. In authoritarian countries, it is also likely that the flaw is used to identify and prosecute media and political dissidents. The decision not to disclose a vulnerability to a manufacturer for mitigation has great risks, including the possibility of malign actors discovering the flaw or stealing code that exploits the flaw.

The paradigmatic government obligation to identify, pursue, and stop crimi-nal and terrorist activities online sometimes depends on tools that exploit vulnerabilities in digital infrastructure. As a White House Cybersecurity

Coordinator explained, "Those exploits produce intelligence for attribution, evidence of a crime, enable defensive investigations, and posture us to respond to our adversaries with cyber capabilities."[74]

The condition under which the U.S. government chooses not to disclose the cybersecurity vulnerabilities it discovers in information and communication technologies is laid out in its Vulnerabilities Equities Policy, which "balances whether to disseminate vulnerability information to the vendor/supplier in the expectation that it will be patched, or to temporarily restrict the knowledge of the vulnerability to the USG, and potentially other partners, so that it can be used for national security and law enforcement purposes, such as intelligence collection, military operations, and/or counterintelligence."[75] Under this process, when a government agency, such as the NSA, Central Intelligence Agency (CIA), or Department of Defense Cyber Crime Center, discovers a software flaw, it should take the information to the interagency Equities Review Board that evaluates the discovering agency's recommendation to either disclose or restrict the security vulnerability.

The decision to leave security flaws in infrastructure (rather than disclosing them) is a critical one and depends on the imperfect assumption that adversarial nation-states and criminal actors will not obtain or discover the same vulnerabilities in technology and carry out attacks on U.S. systems using these exploits.

The trade-offs become more difficult and the risks more pronounced as digital technologies move into the material world. Cyber-physical system security depends not only on the system's own defenses but also on the security of underlying infrastructure. The conditions under which governments allow security flaws to remain, rather than disclosing them to relevant companies, has to be closely scrutinized and reconsidered in light of the rising social and economic importance of cyber-physical system security.

A Case against Encryption Back Doors

Encryption serves as the mathematical foundation for trust in the digital sphere. Financial transmissions remain confidential because of encryption. Private communications between two people rely on cryptographic techniques. Authentication of the identity of devices and websites and people is based on public-key cryptography. Without various types of encryption, there would be no digital commerce, no online financial systems, and no prospect whatsoever for private communications. Democracy is inconceivable without the possibility of private communications between humans. The digital economy is inconceivable without assurance of the integrity and confidentiality of financial transactions. The safety and security of cyber-physical systems is not possible without cryptography. Trust in the online sphere and now trust in the offline sphere require strong encryption.

Yet a cybersecurity debate that has dominated policy discussions for decades is the question of whether governments can compel private companies to build back doors into encryption. A back door is essentially a security vulnerability through which governments can carry out surveillance or access data. The rationale for democratic governments seeking this extraordinary access is intelligence gathering, law enforcement, and national security. The rationale for companies resisting such back doors is that they inherently weaken security and open individuals' private information to malicious hacking, foreign surveillance, and identity theft.

The controversy over pressure to intentionally build weaknesses into technology came to public attention in the aftermath of the terrorist shooting in San Bernardino, California, when the FBI sought to compel Apple to develop software to crack phones that are cryptographically locked. The concern is sometimes called the "going dark" problem. The former FBI director James Comey testified to Congress that "the risks associated with Going Dark are grave both in traditional criminal matters as well as in national security matters."[76] On the basis of contemporary understandings of intelligence gathering of digital information, governments have far greater access to information than ever before, a condition in direct tension with civil liberties and trust in the digital economy. However, the problem is that those who are seeking to carry out malicious online attacks and real-world terrorism employ unbreakable encryption.

History repeats. The tension between the requirement for strong security and the political quest for weaker security has simmered since the rise of the public Internet and in some cases prior to that time.[77] In 1992, debates raged in the United States about an FBI proposal to build "trap-doors." The industry response echoes later debates about smartphone encryption: "The FBI proposal would create an enormous new problem. Any otherwise secure communications system which is made open to FBI surveillance would be vulnerable to others as well. The question is simple—who would guard the 'trap-door' which has been created. . . . This would be a very tempting target itself, and if it fell into the wrong hands could result in a digital Pearl Harbor—the ability to either obfuscate or read all of our mail, all of our telephone communications, all of our sensitive documents."[78] Concern about a "digital Pearl Harbor" was already ensconced in U.S. cyber-policy circles in the early 1990s, even prior to the widespread commercialization of and societal dependence on the Internet. In this nascent web context, the Internet had not yet grown internationally—less than 1 percent of the world's population was online—and large tech companies such as Google had not even been founded. Yet concern existed; and Russia already loomed large as a background threat.

The "digital Pearl Harbor" framing served as a backdrop for the context of U.S. discussions about the threat of foreign theft of corporate intellectual property assets such as commercial trade secrets. The impetus behind government interest in back doors was the billions of dollars lost due to active targeting of U.S. corporations by intelligence agencies from former Soviet-bloc nations and the prospect that such activity could "threaten our nation's long-term economic survival."[79] U.S. technology companies used the framing of a digital Pearl Harbor to express concern about U.S. governmental efforts to erode or impede security by requiring weak encryption or building in, essentially, back doors through which the FBI could crack encryption. Part of the analogy alluded to the possibility of an attack that would be a political wake-up call leading to war, with reference to the vulnerability of the planes that were "lined up wingtip to wingtip and offered the attackers an easy target. . . . A universal trap door in our computer security is precisely such a move, and would leave our critical information just as vulnerable."[80]

The backdrop was the encryption wars of the early 1990s. Completely analogous to more modern debates, the prospect of the FBI or other government agency having access to encrypted digital communication through encryption weakening or back doors was incomprehensible to those who believed that strong encryption was essential for society and the economy.

Encryption serves the same purpose in the contemporary context. It involves the mathematical scrambling of data to keep it private when stored or transmitted over a network. All styles of encryption begin with a cipher (essentially, an algorithm) that encodes information in such a way that only the intended recipient can decode it. The receiving device must know what encryption algorithm encoded the data and also must possess the encryption key—a binary number—to unscramble the data. Private-key, or symmetric, encryption requires all parties to possess the private key in advance, which would be impossible in most cases without sending the key over a network and making it susceptible to interception. Public-key, or asymmetric, cryptography was designed to address this problem by using two keys to encrypt data, one that only the transmitting device knows and one that the recipient device makes publicly available. Then, to decrypt, the recipient uses a combination of the public key and a private key only known to the receiving device. This public-key cryptography approach forms the basis of many security systems online, including the system used to authenticate the digital certificates linked with a site's public key and therefore vouching for the validity of websites.

This question of encryption back doors has historically pertained to digital-only companies, manufacturers that develop information and communication technologies such as smartphones. The trade-offs are already complicated even in digital-only environments. Part of the debate has been framed as the question of when law enforcement and national security authorities should have "extraordinary access" to encrypted communication, sometimes also couched as a back door to encryption. In examining this issue in the United States, the prominent security company run by the former DHS secretary Michael Chertoff concluded that "an extraordinary access requirement is likely to have a negative impact on technological development, the United States' international standing, and the competitiveness of the U.S. economy and will have adverse long-term effects on the security, privacy, and civil liberties of citizens."[81]

As more everyday material objects are digitally connected than laptops and phones, the risks of building in encryption weaknesses for law enforcement rise considerably. The trade-off used to be a conflict between the need to secure the digital economy and the obligation of the state to protect citizens. In the context of cyber-physical environments, strong encryption is necessary to protect citizens. The stakes of cybersecurity have risen considerably as digital technologies integrate into the physical world. Weakening encryption by building back doors into cyber-physical technologies, as well as communication infrastructures, inherently creates a threat to human safety, critical infrastructure, and the digital economy.

The Legality and Importance of Security Research

Security researchers contribute to understandings of technology vulnerabilities (and solutions). Discovering vulnerabilities, especially those with direct consequences for the economy, democracy, and human safety, should be welcome. It can save lives. A Center for Democracy & Technology (CDT) report on the impact of security research in critical areas such as cars, medical devices, voting machines, and consumer IoT concluded that "the efforts of security researchers have been instrumental in finding and fixing flaws in these systems, such as vulnerabilities and bugs that could have resulted in serious harm, economic loss, and loss of trust in digital infrastructure."[82]

Yet security research has been subject to contentious debate because of the question of the legality of these practices. The relevant statutory context varies by country. In the United States, laws restricting research include the Computer Fraud and Abuse Act (CFAA) and the Digital Millennium Copyright Act (DMCA). Indeed, these laws have historically been construed to criminalize research. The DMCA makes it illegal to tamper with technical protections of copyrighted material. The CFAA makes it illegal to engage in unauthorized access.

The CFAA was the statute that federal authorities used to prosecute the Harvard researcher Aaron Swartz, a young computer programmer and Reddit cofounder who downloaded a large repository of academic journal articles via an account he had through the Massachusetts Institute of Technology (MIT). The felony criminal charge for downloading the articles in the manner he did (his account entitled him to access the repository) would carry a maximum penalty of thirty-five years in prison and fines up to $1 million. Swartz committed suicide before the case was brought to trial. The CFAA is not some unused statute made obsolete over time. As the tragic and incongruously excessive case brought against Swartz suggests, it is very much alive, and security researchers are aware of its power. The law was passed in 1986, prior to the invention of the web and in an era in which the ambiguous language made sense. In the contemporary era, it is not always clear, and it has had a chilling effect on security research by criminalizing vulnerability detection in certain circumstances.

The Librarian of Congress, via the U.S. Copyright Office, authorized a temporary security-research exemption to the DMCA prohibitions on circumventing technical controls to copyrighted works. These controls, called technical protection measures (TPM), lock access to software in devices, with criminal penalties for tampering with protections. The exemption allows researchers (and consumers and enterprise users) to search for vulnerabilities. For example, against the protestations of car companies, the exemption temporarily allows researchers to examine car software security without being subject to criminal legal threat.

5

Interoperability Politics

SOME ENGINEERS IN THE INTERNET'S technical design community responded to Edward Snowden's 2013 disclosures about the pervasiveness of NSA surveillance with a call for "hardening the Internet" by shoring up security with greater end-to-end encryption.[1] The Internet Engineering Task Force published a consensus "best current practice" document stating that "pervasive monitoring is a technical attack that should be mitigated in the design of IETF protocols, where possible."[2] These efforts specifically acknowledged that expansive government surveillance presented a serious civil liberties challenge to individual privacy and that protocological approaches could, at a minimum, make it more difficult and costly to enact pervasive monitoring. The Internet Architecture Board (IAB) recommended that end-to-end encryption be the default approach, necessary for restoring trust in the Internet.[3] Extensive surveillance was an assault on privacy.[4]

Internet standards are one of the most technically complex areas of Internet governance but also one of the most politically charged. The idea of the politics embedded in technical standards crystallized in Janet Abbate's *Inventing the Internet* (1999). Referring specifically to the origin of TCP/IP, Abbate wrote, "Standards can be politics by other means. Whereas other government interventions into business and technology (such as safety regulations and antitrust actions) are readily seen as having political and social significance, technical standards are generally assumed to be socially neutral and therefore of little historical interest. But technical decisions can have far-reaching economic and social consequences, altering the balance of power between competing businesses or nations and constraining the freedom of users."[5]

The economic and social consequences of technical standards have become clear over time. Even leading thinkers in the Internet Engineering Task Force, the core engineering community designing Internet protocols, concede that "there is no value-free design."[6] Protocol designers themselves acknowledge the connection between architectural design and social concerns. Economic analyses of standardization emphasize effects on innovation, competition, and global trade.[7] Regarding social policy, web standards determine accessibility for people with hearing, sight, or mobility impairments. As such, studies have examined a range of digital standards from the geopolitics of Internet address standards[8] to global tensions over securing the Internet's Domain Name System via DNS Security Extensions (DNSSEC).[9] Other studies have analyzed—more expansively—the policy implications of Internet RFCs (Requests for Comments), the historical archive of core Internet standards and related informational documents,[10] or examined how Internet design communities can more directly address human rights.[11] Technical specifications have also been closely intertwined with politically charged issues such as privacy and law enforcement, especially in encryption standards.[12] Design tensions between encryption standards and national security and surveillance have existed for decades.

A human analogy is helpful to understand the critical role of standards. In the same way that humans have culturally contingent conventions for communication practices such as greeting each other (e.g., shaking hands, kissing, bowing), language, or addressing a letter to a globally unique physical address, so too do computers require communication standards to be able to exchange information. Technical standards are neither software nor hardware. They are written blueprints for interoperably communicating and interfacing and exchanging data in common formats. The development of technical standards, instantiated as protocological rules, constitutes one of the core cyber-governance functions enabling networks and products built by different manufacturers to interoperate and incorporate the necessary encryption, formatting, error checking, addressing, and other functions.

The design of algorithms is closely related and similarly powerful. Algorithms play a central, if obfuscated, role in society because they rank, sort, discriminate, predict, and rate all aspects of life.[13] Computing devices are not useful unless they are provided with programming instructions telling them what functions to perform and how to perform them. Algorithms perform tasks related to encrypting, routing, ranking, filtering, searching for, and compressing information—permeating every aspect of information and communication technology infrastructure. They also make consequential decisions related to how to value, score, or tailor political speech to people online. Cyber-physical system algorithms that serve as portals between virtual and material worlds may have even greater consequences in their design. This is especially the case for collision-avoidance algorithms in autonomous vehicles and control algorithms for real-world infrastructure systems in critical energy, health, and transportation sectors. Machine-learning algorithms aggregate historical data from the real world and make predictive decisions accordingly.

Examining the implications of technical protocols and algorithms alike requires peering inside of these specifications. The computer scientist and Internet pioneer David Clark, via his control point analysis approach, explains that understanding the actors, control points, and implications requires the extraction and cataloging of technical workings, again opening the black box.[14] Understanding the politics of technical architecture is also well served through the concept of code as law. Lawrence Lessig's influential book *Code and Other Laws of Cyberspace* explained that online and offline behavior is regulated by four modalities. These include laws, such as being held legally responsible for theft in the real world or theft online; norms, such as cultural expectations about what clothing to wear in the real world or how to behave in an online forum; and markets, such as economic forces of supply and demand. Architecture is another constraining modality, such as lack of accessible architecture for the disabled. As Lessig explained, "To understand a regulation then we must understand the sum of these four constraints operating together. Any one alone cannot represent the effect of the four together."[15]

If architecture is part of politics, changes to arrangements of technology are changes to arrangements of power. Who is in charge of cyber-physical system architectures, and what interests and values are embedded in emerging designs? Who are the technical communities that design and administer cyber-physical systems, and are they different from traditional technical communities? Are these new architectures incorporating adequate security features to address the rising stakes of cyber-physical systems for public safety and critical industrial infrastructure? In what ways are emerging architectures able to be exploited for political power on the international security stage? The behind-the-scenes frameworks, power structures, and standards institutions are changing as the Internet diffuses into the real world, co-constructing politics and technical architecture.

Anyone packing power adaptors for an international trip understands the inconvenience of incompatible standards. Plug configurations vary by region, so a laptop from Australia does not directly plug into an electrical outlet in Canada. Individuals have to use an adaptor to plug their computing device into an outlet in another country. The opening years of IoT innovation have lacked both interoperability and adaptability.

Individuals using different brands of smart lightbulbs in their own homes do not necessarily have the option to interconnect them via a common platform. One company's IoT devices are not always compatible with another company's devices or intelligent home assistant. This is a departure from the norm of interoperability by design in the Internet era. Common Internet standards allow someone to access a website from any browser (e.g., Chrome, Edge, Firefox, Safari). There are always forces of enclosure, such as smartphone-app gate-keeping or lack of data portability and universal search in proprietary social media platforms, but the Internet has generally privileged content interoperability. This is not a norm in cyber-physical systems.

In the contemporary context, interoperability is waning, not waxing. The state of standardization in these emerging spaces is chaotic and fluid. The shift from digital information systems to cyber-physical systems is creating unique challenges that call into question long-established understandings of competition, consumer choice, universality, fragmentation, and open standards. The lack of product compatibility in the cyber-physical space may just be following the trajectory of information systems, which required the development over time of common technical standards. Alternatively, proprietary approaches could become dominant.

Cyber-physical standardization faces unique challenges. Real-world interfaces via sensors and actuators require both higher security and lower energy consumption. Companies as diverse as John Deere and Caterpillar or Google and Microsoft produce technology products requiring standardization. Internet standards once created specifications primarily for digital-only environments for communications and sharing of content. Now they involve physical control interfaces and transductive exchanges in hybrid online and offline spheres. Standards have to address autonomous networking exchanges between objects rather than communication between people.

Constrained architectures have unique requirements. Cyber-embedded objects have physical and logical space constraints, have esoteric rather than general-purpose application, and often operate in low-power environments. Interoperability standards for a wireless, battery-powered device are completely different from the network protocols, data formats, and security specifications for a general-purpose computer.

A controversial but important question is whether interoperability is still necessary to the same extent. Implementations are more ad hoc rather than general purpose. There is considerable heterogeneity, in usage, in industry sector, and in required functionality. On the one hand, interoperability and open standards enable innovation, network universality, and market competition. Open and widely implemented security standards can also be more secure than closed specifications that are not scrutinized and vetted.

On the other hand, lack of interoperability is sometimes beneficial in the cyber-physical space. Designing a medical monitoring device to communicate directly with a door lock is both unnecessary and undesirable, especially from a security standpoint. Having some inherent lack of interoperability between different implementation settings, particularly by sector, assuming each environment itself develops sufficient stability and security, seems preferable to a wide-open plane of attack for cross-sector and cross-border security incursions.

At the same time, a shared underlying infrastructure based on common technical standards underlies all information systems and cyber-physical systems. Network operators make decisions to interconnect their networks using standard protocols. A common universal address space allows for the choice of global reach when applicable. All systems require a stable and secure common routing infrastructure over which data is transmitted. The requirement for strong security standards exists at many layers of this common infrastructure. Spectrum is managed. The standards landscape has to evolve to address entirely new requirements but also strengthen and extend existing common standards to support constrained cyber-physical architectures.

The stakes of standardization are high, with consequences for economic competition and innovation, privacy, infrastructure stability, and security. Yet the current state of Internet of things standards is unsettled, heterogeneous, and involving many different organizations, sometimes in direct competition. The IoT standards environment has developed over time into a diverse and fragmented space. Open standards are still necessary, even if applying narrowly within industry sectors rather than universally, and cyber-physical architectures actually raise the economic and social stakes of maintaining interoperability and common security standards in shared underlying network infrastructure.

The IoT Standards Landscape: Heterogeneity and Fragmentation

The term "Wild West" captures the frenetic pace and overlapping complexity of standards development for cyber-physical technologies. Many cyber-physical areas have numerous, competing standards in the same space. In some cases, entirely new protocols are emerging. In other cases, standards development adapts entrenched communication standards to the unique requirements and constraints of cyber-physical architectures. The number of standards-setting consortia is rising, some newly formed around the IoT. Established standards-setting institutions have moved into this space as well. Real-world companies are now involved; digital-only companies participate. It is not yet clear which standards will become dominant or even what standards-setting institution or institutions will be authoritative. In some areas, monocultures are developing, in which only one brand of connected object is able to communicate with an intelligent controller made by the same company. This condition invokes the proprietary computer networking environment of the 1980s, when only one brand of computers could interconnect and only by using that company's proprietary network operating system. In other cases, common standards are emerging but compete with other specifications in the same technical layer.

What are some evolving standards in this space? Figure 3 is a completely nonexhaustive snapshot but does serve to illustrate the wide variety of newer standards, in alphabetical order and spanning a variety of functional areas of standardization.

Any exchange of information—whether communication between people or control signals between things—simultaneously uses numerous standards. Using the public Internet has always involved hundreds upon hundreds of technical standards, or blueprints, that software and hardware manufacturers use to ensure that their products and services interact with those created by other developers. For example, HTTPS (Hypertext Transfer Protocol Secure) standardizes secure information exchange between browsers and websites; Voice over Internet Protocol (VoIP) is the underlying standard for making calls over the Internet.

6Lo	6LoWPAN	6TiSCH
Aeron	Alljoyn	AMQP
ANT	Bluetooth Low Energy	CARP
CoAP	CORPL	DASH 7
DDS	DECT	DigiMesh
DTLS	EnOcean	EPC
G.9959	HomePlug	HyperCat
IEEE 1377-2012	IEEE 1888.3-2013	IEEE 802.11
IEEE 802.15.4	IEEE P1856	IoTDB
IoTivity	IPSO	IPv6
IPv6 over Bluetooth	ISA 100.11a	LLAP
LoRAWAN	LsDL	LTE-A
LTE-M	LWM2M	mDNS
Mosquitto	MQTT	MQTT-SN
NanoIP	NB-IoT	NFC
LightweightM2M	OTrP	P2413
QUIC	RAML	REST
ROLL/RPL	RPL	RPMA
SENML	SensorML	SMCP
SMQTT	SSI	STOMP
Telehash	TSMP	uIP
UPnP	Weave	Weightless
WirelessHart	Wolfram	X.509
XMPP-IoT	Z-Wave	Zigbee

Figure 3. Nonexhaustive sampling of IoT standards

Network engineering processes have always approached standardization by divisions of specifications into layers, with each layer building on other layers. A layer is a conceptual tool for delineating groups of standards. The actual protocol is a defined, agreed-on (or proprietary) specification providing rules for interoperability and other functions. Further still into actual deployment, an implementation of these protocols is the instantiation of a standard into an actual manufacturer-specific hardware or software process.

The Open Systems Interconnection (OSI) reference model, dating back to the 1980s, provides a tradition of conceptualizing standards in seven functional layers. The model originally represented a set of protocols that were in contention

with the Internet's TCP/IP suite to create interoperability among previously proprietary systems. Now it is only a conceptual taxonomy, but it is still helpful for
developing and understanding various types of protocols. These conceptual layers include the physical layer, specifying mechanical, optical, or electrical interfaces between a device and a transmission medium (e.g., fiber-optic cable,
coaxial cable, wireless); the data-link layer, such as Ethernet, providing logical
specifications (frame formats, access techniques) for connecting to a network;
the network layer, such as IP, specifying how a network should route information; the transport layer (e.g., Transmission Control Protocol, or TCP, and User
Datagram Protocol, or UDP), handling the assurance that packets successfully
move from origination to destination point on a network; the session and presentation layers (e.g., Joint Photographic Experts Group, or JPEG, and Motion Picture Experts Group, or MPEG) for encoding and compressing information; and
the application layer, which includes high-level protocols for email, file transfer,
and web standards such as HTTP. Issues of security transcend all layers. There
are other layered conceptual taxonomies, most notably the four-layer TCP/IP
model, which combines the physical and data-link layer into one link layer and
aggregates the session, presentation, and application layer into a single functional application layer. There are many layered architectures for understanding
the relationship of protocols in the IoT, such as the ITU four-layer reference architecture.[16] For illustration purposes, figure 4 suggests a layered architecture
prototype for organizing relevant standards that combines consensus elements
from various models.

This customary approach of dividing myriad specifications into functional
groupings extends into cyber-physical systems. It also helps acknowledge that
these systems involve far more than just the end objects and extend into communication networks, switching systems, back-end analytics, applications,
controllers, and cloud-computing offerings. Of course, end devices themselves
embed an entire class of standards.

At any layer of IoT standards, some cyber-physical implementations use protocols that are already in wide use in information systems, while other implementations use specialized standards that address the unique requirements and
constraints of embedded systems.

Examining even one standards area—the local consumer IoT communication
area (device and network layers)—helps to elucidate this interplay between existing and new protocols, as well as the contention and competition that exists in

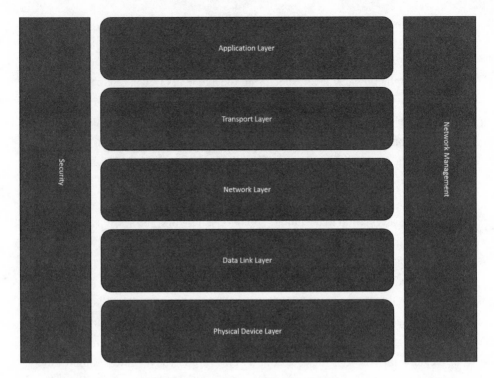

Figure 4. Cyber-physical layered architecture

even one space. Ethernet has served as the traditional approach to connecting laptops or smartphones in homes and offices: formally the IEEE 802.3 standard for a wired network or Wi-Fi, a wireless local area networking standard built on the IEEE 802.11 standard. Both of these are deployed to connect cyber-embedded objects in industrial and consumer settings. In other cases, smart communication devices, and especially phones, rely on cellular networks.

Because many cyber-physical devices have power and processing constraints, companies and standards institutions have worked to develop newer ad hoc specifications to more efficiently and resiliently accommodate these leaner environments. End devices often rely on battery power. They sometimes have a low transmission throughput, and their limited capacity restricts packet size and therefore address size within each packet to be transmitted. Some devices, by design, have intermittent connectivity or turn on and off to conserve battery resources.

With apologies in advance for the acronyms, the following are some examples of IoT-specific local or personal area communication standards. Bluetooth Low Energy (BLE)[17] provides a low-power variation of the Bluetooth 2.4 GHz short-range wireless communication protocol. Near Field Communication (NFC) protocols provide very-short-range (within four centimeters) communication for applications such as warehouse tracking of products or contactless payment systems and building-access keycards. A variety of organizations are involved in standardizing NFC protocols, including ISO/IEC (a joint initiative of the International Organization for Standardization and the International Electrotechnical Commission), European Computer Manufacturers Association (ECMA), the NFC Forum, GSMA, and others. Various RFID-based standards, such as the DASH7 wireless sensor and actuator protocols, serve primarily industrial and commercial environments. Zigbee and Z-Wave are somewhat-longer-range home and building wireless protocols, based on the IEEE 802.15.4 standards. Some of the different standards for short-range, inexpensive, low-bandwidth, low-power device connections rely on IEEE 802.15.4 low-power wireless personal area network (LoWPAN) standards. Standards organizations have designed these protocols specifically for IoT environments.

In other cases, protocol development in the cyber-physical space retrofits established protocols to constrained architectures. For example, to communicate, objects require unique addresses. The sheer volume of connected devices accentuates the need for global deployment of IPv6, the Internet Protocol standard that provides orders of magnitude more addresses than its predecessor IPv4 (Internet Protocol version 4). Some standards efforts have focused on the adoption of IPv6 addresses to constrained environments, which in some cases might not have the power or space for widely deployed protocols designed in the context of personal computers and other powerful platforms. For example, the IETF has worked on 6LoWPAN,[18] IPv6 over low-powered wireless networks, to use header compression to allow IPv6 to work in constrained environments. The IETF has also developed a routing standard called RPL, short for IPv6 Routing Protocol for Low-Power and Lossy Networks,[19] and other standards that adapt IPv6 over Bluetooth Low Energy (RFC 7668), Z-Wave ITU-T G.9959 (RFC 7428), and others.

These are just a few examples of the numerous standards developed over many years at the link and network layers. Many other standards exist in other functional categories all the way up to the application layer. Some environments are industry specific. Others are more general. The IETF has launched a number of initiatives to this effect, such as the Constrained Application Protocol (CoAP), which addresses application-level specifications and is modeled after HTTP.

Many competing organizations, frameworks, and standards exist in each space. The Internet engineer Patrik Fältström has used IP-based lighting-control systems as an example of less interoperable, even closed consumer electronics approaches whereby device manufacturers create products that speak to other products in the same manufacturer's line but are not able to interoperate with connected objects sold by other companies. He explains, "each company imagines that its proprietary approach will become widely adopted as the 'de facto' standard, with respect to which it will have an obvious competitive advantage over other companies pursuing the same 'maybe it will be me' strategy."[20]

Who is in charge? In other areas of digital interoperability, certain standards organizations have had clear expertise-based jurisdiction over the trajectory of protocols. Dozens of dominant organizations have carved out important areas of innovation and influence in establishing standards that collectively constitute the technical architecture of the Internet. The IETF is the primary institution setting core Internet protocols (e.g., TCP/IP). The World Wide Web Consortium (W3C), founded in 1994 by the web's inventor, Tim Berners-Lee, establishes standards (called Recommendations) for the web;[21] the Institute of Electrical and Electronics Engineers (IEEE) sets Ethernet LAN (local area network) standards and Wi-Fi specifications; and the ITU historically provides telecommunication specifications in areas such as Internet telephony. The International Organization for Standardization (ISO) serves as an international body composed of national bodies from more than 160 nations. The United States has NIST and the American National Standards Institute (ANSI). There are numerous others.

All of these long-standing standards organizations are squarely working in the cyber-physical space, with the addition of other alliances, industry consortia, and organizations arising specifically to address this area, such as the Industrial Internet Consortium, OneM2M, the Open Connectivity Foundation, Fairhair Alliance, the Zigbee Alliance, and many others.

One barrier to standardization is that, as one established technical organization describes it, "Most current standardization activities are confined to very specific verticals and represent islands of disjointed and often redundant development."[22] Fragmentation exists among different industries. Some standards are specifically designed for smart-city environments, others for manufacturing, others for health-care environments, others for utility meters. There is fragmentation at specific functional protocol layers and multiple competing efforts by different stakeholders, industry groups, and established standards-setting institutions.

Several efforts also seek to create a unified, multilayered approach, but even these are in contention. Some are open-source projects. Some are emphasizing royalty-free standards. Others are more closed. The initiatives sometimes focus on different layers of the protocol stack, such as data formats versus data-link interfaces. Standards for connected objects are unsettled. This is a significant concern considering the stakes of cyber-physical systems.

The trend toward closed (proprietary) ecosystems has accelerated in the area of IoT markets, whether due to the need to rapidly introduce products rather than adopt codeveloped standards frameworks, due to the dominance of companies arising in industries that are not historically part of ICT standards cultures, or due to market forces opposing interoperability to gain competitive advantage via proprietary implementations that can lock in users and discourage competition. One indication of fragmentation is the proliferation of efforts on the part of standards organizations to try to solve fragmentation:

> "The adoption of a unified approach to the development of IoT systems will reduce industry *fragmentation* and create a critical mass of multi-stakeholder activities around the world."
> —IEEE[23]

> "The Zigbee Alliance and Threat Group Address IoT *Fragmentation* with the Availability of the Dotdot Specification over Thread's IP Network."
> —Zigbee Alliance[24]

> "There are huge, transformative opportunities not only for mobile operators but for all businesses if we can overcome the *fragmentation* of the IoT."
> —W3C announcement about Web of Things working group[25]

> *"Fragmentation* of IoT standards locks consumers into an ecosystem where they become dependent on one vendor to meet their smart home needs."
> —Open Connectivity Foundation[26]

> "The IoT is the natural evolution of computing and it brings its own challenges— an immature ecosystem bearing a *fragmentation of standards and security concerns* in a non-homogeneous IoT market, as at the moment each industry and application is different."
> —ENISA[27]

Fragmentation exists in many areas, from network interfaces to wireless protocols to controller standards. What would constitute a positive outcome? The IETF at one point published an informational RFC on just this question of "what makes for a successful protocol?"[28] The two success indicators are scale, meaning widely deployed, and purpose, meaning meeting its original design objective. In other cases, the RFC suggests, some standards, such as IPv4 and HTTP, are perhaps too successful, implemented far beyond their intended scale or intended use.

The limitation of this definition of success in the IoT space, based on level of deployment and adherence to originally intended purpose, is that it assumes that the original design objective is always inherently appropriate and it assumes that wide deployment is desirable. Neither of these characteristics can be applied to cyber-physical systems with such certainty. Objectives are sometimes problematic or at least contentious; wide deployment of an individual specification is not necessarily desirable. When viewing the Internet as a communication system, wide deployment of standards has obvious salutary effects such as creating an interoperable digital economy and a global public sphere. When viewing the Internet as a control network connecting things, having industry-specific segmentation might actually have utility from the standpoint of consumer safety and critical infrastructure security. Fragmentation by industry might be desirable so that, considering the serious security threats and vulnerabilities addressed in chapter 4, a lack of cross-industry interoperability can serve as a check on security problems. This case for some fragmentation emanates from not only the concern about global attacks on cyber-physical systems but also the concern about global attacks originating from insecure IoT devices whose vulnerabilities are exploited and then used to launch distributed attacks on major online sites.

On the issue of "purpose," the design objectives for standards are not always fixed or settled. Shoring up the many dimensions of cybersecurity—authentication, availability, integrity, confidentiality—is a clear purpose of technical communities but not always of law enforcement and intelligence communities. Furthermore, some of the objectives of IoT standards are arguably not virtuous from the standpoint of accountability or market competition. Indeed, many constitute a reversion back to proprietary enclosure and anticompetitive practices.

What is hopefully clear from this brief treatment and snapshot of only a few areas of IoT standardization is that a high degree of heterogeneity and competition exists in this quickly evolving and lucrative industry area. Not surprisingly, media articles on the subject have such creative titles as "Grab a Fork! Unravelling the Internet of Things Standards Spaghetti."[29]

A Case for Open Standards in the IoT

Protocol diversity and fragmentation have become a norm in the Internet of things, a departure from the expectation for common standards for communication systems so that all devices and systems can interoperate. This fragmentation exists between industries, between standards organizations, and in specific functional areas. Products often use proprietary specifications that, by design, limit or prevent interoperability with competing products. Trends are pushing against the norm of common, open standards that historically have served as baseline blueprints for many communication layers, from securing web queries to specifications for how network operators exchange routing information at autonomous system borders.

There are many explanations for the preponderance of closed specifications. First, companies in the IoT space do not necessarily have a history of involvement in digital-standards-setting organizations. Additionally, the accelerating pace of innovation and economic incentive to be first to market does not comport with the slower pace of collaborative standards setting. Finally, commensurate with the historical trajectory of communication standards, companies sometimes have an interest in proprietary specifications for anticompetitive effects and to lock in customer bases to a monoculture.

Private ordering of embedded objects, often through proprietary enclosure, raises questions about interoperability and competition policy and the right to innovate or right simply to function.

American farmers have taken the lead in highlighting and protesting one layer of private-industry control: how the intellectual property rights within connected objects enable manufacturers to control the flow of data and the autonomy and rights of individuals even after an object is purchased outright. These rights are often affected by trade-secrecy laws that protect formulas and algorithms, copyrighted software, and standards-embedded patents. Private property is no longer truly private property but rather hybrid owned-licensed property. Does someone ever own a connected object in the same way one can own a purely mechanical object? At best, property ownership is a gray area in cyber-physical systems. Embedded intellectual property rights can impede the right of users to repair or upgrade the devices they have already purchased. Who owns or may access the data collected from connected objects? Without the historical data from a car, for example, third-party mechanics may not be able to diagnose and repair the vehicle.

Tractors are no longer just tractors but digitally connected computer-tractor hybrids. John Deere's license agreement for machine-embedded software applies to, essentially, any digital components of farm equipment including actuators, sensors, and controllers and explicitly prohibits the purchaser from circumventing any technological measures (e.g., "passwords, key codes, encryption or other security device") that protects embedded intellectual property rights.[30] Farmers have historically fixed their own equipment, but in the era of digitally embedded farm machinery, they can be prohibited from accessing code or having open access to diagnostic information and tools. The legislative efforts to address this point of control proceed under the banner of the "Right to Repair."

Throughout the world, laws prohibit the circumvention of technical barriers designed to protect copyrighted material. Internationally, these anticircumvention laws were codified in the World Intellectual Property Organization's (WIPO) Copyright Treaty. In the United States, the DMCA defines technological measure circumvention as, among other things, bypassing, deactivating, decrypting, or otherwise unlawfully accessing copyrighted work. These treaties and laws have primarily applied to purely digital products such as movies, books, video games, and music. Now these same laws apply to physical objects used in the real world that happen to have embedded digital components. The implications are quite different and potentially interfere with the ability to carry out everyday tasks in the real world with purchased objects that require modifications or repair. This virtual-material hybridization changes the nature of object ownership. Paying $100,000 to purchase a physical artifact no longer means gaining control of the object. The manufacturer retains some control.

Traditional principles of Internet architecture and governance are being challenged. New hybrid physical-digital intellectual property rights issues, such as how copyright-embedded software or standards-based patents might conflict with the ability of consumers to use or repair material objects, foreshadow how traditional norms and statutes around intermediaries and Internet governance become clearly challenged by new control dimensions within cyber-physical systems. Are norms of open standards, always contested and in tension with other values, further eroding?

Open standards very much matter in the cyber-physical space, even if a requirement for interoperability among any and all industry spheres is not self-evident. Industry-sector fragmentation can coexist with open standards within sectors and application areas. Open standards—those that allow for participatory development processes, that are openly published, and that are unencumbered in their use—have important political, technical, and economic implications.[31] For example, the safety of autonomous transportation environments will require data interoperability among connected cars made by different manufacturers, as well as interfaces with traffic management systems and roads.

Open standards communities also matter in that they are important stakeholders and influencers in public policy debates related to national security, surveillance, and privacy. For example, design tensions between security and surveillance have confronted the Internet Engineering Task Force for decades, whether deflecting requests to build wiretapping capability into protocols or entering broader debates about government efforts to weaken encryption strength to enact pervasive surveillance. The Internet's engineering community has historically served as a constraining force on invasive government surveillance. In 1996, the Internet Architecture Board—an IETF committee with oversight of Internet standards—addressed the issue of encryption strength in the context of politically charged policy discussions seeking to limit or weaken encryption for government access to communications. RFC 1984, for example, provided a consensus position of the engineering community on the need for strong encryption, both for privacy and for securing commercial transactions.[32]

If one believes that standards setting has public policy effects, then a procedural governance question arises. What is the basis of legitimacy for this policy-making role? Open standards have served, to a certain extent, to provide the transparency and participatory openness that help to legitimize governance functions that are not carried out by traditional nation-states but by institutions of experts largely from the private sector. The IETF is an example of an institution that adheres to procedural openness, in that anyone may participate in the development process or view the deliberations of working groups in which design discussions occur. Procedurally, there are well-defined rules and procedures. Even though the IETF development process is open to anyone, there are still inherent barriers to participation. In practice, the individuals involved in standards setting have been affiliated with corporations with a stake in the outcome of deliberations. Participation, while open, requires technical expertise and, often, funding to meaningfully engage. But many organizations do not at all meet the standard of allowing for free and open participation. In the cyber-physical space, some organizations are more closed industry consortia than standards organizations.

Another measure of openness involves whether the standard is freely published and the extent to which it is encumbered by intellectual property rights restrictions on its use. Similar to W3C specifications, IETF standards are freely published and historically unconstrained by intellectual property rights. The transparency surrounding the development process and the ability to view the standards themselves help to provide some accountability and oversight. The IETF has been one of the most open standards organizations with regard to its tradition of making specifications openly available in its electronic archive known as the Requests for Comments (RFCs) series documenting standards (and procedures and supporting technical information) dating back to 1969.[33] One historic contribution of the Internet of the late twentieth century, relative to its predecessor networks, was that it enabled devices to communicate without regard to the manufacturer of the device, the owner of the device, or the location around the world. Prior to the development and implementation of the TCP/IP protocols and other open standards underlying the Internet, a network of computers using one manufacturer's products was not intrinsically able to exchange information on a computer network made by a different manufacturer. People using email on one platform could not exchange messages with a friend on another platform. It is important to note the history of the TCP/IP protocol suite and how its technological affordance of openness and interoperability created a global Internet in which all devices could interact.

This degree of interoperability and unencumbered availability and use of standards speaks to the economic implication of openness. Standardization connects to innovation policy and markets to the extent that it enables product competition and creates network effects related to interoperability.

This level of openness in standards has always been under pressure from proprietary enclosure. But historical traditions of openness are especially not conveying to the IoT development world. Instead of royalty-free standards, standards are embedded with patents that significantly restrict their use or are available under what is sometimes called "Reasonable and Non-Discriminatory" (RAND) licensing. Processes are not necessarily openly and freely available to anyone, and specifications are not always published. For example, the Zigbee Alliance offers tiered levels of participation that require paid fees. Becoming a "participant" who can attend face-to-face meetings or engage in online discussion, vote, and "gain early access to Zigbee Alliance specifications," costs $15,000 per year.[34]

A lack of standards is also not neutral. Completely proprietary approaches are a public policy issue of a different kind. Closed specifications that are not available for use by others have political and economic effects. In communication environments, they create a fragmented or closed-speech environment that restrains expressive freedom. They often serve as technical barriers to global trade and prevent economic competition. In other cases, proprietary approaches develop into de facto industry standards.

Many efforts to create broad standards architecture frameworks for cyber-physical systems are simultaneously under way. Some compete with each other. Some are in different vertical areas. Some are all-encompassing. The area has rapidly developed and continually changed. The W3C, in 2017, launched a working group on the "Web of Things" to try to bring standardization to data formats and application programming interfaces in the IoT that is commensurate to the standardized linking of data in the web.[35] The W3C advocates for royalty-free and platform-independent solutions and has brought these design and market philosophies into its IoT standardization effort. The IEEE is doing work on a common architectural framework for the IoT.[36] ISO has the ISO/IEC IoT Reference Architecture initiative.[37] Some initiatives focus primarily on the industrial domain, such as the Industrial Internet Consortium (IIC) Industrial Internet Reference Architecture.[38] These are a few examples and only a snapshot in time in a very rapidly moving standards area. In some cases, different institutional efforts have agreed on liaisons with each other.

Open standards matter, but even attempts to develop an open architecture framework for the IoT are in competition, highlighting the need for greater cooperation among standards organizations in this area.

The Ongoing Need for a Common Underlying Infrastructure

Why does traffic associated with high-profile websites or financial companies sometimes suddenly reroute through Russia?[39] There is no one cloud. There are only private-sector-owned networks, routers, servers, buildings, switches, and fiber-optic cable. Cyber-physical systems and communication systems alike run over a common cross-border infrastructure that is sometimes taken for granted. Security and stability of a connected medical device depend on infrastructural arrangements that are far removed from the device and systems that support the device.

Interoperability agreements—for routing, addressing, and interconnecting—are at the core of the security and stability of the common infrastructure enabling communications among and even within cyber-physical systems. From an engineering perspective, there is not a single global network that supports Internet of things communication but rather a collection of interconnected networks operated by different network operators and interconnected via technical and economic (and sometimes political) agreements to interconnect and exchange information.

The security of local cyber-physical systems generally depends on the security of global routing systems. The security and reliability of cyber-physical systems are only as strong as the security and reliability of the networks over which control data from sensors and actuators flow. These individual networks have a physical infrastructure presence but also a logical (software-defined) infrastructure. These networks, more accurately called "autonomous systems," collectively shape the global routing table that lists all IP address prefixes and paths available to access these addresses. Some network providers (large telecommunication companies such as AT&T, content distribution networks such as Akamai, and content companies such as Google) operate multiple autonomous systems.

Autonomous systems are best understood as routing domains. Each one manages a collection of routers and IP addresses that point to resources that reside in that domain or that are located in a domain in which the autonomous system can route information under a transit agreement. Each autonomous system has a globally unique 32-bit number—an autonomous system number—assigned by a Regional Internet Registry (RIR), which in turn receives allocations from the Internet Assigned Numbers Authority (IANA).[40] As of 2018, there were more than eighty thousand autonomous system numbers assigned to network operators.[41] The defining feature of an autonomous system is that it manages a group of IP prefixes and has a clearly defined routing policy.[42] Each of these systems uses an interior routing protocol (called an interior gateway protocol) to guide routers within the domain regarding the path over which to forward packets of data. Each uses an exterior routing protocol called Border Gateway Protocol (BGP) to communicate between autonomous systems.

BGP, one of the most important standards facilitating the global exchange of information, allows networks to advertise to other networks information about what set of routes (paths to virtual resources) are accessible via that autono-mous system.[43] Internet history has been replete with examples of outages due to false routes advertised by a network or problems created by route leaks. The Internet Engineering Task Force defines a "route leak" as "the propagation of routing announcement(s) beyond their intended scope."[44] This type of unau-thorized propagation, whether malicious or due to an inadvertent misconfigura-tion, results in the routing of information through a path that can enable traffic eavesdropping or overload.

The routing of packets of data among network operators has historically relied on trust, creating a de facto infrastructure vulnerability in which it is relatively easy to reroute traffic intended to reach a legitimate destination, whether inadvert-ently or with malicious intent. This rerouting, in effect, creates a temporary outage during which a legitimate site becomes unreachable. Routing-induced outages have occurred for years, with one of the most infamous historical examples occur-ring in 2008 when YouTube was temporarily blocked in much of the world. The Pakistan government directed Pakistan Telecom to censor (block access to) YouTube due to a video that violated the country's blasphemy laws. YouTube ad-ministrators blocked access within the country by redirecting the IP addresses as-sociated with YouTube servers into, essentially, a black-hole site. But the company also advertised these redirected routes, whether intentionally or not, to neighbor-ing networks to which it connected, resulting in the routes being replicated throughout the global Internet router tables. The end result was that YouTube was unreachable in much of the world until the false routes were corrected globally.

Outages due to routing problems, although not always covered by the main-stream media, are common. The network monitoring firm BGPmon, which spe-cializes in routing security, tracks incidents of hijacked or leaked routes, such as the December 2017 incident in which some of the most popular online resources—including routes associated with Apple, Facebook, Google, and Microsoft—were rerouted to Russia.[45] Some characteristics of this event sug-gested that the short-lived outage was intentional: it affected a collection of very high-profile sites, and the routes were redirected to a Russian network that had been dormant until this incident.

Improving the security of BGP is a critical part of improving the security of the Internet of Everything. The IETF has developed protocols to apply public-key cryptography to interdomain routing, including a technique called Resource Public Key Infrastructure (RPKI). This technique, essentially, authenticates IP routes. While it is too involved of an initiative to explain here, the system of interdomain routing between networks is a core part of the infrastructure underlying everything, and implementing route authentication, while creating additional complexity, is a critical need.

The advent of physical-world connected devices and the proprietary approaches that sometimes support them raise the question of whether the Internet Protocol is necessary anymore as a universal address system. More broadly, is it even necessary for connected objects to natively use Internet protocols (e.g., IPv4, IPv6, HTTP, UDP, TCP), and does it matter? This is a much more complicated question than it sounds, and it is surprisingly difficult to demarcate between devices that adhere to Internet protocols versus those that do not. Technical experts in the Internet's traditional design community emphasize that "the deployed Internet matters" and that "most smart object deployments can make use of the already-standardized Internet Protocol Suite."[46]

The Internet Protocol, in particular, and the Internet address space (both IPv4 and IPv6) are certainly part of the common core infrastructure of the Internet, and there are many reasons to apply IP in cyber-physical environments, whether via a gateway or natively in devices. It would be relying on existing, well-understood, and proven infrastructure and is an open standard.[47] Many IoT applications connect directly to the public Internet, so it is a given that they will be using IP and other core Internet protocols.

Cumulatively, the sheer explosion in the number of embedded objects that are interconnected requires global adoption of IPv6. The Internet address standard in widest use is called IPv4, short for Internet Protocol version 4, which specifies a unique combination of thirty-two bits (zeros and ones) for each address, such as 00010011001010001000000100100001. This number is a unique address that tells devices, called routers, how to route information to its destination. Although computers read this long binary number, it is customary for people to represent this number using shorthand notation called dotted decimal format. The shorthand notation of the preceding number is 19.40.129.33.

These IP addresses are a basic building block of how the Internet works because they are used by Internet routers to transmit packets of information to their appropriate destinations. This 32-bit format provides roughly 4.3 billion unique addresses. Because of the Internet's rapid growth, engineers developed a new standard called IPv6 (Internet Protocol version 6) that expands the address length to 128 bits, providing an Internet address pool of 2^{128}, or 340 undecillion addresses. IPv4 addresses have all been allocated; this newer standard has been available in products for years, but universal migration has been relatively slow, a much more involved situation than can be addressed here.[48] However, IPv6 will be a critically important logical resource for supporting the cyber-physical world.

The stability and security of emerging systems depends on the stability and security of the global network infrastructure on which they operate. They are also only as resilient as the energy grid on which everything depends. Making industrial IoT systems themselves secure will have no impact whatsoever if the distributed networks, switches, routing and addressing systems, and energy grid they depend on are not stable and secure. This network and systems dependency is analogous to a train having no utility without tracks, switches, conductors, engineers, and natural resources. The IoT runs on existing, distributed, globally entrenched infrastructure. This foundation—the global collection of interconnected, largely private networks and exchange points—cannot be taken for granted.

There is an irony. Cyber-embedded physical systems do not necessarily themselves adhere to open standards that support interoperability. But they are able to be built on existing architectural frameworks because these architectures do enable interoperability. Emerging systems are not usually general-purpose systems but rather more esoteric to a specific task, but they depend on a global network that works precisely because it is a general-purpose system with global reach. The edges of networks are far more heterogeneous and complex than they have been since the early 1990s. The core of the globally interconnected digital domain runs on interoperability. The cyber-physical disruption depends on core, common infrastructure built on shared protocols for formatting, addressing, and routing data.

Future Proofing Standards from Blockchain to Quantum Computing

Technologies continually evolve. The original design of the Internet was itself a radical rethinking of existing architecture. Standards can sometimes ossify. They become entrenched in large-scale systems and sometimes have, as the historian of technology Thomas Hughes described it, a conservative momentum that can only be dislodged by tremendous events.[49] The entrenched protocols of the Internet, as originally designed, have had great staying power because of this conservative momentum and legacy installed base. The term "infrastructure ossification" sometimes arises in technical discussions. The tenacity of IPv4 and the protracted delay in implementing IPv6 is an example of this legacy feature of protocols. So are the DNS protocols and large suite of web standards from HTML (Hypertext Markup Language) to XML (Extensible Markup Language) and beyond. The broad and rapid diffusion of the Internet into the material world might serve as such a tipping point that churns dominant architectures. It is also possible that other, more technology-specific flashpoints will prompt changes.

IoT is at a standards-development inflection point. Because cyber-physical standards are in flux, with competing, heterogeneous efforts and no dominant framework, there is an opportunity to anticipate technologies of the future that need to be accounted for in their design and implementation. Quantum computing and blockchain are examples of two technologies that, at this writing, are in an untested hype stage but whose possible impact and (ir)rational exuberance standards must anticipate.

Technical communities already acknowledge quantum-computing entanglements with cybersecurity standards as an area of interest, even though it is still unproven territory. The success of cryptographic approaches that secure digital transactions is predicated on the assumption that there is not sufficient computing power to crack entrenched encryption, or at least that encryption deters hacking by making it either too expensive or too time-consuming to crack. The promise of quantum computing is that it could be orders of magnitude more powerful than digital computers, calling into question whether some strong cryptographic approaches might be cracked by this sheer processing power.

Advances in microprocessing power have, as Moore's law suggested more than a half century ago, leapt forward at dramatic rates. However, even a continuation of the rapid rate of advancement in digital microprocessors that has accreted over decades is still insufficient to anticipate overtaking strong encryption. But what could overtake encryption, and public-key cryptography in particular, is a complete transformation of computational processing that moves the world from digital (discrete processing based on binary) to quantum computing.

Quantum computing, as the name suggests, is based on quantum mechanics, a subfield of physics that studies how particles in the natural world simultaneously occupy more than one state and how these states interact with and depend on the state of other particles. Two natural affordances of quantum physics structure the idea of quantum computing. These are superposition and entanglement.

Superposition refers to the ability of particles to occupy more than one state at a time. Entanglement refers to the ability of the state of one particle to influence the state of another particle.

These characteristics of quantum computing—superposition and entanglement—potentially suggest a sweeping departure from digital computing. Digital computers encode all information—video, text, numbers—in zeros and ones, and the minuscule switches in silicon chips switch on and off to represent these two states, which we call zero and one but could be just as easily called True and False or anything that conveys the representation of two discrete states. These are binary digits, or "bits" for short. Bits have exactly two states, zero and one, and can occupy one of these states at a time. Quantum computing uses quantum bits, "qubits," which can occupy two states at the same time. The end result, should quantum computers be proven successful, is that processing power would exponentially increase.

The processing power of quantum computing, if it successfully advances, would have possible direct effects on everything from the speed of online searches to genomic medicine. History has indicated that paradigmatic transformations in computing occur. For example, the replacement of vacuum tubes with the transistor was one of the most consequential technological transformations of the twentieth century, ushering in the era of modern silicon microprocessors that have shaped the digital era.

This same advancement threatens prevailing security approaches, especially public-key cryptography. Quantum algorithms could solve approaches that rely on the length of public encryption keys to make mathematical calculations impossible (or prohibitively costly) to solve. Standards organizations—including IEEE, NIST, and the European Telecommunications Standards Institute (ETSI)—are beginning to address quantum computing,[50] both from the standpoint of future proofing modern cryptography and also from the standpoint of anticipating the need for common frameworks and standards in quantum-computing applications.

History has demonstrated that no security measures are impenetrable and that paradigmatic changes occur. This leads to the problem of blockchain standards governance. Blockchain is a decentralized public ledger system that tracks and manages transactions via cryptography and mathematical calculations rather than through a central authority. Probably the easiest way to characterize the blockchain architecture is to think about it as a distributed system that tracks a continuously growing set of records, or connected blocks, that are cryptographically linked as a way to secure them against modification, fraud, or tampering. Blockchain's usual description as a "distributed ledger" sounds like a Charles Dickens–era record-keeping term but just means a database of information shared and synchronized among participants in a network. Ledgers can keep track of any transaction, from recordation of business assets to real estate transactions to contracts.

Blockchain is a technology described as having unbreakable security, as well as being proposed as a solution for many problems (including many having nothing to do with what the technology actually does). It is the underlying architecture of Bitcoin and other cryptocurrency. Blockchain is already promised as a solution for every conceivable area of human activity including voting, health-record storage, and genomics, as well as in many areas of Internet governance including intellectual property rights protection, decentralized Domain Name System, and any network elements that require a digital identity system, including IoT systems.[51]

The technology already underlies a variety of mainstream financial and industrial service implementations such as supply-chain management, insurance-claims management, and settlement clearing. There are also many applications for which blockchain would never make sense. Not every application requires a record that can never be deleted. Many transactions are quick and transient. But it is a real technology that requires examining from the standpoint of IoT public policy and standardization.

Understanding blockchain governance considerations is aided by a comparison with cryptographic trust systems that require an intermediary—"trusted third party"—to perform some certification or authentication function. In the online world, almost every transaction requires trust in a third party. Websites require authentication by a third-party system to ensure that they are legitimate, via the Certificate Authority (CA) process. Financial transactions (or any transactions) online require trust that the site accessed, such as an online banking or retail site, is the actual site and not a counterfeit system designed to illegally appropriate information, money, or a customer's identity. Encryption, and specifically public-key cryptography, is at the heart of many authentication processes.

These third parties are sources of trust but also sources that can be hacked or otherwise subject to exploitation. A significant problem of Internet governance is the infinite-regress question of how to certify the authority that in turn certifies an online site. The governance problem of how to trust the trusted intermediaries is exactly the problem that blockchain is poised to address. The idea behind the peer-to-peer decentralization of blockchain transaction validation is to reduce the risk of fraud and tampering or to avoid endowing centralized intermediaries, whether governments, corporations, institutions, or individuals, with outsized power. Centralized intermediaries become unnecessary because public ledger transactions are instead vouched for by the other participants in the system. It is a system of distributed consensus authenticating that a transaction has taken place rather than relying on centralized authority.

Blockchain-based cryptocurrency implementations seek to ensure that the entity spending the cryptocurrency actually owns it and that it holds sufficient resources for the transaction. The security associated with blockchain-based cryptocurrency is based on encryption technologies. Digital signatures signed with encryption keys authenticate sources of information. This authentication feature is roughly commensurate with other cryptographic approaches that vouch for sites or devices/participants in a network. The other cryptographic feature—cryptographic hashes—is designed to ensure that there are no alterations to records. Records added to the ledger each have a unique cryptographic affordance that enables verification and auditability.

In short, blockchain is an information technology. But it has many unique technological affordances:

- *Disintermediation.* A central intermediary is not necessary because decentralized nodes becomes the intermediating network. Centralized authorities are replaced by distributed consensus mechanisms.
- *Record Permanence.* Once a record is added to the public ledger, it can (theoretically) never be removed from the database.
- *Record Immutability.* Records, once validated, can never be altered.
- *Decentralized Authority.* Transaction verification occurs by distributed consensus rather than centralized authority.
- *Peer-to-Peer Networking.* The logical infrastructure underpinning is peer-to-peer rather than hierarchical.

The central authority is designed to be computation rather than people or institutions. From the disciplinary standpoint of science and technology studies, such a statement is inconceivable. The design of technology itself embeds power relations and produces socioeconomic effects. Historically, it has also almost never worked out to say that a technology is unbreakable.

An open question is security. The technology is described as "uncrackable." Perhaps certain implementations can be hacked but not the underlying mathematical underpinning. Strong security is one of the promises of this cryptographic technology, but already there are questions about what happens if a single entity controlled or compromised enough of the disintermediated computing systems (the 51 percent problem). Quantum-computing advances would also necessitate a reconceptualization of the promised security of blockchain. Regardless, blockchain technology has many potential applications in the Internet of things and has to become a consideration, ab initio, in standardization architectures.

A Historical Perspective on the Power and Limits of Standards

Interoperability is not a given. Interoperability among devices, via common protocols, is a key technical enabler of interconnection, commensurate with the role of standards in all interconnection. However, IoT implementations have not adopted the same approach to open standards as traditionally have arisen in Internet communication applications such as the web and email, for example.[52] This is why the British computer scientist Dame Wendy Hall has presciently said, "The Internet of Things is not yet an Internet."[53]

There has always been a tension between proprietary enclosure and open and interconnected common markets for innovation.[54] At one point, proprietary computer network systems were the norm. For example, IBM (International Business Machines) computers ran on a protocol architecture called Systems Network Architecture (SNA), and these computers could not natively interoperate with Apple computers connected via AppleTalk protocols. Business models were based on proprietary and closed systems that created what was then often referred to as islands of automation or walled gardens. Devices on one vendor's network could not communicate with devices on another network. Even into the 1990s with the advent of home online systems like America Online, Prodigy, and CompuServe, these systems were based on proprietary standards and were designed not to interoperate.

This tension is tipping somewhat toward proprietary, closed standards. This trend applies broadly and not only in cyber-physical systems. For example, social media platforms are, in some ways, closer to the proprietary online systems of the 1990s in which users of one online service could not communicate with users on other systems. There is not necessarily compatibility among platforms, there is not Uniform Resource Locator (URL) compatibility, there is not data portability, and there is not universal searchability. It is not that standards approaches are not available. It is that the companies operating these platforms have engineered open standards and interoperability out of these microcosms. The analog would be an email user of Gmail unable to send email to a user of Microsoft's Outlook email.

Without open standards, there would not have been the same competition, innovation, and growth in applications connected to the Internet. There is already a resurgence of proprietary standards in some areas of information and communication technology. This is what markets are selecting, certainly in the consumer IoT space, with the consequences still to be determined even while open architectures are in development. Because of the economic and political implications of standards—on security, stability, economic competition, and human rights—standards governance is an important part of cyber-physical systems.

It is also important to keep some perspective on the limitations of protocols. Just because a standard is developed, the specification does not spontaneously or automatically become implanted in the devices manufactured by private industry, nor does it guarantee the usage of these standards-embedded products in markets. There is also no guarantee that the intended effect of a standard occurs. For example, even if protocol formulation resists governments' attempts to weaken encryption to enable surveillance, governments can carry out surveillance by many other means, such as requesting that a manufacturer build it into specific network switches, carrying out surveillance at interconnection points, or asking information intermediaries to divulge subscriber or device information. Technical-standards-setting institutions, already a diverse and sometimes competing arena of many institutions, are only part of a broader mosaic of technical governance. The cyber-governance regime includes industry, policymakers, market forces, Internet governance institutions, and many other actors. But standard setting is a powerful force. How cyber-physical standards develop will help to shape interoperability, rights, and competition for the next generation.

PART THREE

RETHINKING INTERNET FREEDOM AND GOVERNANCE

6

The Internet Freedom Oxymoron

PRESERVE A "FREE AND OPEN INTERNET." This mantra has remained the dominant Internet governance vision of the twenty-first century in democratic societies. Google public policy statements have cited "preserving a free and open Internet" as a rationale for encouraging the U.S. government to relinquish its historical oversight of Internet names and numbers.[1] The former Federal Communications Commission (FCC) chair Jules Genachowski announced FCC open Internet net-neutrality rules under the mantle of "preserving a free and open Internet."[2] And former secretary of state Hillary Clinton delivered two celebrated Internet freedom speeches promoting the need to "protect and defend a free and open Internet."[3]

These freedom aspirations, on the surface, comport with U.S. First Amendment traditions, the objective of maintaining the dominance of U.S. multinational tech companies, and a host of foreign-policy interventions contingent on spreading democratic values and attenuating the power of authoritarian regimes. Discourses around Internet freedom have served a variety of interests and ideologies.

However, the diffusion of digital technologies into the material world necessitates a radical reconceptualization of freedom and human rights. Traditional notions of Internet freedom are disconnected from actual technical, political, and market conditions. "Internet freedom" usually pertains to content, especially freedom of expression, intellectual property rights, and freedom from government regulation of content. Rarely has it involved technical architecture itself, although interestingly the philosophical principles of freedom and openness have some historical roots in the Internet's engineering design community. When human rights concerns do invoke infrastructure, this connection has primarily focused on access rights that affect the flow of content, such as broadband penetration rates or net neutrality, both infrastructure issues that reside very close to human users rather than embedded in technical architecture.

Of course, the Internet was never completely free or completely open, even viewed through the lens of content. While activists and technologists have sought to defensively preserve a free and open Internet, authoritarian and democratic governments alike have turned to digital technologies to constrain human freedom and enact invasive surveillance of citizens, sometimes under the mantel of preserving social order.

Science fiction imaginaries about pervasive surveillance, digitally meddling in democratic elections, and cyber infrastructure disruptions that once seemed unthinkable have wholly materialized. In a span of a few years, the Egyptian government was able to sever citizens' Internet and mobile phone access for days; a hacker obtained the personal data of seventy million customers of an American retail giant; and the U.S. intelligence community exposed Russian attempts to intervene in elections.

For those who access the Internet in democratic societies, it is sometimes difficult to absorb how illusory are digital speech rights in other cultures. A Saudi Arabian court sentenced a father of three to ten years of imprisonment and corporal punishment of two thousand lashes for posting atheistic tweets criticizing religion in 2016.[4] The Committee to Protect Journalists, in a recent prison census, recounted a record number of Internet-based journalists jailed in Egypt, ranked only behind China in the imprisonment of journalists.[5] The Turkish government has ordered a succession of Internet blockages. A great enduring mythology in the history of the Internet is the notion of a social-media-fueled Arab Spring that has brought about democratic revolutions.

Two incommensurable Internet worldviews coexist: preserving a free and open Internet versus preserving an invasive system of efficient censorship and surveillance. One presents utopian possibilities for freedom of expression and access to knowledge, and the other presents a chilling vision of information control and personally invasive private and public scrutiny. As with all tenuous binaries, the reality is much more complicated, and the same exact technologies that enable individual freedom can be used by authoritarian governments for repression. Problematically, both framings focus primarily on content.

Competing notions of utopian possibility and dystopian admonition have many historical antecedents in times of rapid technological change. The nineteenth-century introduction of the telegraph radically altered possibilities for communication. The novel invention suddenly enabled information to flow orders of magnitude faster than the mail-delivery speed limitations of real-world transportation systems like railroad and shipping technologies. The telegraph's globally spanning network of cables and network operators using Morse code to transmit and receive messages disordered economic and social life. As the historian Tom Standage describes the telegraph in *The Victorian Internet,* "It revolutionized business practice, gave rise to new forms of crime, and inundated its users with a deluge of information. Romances blossomed over the wires. Secret codes were devised by some users and cracked by others. The benefits of the network were relentlessly hyped by its advocates and dismissed by the skeptics. Governments and regulators tried and failed to control the new medium. Attitudes toward everything from news gathering to diplomacy had to be completely rethought."[6] The advent of radio and television prompted similar rhetoric about the democratic possibilities of mass broadcasting, albeit using a one-to-many rather than two-way transmission flow.[7] Each new technology similarly resulted in regulatory tussles and conflicts between stakeholders' interests. So it is with cyber technologies.

How does Internet freedom require rethinking in the context of the cyber-physical disruption? This chapter offers an evolutionary history of different Internet freedom framings and their stakeholder implications. It then compares the promise of Internet freedom against what has occurred in practice. Finally, it sets the stage for the complications that the Internet's transformation into the physical world presents for the future of individual cyber freedom. Internet freedom framings have not at all encompassed concerns about basic security and stability, and this must change. Digital rights framings must evolve again to reflect the high stakes of contemporary technological transformations.

The Engineering Roots of Freedom from Top-Down Control

Before there were Internet freedom advocates, there were engineers in the Internet Engineering Task Force who created traditions of bottom-up technical design based on participatory processes and rough consensus. The IETF as an institution was formally established in 1986 and more recently placed under the umbrella organization that is the Internet Society, but its functional and institutional lineage traces back into the 1970s. As the historian of technology Andrew Russell explains, "The Internet standards community not only introduced technological innovations; it also pioneered organizational innovations such as the use of electronic mailing lists to build consensus around technical work, a process open to all interested stakeholders, and the free and unrestricted distribution of standards."[8]

A 1995 *Wired* magazine article portrayed the emerging culture of the IETF: "in the cyber '90s . . . the True Masters of the Universe are not freemasons, mergers-and-acquisitions specialists, or venture capitalists but the members of a voluntary association of tech wizards that create and oversee the technological future of the Internet."[9]

The Internet's engineering community pioneered democratic design traditions. Historically, anyone could participate in in-person meetings or electronically mediated working groups. The standards themselves were made freely and transparently accessible to anyone, enabling both open innovation and also the possibility for public accountability over the specifications. Dominant standards have traditionally had minimal or no intellectual property restrictions on their use, reflecting the values of designers. Whereas the goal of many standards is to extract royalties via underlying patents or to gain market advantage by limiting access to specifications, the openness of IETF specifications has supported the institution's objective of having them widely adopted.[10]

One of the most enduring design philosophies of the Internet engineering community came from David Clark's 1992 plenary talk "A Cloudy Crystal Ball, Visions of the Future," and it became an articulation of the IETF's core philosophy:

> We reject: kings, presidents, and voting.
> We believe in: rough consensus and running code.[11]

This statement was not a response to government intrusion into the Internet design process. It reflected concern that IETF working group members felt about hierarchical pressure within the IETF itself. In the context of decisions that would eventually lead to the development of IPv6, designed to expand the number of available Internet addresses by replacing its predecessor standard IPv4, the IETF's leadership body, the Internet Architecture Board (IAB) had recommended a specific protocol as a replacement. Clark and other engineers believed the most effective solutions would emanate in a bottom-up approach from IETF working groups that adopted working, tested solutions. The phrase "rough consensus and running code" became the institution's de facto operating credo that endured for decades. Although not employing the term "Internet freedom," this pragmatic philosophy reflected values of democratic participation and transparency and the rejection of top-down control, all values that would shape future Internet freedom epochs.

The Evolutionary Politics of Internet Freedom

The normative stance of promoting Internet freedom has malleably responded to almost any problem or stakeholder interest related to cyberspace. Self-described conceptions of Internet freedom have evolved over decades and certainly since the early 1990s inception of the web. Each historically specific formulation is value laden and shaped by its own set of stakeholders and incentives. Each arises contextually around particular ideologies, infrastructures, and usage norms.

One potent and durable Internet freedom framing arose from cyber-libertarian opposition to regulatory interventions in cyberspace, from the Communications Decency Act (CDA) of 1996 to the Stop Online Piracy Act (SOPA) proposed in 2011, among numerous others. Separately, the U.S. Department of State conceptualized Internet freedom as a foreign-policy intervention to promote democracy during the Obama administration. Large corporate intermediaries have adopted a similar Internet freedom conception opposing censorship and promoting the free flow of information. A completely distinct framing addresses Internet access as a human right, spanning concerns such as broadband penetration rates around the world and the nondiscrimination principle of net neutrality. A more recent and globally influential Internet freedom formulation views multistakeholder governance models as a mechanism for democratic ideals in cyberspace.

These five rhetorical conceptions of Internet freedom share one common feature. They are centrally about *content* and, more specifically, communicative expression—free speech, the right to access knowledge, the free flow of information, the ability to communicate with others. Rethinking rights in the context of the Internet as a control network enmeshed in cyber-physical systems first requires a historical understanding of content-centric Internet freedom conceptions and what is at stake for various stakeholders who construct these formulations.

Freedom from Government Regulation: From Decency to Piracy

Concern about sexually explicit content online has often come into conflict with freedom of expression. One of the first formal references to the term "Internet freedom" emerged in 1995 in the context of U.S. government attempts to censor speech that it deemed immoral. There was not sufficient broadband access to easily stream video in this technological context. The concern was primarily about what was deemed by some people as obscene or indecent text and images. FCC restrictions on offensive language on television already existed, but the question was whether the government would turn attention to regulating Internet content.

In the early 1990s, the Internet was called the "information superhighway." Internet access services leveraging new browser technologies to enable easy navigation of the web were supplanting the dominant proprietary online systems like America Online, Prodigy, and CompuServe. Rather than accessing curated services in which content was provided by the network provider or heavily moderated, the web allowed anyone to post information, including sexually explicit material.

In this context, the United States established a law designed specifically to enact government regulation of online content related to "indecency." Passed by Congress and signed into law by President Bill Clinton, the Telecommunications Act of 1996 included a controversial Title V provision known as the "Communications Decency Act." The CDA amounted to government regulation of online content specifically related to "indecency." It criminalized, by punishment of fines or imprisonment, the use of "any interactive computer service to display in a manner available to a person under 18 years of age, any comment, request, suggestion, proposal, image, or other communication that, in context, depicts or describes, in terms patently offensive as measured by contemporary community standards."[12]

Advocacy organizations—including the American Civil Liberties Union (ACLU), the Electronic Privacy Information Center (EPIC), and the Electronic Frontier Foundation (EFF)—viewed the CDA as a threat to Internet freedom. Free-speech advocates interpreted the reach and vagueness of the law as an unconstitutional restriction on speech that would have chilling effects on expression and possibly even restrict discussions about abortion, birth control, human sexuality, medical procedures, and human anatomy. Hundreds of website operators blackened their background screens to protest the law's passage.[13] The

World Wide Web was then only a few years old, so this online protest was one of the first instances of a web boycott.

One short publication symbolically epitomized cyber-libertarian perspectives on a limited role for governments in regulating Internet content: "A Declaration of the Independence of Cyberspace" by the late John Perry Barlow, an original thinker about the Internet and civil liberties online. A former Grateful Dead lyricist, Wyoming rancher, and cofounder of EFF, Barlow published the roughly 850-word treatise in 1996 in the context of the passage of the Telecommunications Act of 1996.[14] An excerpt from the opening of the declaration follows:

> Governments of the Industrial World, you weary giants of flesh and steel, I come from Cyberspace, the new home of Mind. On behalf of the future, I ask you of the past to leave us alone. You are not welcome among us. You have no sovereignty where we gather.
>
> We have no elected government, nor are we likely to have one, so I address you with no greater authority than that with which liberty itself always speaks. I declare the global social space we are building to be naturally independent of the tyrannies you seek to impose on us. You have no moral right to rule us nor do you possess any methods of enforcement we have true reason to fear.[15]

Barlow's piece specifically referenced the Telecommunications Act and warned about content "guard posts" erected in other countries. It also took aim at increasing attention to intellectual property rights enforcement approaches online, criticizing laws prohibiting the dissemination of ideas from "increasingly obsolete information industries" in a technological world in which ideas "can be reproduced and distributed infinitely and at no cost."[16]

After moving through the courts, a 9–0 Supreme Court ruling struck down part of the CDA—specifically its anti-indecency provisions—in *Reno v. American Civil Liberties Union* on the grounds of violating the First Amendment of the United States Constitution. The 1997 ruling described the Internet as a network of computers enabling "tens of millions of people to communicate with one another" and constituting "a unique and wholly new medium of worldwide human communication."[17] The court viewed the Internet as distinct from broadcasting in that children could access broadcast material with little or no difficulty or action. Most notably, the ruling noted that the undefined terms "indecent" and "patently offensive" were sufficiently vague to raise First Amendment concerns about the law's chilling effects on free speech.

This tension between the public interest of protecting children and promoting conditions of free expression is an example of the enduring values conflicts that exist at cyber control points. A lasting and influential legacy of the CDA is its Section 230 provision, which provides immunity from liability for Internet providers (called in the context of the CDA "providers of interactive computer services") for information published by others on their services. Fast-forwarding decades from the inception of this law, a social media service, for example, is generally not liable in the United States for the content its subscribers post on the service, whether it is hate speech or political propaganda. Contemporary questions about the obligations of private intermediaries to perform content moderation around everything from cyberbullying to foreign political propaganda raise the question anew about service providers not treated as the speaker or the publisher. The safe harbor provision of this law also immunizes intermediaries from liability for good-faith attempts to address objectionable content.

Another legacy is Barlow's declaration itself. Even though scholars have retrospectively criticized his essay as ideological and oversimplified,[18] and even though Barlow rethought it himself over the years, it was a visionary response that admirers and detractors alike have reproduced on tens of thousands of websites, cyber activists have referenced, and Internet policy scholars have extensively cited. The underlying philosophy rests on principles of limited government regulation of content and the expansion of cyberspace—both infrastructure and content—as a precursor for growth and innovation of the digital economy and online creativity.

Similar concerns about the consequences of government regulation fueled the 2011 and 2012 web blackouts over two intellectual property rights bills moving through the United States Congress, the Stop Online Piracy Act (SOPA) and the Preventing Real Online Threats to Economic Creativity and Theft of Intellectual Property Act (PROTECT IP Act, or PIPA). Drafters designed SOPA and PIPA, rare examples of bills with full bipartisan support, to target intellectual property rights violations, such as the illegal digital sharing of copyrighted media (e.g., music and videos) and trademark and trade-secrecy violations such as the online sale of counterfeit pharmaceutical products or knockoffs of luxury goods. Not surprisingly, the bills had the support of powerful mainstream media content corporations, the pharmaceutical industry, and the motion picture and music lobby. Both bills would have increased criminal penalties for downloading pirated media. They would have enabled law enforcement and intellectual property rights holders to demand that private intermediaries block services to infringing sites, such as search engines not returning links to these sites, Internet service providers blocking access, financial intermediaries not directing payments, and advertising companies not serving ads to these sites.

The two piracy bills prompted the largest online boycott and petition effort in the Internet's history, at least up until that time. The response, led by large technology companies and advocacy organizations, included dramatic coordinated blackouts of popular online sites. For twenty-four hours, Wikipedia blacked out its English-language site with a banner reading, "Imagine a World without Free Knowledge." Reddit similarly disrupted access to its own site. Google blacked out its opening Google doodle (its daily alteration of its search-screen logo). EFF, among other prominent advocacy organizations, facilitated millions of petition signatures and calls to Congress.

The boycott and petition effort was not necessarily resistance to antipiracy efforts but a protest over specific provisions of how antipiracy efforts would be carried out, such as heightening criminal penalties, possibly holding intermediary companies liable for copyright infringement on their sites, and the prospect of blocking access to an entire site for containing a hyperlink to other sites hosting pirated content. Concern centered on free speech and the ability for the tech industry to innovate or even transact business as usual.[19] As Reddit cofounder Alexis Ohanian warned, the legislation would "obliterate an entire tech industry."[20]

The Internet's technical community expressed concern about a more complicated and alarming provision of the bills, the possibility of enforcing intellectual property rights by altering the Domain Name System's universally consistent mapping of domain names into associated IP addresses. It had already been common for national governments to order Internet registries within their borders to block access (not resolve domain names into IP addresses) to sites with domain names under their jurisdiction. The additional provision would have addressed the problem of piracy taking place extraterritorially, such as originating in Russia and involving a domain name that a foreign registry controlled, and would have required intermediaries to locally modify the global mapping of names into numbers. This suggestion of shifting from a universally consistent domain name mapping to one that would be locally modified raised concerns about how this change would complicate DNS security and erode the universality of the Internet.[21]

This attention from the Internet technical community helped discursively position the debate as a "don't break the Internet" framing as well as one of

"Internet freedom." But it was the media attention from the online blackouts and petition efforts that attracted the attention of policymakers, leading to sponsors of the bill withdrawing their support for the bill as crafted. Over time, Internet freedom concern about regulatory overreach encompassed three primary concerns: limiting freedom of expression, impeding the ability of tech companies to thrive, and, to put it simply, breaking the Internet.

Internet Freedom as U.S. Foreign Policy

A conception of Internet freedom that is more tightly embroiled in the global political system began roughly with Hillary Clinton's famous 2010 speech on Internet freedom at the Newseum in Washington, DC. As secretary of state, Clinton delivered formal remarks outlining the new Obama administration's policies on Internet freedom. This first major speech by a U.S. government official on the Internet described the spread of cyberspace as enabling the free flow of information while also acknowledging its role as a platform for widespread government censorship, such as in China, Tunisia, and Uzbekistan, as well as the Egyptian government's detention of bloggers and activists. Her speech directly referenced Franklin Delano Roosevelt's 1941 "Four Freedoms" speech and Winston Churchill's "Iron Curtain" speech to introduce basic digital rights including freedom of expression and the freedom to connect. The short speech used the word "freedom" forty-six times. Secretary Clinton directly criticized censorship by China and called on industry to push back against the efforts of authoritarian governments to restrict or block speech.[22] Policy scholars and activists immediately immortalized her address as a "historic speech."[23]

Internet freedom became part of U.S. foreign policy in rhetoric but also more actively in programmatic activities, partnerships with civil society and the private sector, foreign funding, and bilateral and multilateral policy engagement. During the Obama administration, the U.S. Congress appropriated hundreds of millions of dollars to the United States Agency for International Development (USAID) and the State Department to support activities related to the advancement of Internet freedom. Described as a "venture capital approach" to Internet freedom, the State Department's Bureau of Democracy, Human Rights, and Labor provided financial support for a wide range of programmatic approaches—technological innovation, advocacy, education, research—in support of global Internet freedom.[24]

The Internet governance scholar Madeline Carr suggests that U.S. foreign-policy advocacy for Internet freedom could be understood not only "as the promotion of human rights or of a normative 'public good' but also as an expression of state power."[25] In other words, the liberal democratic values embedded in most Internet freedom conceptions, and certainly the U.S. State Department's technological vision during Secretary Clinton's term, accomplished multiple distinct goals of promoting human rights, bolstering the legitimacy of the state, and establishing the conditions for both how the Internet functions and the institutional power structures around these functions.

Global political controversies over cyber control also increasingly entered the public consciousness during this era. The same year as Secretary Clinton's first Internet freedom speech, WikiLeaks began releasing into the public domain classified diplomatic cables sent between the State Department and consulates, diplomatic missions, and embassies. Exactly one year after Clinton's first Internet freedom speech, on January 27, 2011, in a political phenomenon without historical precedent, the Egyptian government cut off phone and Internet access to its citizens. The five-day outage was carried out by private industry at the behest of the Egyptian government under President Hosni Mubarak in the context of political unrest directed against the state. Shortly thereafter, Secretary Clinton made a second Internet freedom speech, this time at George Washington University in Washington, DC. Clinton addressed the WikiLeaks State Department cable breach head-on and emphasized the need for security as well as liberty and principles of confidentiality, including for government online communications. Still, freedom of expression and the promotion of democratic freedom around the world remained primary principles.

Narratives about the so-called Arab Spring certainly fall into this linkage between Internet freedom and democratic values. The term generally referred to a wave of protests and uprisings against primarily authoritarian governments in the Middle East and North Africa, beginning in Tunisia in 2010. The role of the Internet in organizing protests and promoting change during this time was one of the more utopian and technologically deterministic views of cyberspace since its inception, especially considering the regional instability that has ensued in the intervening years, such as civil war in Libya, political turmoil and media censorship in Egypt, and nearly complete societal breakdown in Syria.

Nevertheless, U.S. foreign-policy concerns about Internet freedom have included, as scholars at the Center for a New American Century explain, two reciprocal dimensions: (1) extending freedoms of expression, assembly, and association into online realms; and (2) the idea that the Internet and new information technologies promote democratic freedom offline.[26] Corporate economic interest in the free flow of information is an additional dimension of foreign policy because of the enormous importance of large media companies to global markets and to the U.S. economy.

Internet Freedom and Corporate Interests

The United Nations' conception of human rights on the Internet affirms that "the same rights that people have offline must also be protected online, in particular freedom of expression, which is applicable regardless of frontiers and through any media of one's choice, in accordance with articles 19 of the Universal Declaration of Human Rights and the International Covenant on Civil and Political Rights."[27] Private information intermediaries, such as Google and Facebook, have an obvious and significant stake in the promotion of freedom of expression around the world.[28] Online platform intermediaries drove the Internet boycotts and petitions responding to the perceived regulatory overreach of the antipiracy bills SOPA and PIPA. These companies have similarly sometimes pushed back against Internet censorship and blocking around the world. These efforts are not only statements of corporate principles but efforts to preserve the companies' business models.

Government censorship of corporate media platforms such as YouTube is also a blockage of the ability of these companies to generate revenue, which they do primarily through serving targeted online ads to users. As a characteristic example of the free expression commitment of online intermediaries, the following was a 2008 statement from a Google Policy Counsel on "Promoting Free Expression on the Internet": "Google's commitment to freedom of expression is at the core of everything we do—whether it's independent media organizations using YouTube to express themselves in Venezuela, or citizen journalists using Blogger to chronicle Myanmar's crackdown last year on Buddhist monk protests. Unfortunately, many governments around the world impose limits on their citizens' freedom of speech, and that often leads them to block or limit access to our tools and services. This is one of the largest challenges we face as a company."[29] Ironically, governments are rarely able to censor information and block access or monitor communication on their own but do so via private companies that own and operate the infrastructure and platforms over which information flows.

Shutting down access requires the cooperation of private companies, whereas governments order service providers to shut down cell phone and Internet service. Therefore, private companies are both a mechanism for and also a source of resistance for pushing back against restrictive information policies. Private information intermediaries, like companies in other industries such as energy, often have statements of corporate social responsibility that lay out operating principles that comply with a particular set of values.

Large Internet companies including Microsoft, Google, and Yahoo!, along with CDT and other advocacy organizations, formed the Global Network Initiative (GNI) as a coalition expression of corporate principles on freedom of expression and privacy. Drawing from international standards such as the Universal Declaration of Human Rights, the coalition sought to promote common principles for freedom of expression, privacy, and transparency, to provide accountability via independent assessments of adherence to these principles, and to engage in shared policy engagement and information sharing. Multistakeholder coalitions such as GNI have not been without conflict. For example, EFF withdrew its membership after the revelations about the expansiveness of NSA surveillance and the extent to which private companies have cooperated with this surveillance.[30]

In *Consent of the Networked: The Worldwide Struggle for Internet Freedom*, Rebecca MacKinnon sorts through the complex dynamics between democratic freedom and political control online, making visible the shift in governance functions from the state to private networks and conceptually explaining the types of political control possible online. For example, the same technologies enabling democratic openness can be used to repress, even while making censored people feel freer (e.g., the "networked authoritarianism" of China) or to manipulate, such as the "digital bonapartism" of how Russia is perfecting public-opinion manipulation via direct and indirect control of digital networks.[31] In light of these political control approaches and the role of the private sector in intermediating everything, MacKinnon views corporate accountability as a precursor to what she also terms a "free and open Internet."[32]

Internet Freedom as Access Rights

Internet freedom has sometimes been synonymous with "net neutrality" and conceptions of access as a fundamental human right. Access rights fall into several overlapping categories: net neutrality and the principle of nondiscrimination by Internet service providers; broadband penetration rates and similar digital-divide issues; and a hybrid of the two in which free services (zero rating) help bridge the second category (broadband penetration) but potentially violate the first category (net neutrality) because the free services only allow access through proprietary portals that limit what can be freely accessed.

This conception of Internet freedom resides close to human end users, focusing on edge-of-the-network access technologies and policies, and is rooted, particularly among U.S. legal scholars, in First Amendment rights. As the Internet law scholar Marvin Ammori explains, "There should be no doubt that access to high-speed Internet service is even a First Amendment issue—as is the question of whether or not that access is limited by telecoms, cable companies, Hollywood, devices, or large tech companies."[33]

Many depictions of Internet freedom have singularly focused on net neutrality, a narrow but important policy issue that is geographically local but has global implications. The basic policy question of net neutrality is whether network operators should be legally prohibited from discriminating against certain types of traffic, content, applications, or sites for political, economic, technical, or other reasons. Discrimination can entail blocking, prioritizing, or throttling (slowing). The types of affected traffic can include specific applications such as BitTorrent clients or Skype, protocols such as VoIP or peer-to-peer (P2P) file-sharing protocols, services such as YouTube or Netflix, or specific websites or user accounts such as those that are critical of government or illegally selling pirated or counterfeit products.

Positions for and against net neutrality have equally been characterized as preserving a free and open Internet. The Obama White House often framed the regulatory push for net neutrality as "President Obama's plan for a free and open Internet." FCC orders during this time were cast as "Preserving a Free and Open Internet," calling on providers to transparently disclose their network management practices; to refrain from blocking lawful content, devices, applications, and services; and to refrain from unreasonable discrimination.[34] Those who were against net-neutrality regulations also described their position as advocating for a free and open Internet. For example, the network service provider Comcast opposed regulatory frameworks designed to legally enforce the nondiscrimination principle (e.g., the FCC reclassification of broadband Internet access as a utility under Title II of the Communications Act of 1934) on the grounds of thwarting a free and open Internet and also discouraging investment and innovation.[35]

The net-neutrality issue, as historically constructed, is limited in scope to what is usually described as "last mile" connections of a network service to individuals or homes, such as the link between a cellular antenna to a mobile phone or a coaxial cable or fiber connection to a home. Even though this represents a small segment of broader Internet infrastructure, this concern about last-mile access discrimination is appropriate because it serves as a choke point providing entrée to the broader Internet and because subscribers often do not have considerable choice of providers, especially in rural areas. The complexity of the issue is far greater than it is often simplistically portrayed in the media and by policymakers, and it is one that speaks to the right to innovate and compete in markets, the freedom of individual customers to access lawful content, and the pragmatic engineering need to undertake routine network management that addresses performance, latency, and quality of service.

Beyond the narrow net-neutrality issue is the broader view of access as a right and as the core building block of a free and open Internet. The United Nations Human Rights Council resolution "The Promotion, Protection, and Enjoyment of Human Rights on the Internet" "recognizes the global and open nature of the Internet as a driving force in accelerating progress towards development in its various forms" and "calls upon all States to promote and facilitate access to the Internet and international cooperation aimed at the development of media and information and communications facilities in all countries."[36] Large cities from New York to New Delhi have identified affordable broadband access as a policy priority related to Internet freedom. In some cases, this vision includes the development of municipal high-speed Wi-Fi networks. In other cases, it involves policy approaches that provide inducements for private industry to build infrastructure into rural and underserved areas.

A newer set of access debates about a free and open Internet arose at the intersection of net neutrality and broadband policies. New business models known as zero rating services—such as Facebook's Free Basics program—were designed to provide free Internet access in underserved markets but raised questions about whether people would have free and open access to the broader Internet or access only to a "walled garden" segment of the Internet, as well as concerns about the potentially anticompetitive effects of this model.

Multistakeholder Governance and Internet Freedom

Multistakeholder governance, itself a fetishized ideal, has also become closely associated with the preservation of a free and open Internet. A system of administration distributed among the private sector, governments, and global coordinating institutions, multistakeholder governance increasingly emerges in cyber-policy discourses as a precursor for a variety of democratic rights online, including freedom of expression and privacy.

The multistakeholder Internet governance principle crystallized in the immediate aftermath of the 2003 World Summit on the Information Society (WSIS), when then-secretary-general of the United Nations Kofi Annan tasked a Working Group on Internet Governance to resolve open issues over control of the Internet. The open issues primarily involved global contention over the U.S. government's historical oversight of Internet names and numbers, especially its contractual relationship with the Internet Corporation for Assigned Names and Numbers (ICANN) and its authority over changes to the Internet's root zone file that tracks the names and addresses of top-level domain root servers. The working group devised a definition of Internet governance as follows: "Internet governance is the development and application by Governments, the private sector and civil society, in their respective roles, of shared principles, norms, rules, decision-making procedures, and programmes that shape the evolution and use of the Internet."[37]

"Multistakeholder governance" has since become a term that captures some characteristics of how the Internet is governed, albeit in specific technical coordination areas such as standards setting and the administration of names and numbers. The term is often mischaracterized as *the* multistakeholder model of Internet governance, as if Internet governance were a single system rather than an entire constellation of distinct functions necessary to keep the Internet operational, with some functions carried out by the private sector, some by governments, and some by new global institutions with varying degrees of participation by two or more classes of stakeholders.[38]

The interpretive flexibility of this governance ideal helps endow it with context-specific political utility. For example, the global multistakeholder ideal was deployed for years as a rationale for diminishing U.S. hegemony over Internet governance functions. Indeed, the U.S. government's own announcement about its intention to relinquish its historical oversight role embraced this framing: "To support and enhance the multistakeholder model of Internet policymaking and governance, the U.S. Commerce Department's National Telecommunications and Information Administration (NTIA) today announces its intent to transition key Internet domain name functions to the global multistakeholder community."[39] The Internet's technical community, among others, viewed the transition process as "one more step to ensure the long-term health of a free and open Internet."[40] Even those who opposed the transition to multistakeholder governance cited concerns about relinquishing control to Russia and China and other governments with authoritarian Internet-governance approaches that could weaken Internet freedom.

This framing serves as a preemptive barrier to the possibility of oversight of the Internet by the United Nations (and therefore by its nondemocratic-government constituency). China is a powerful player in United Nations multilateral discussions and has a track record of enacting widespread systems of censorship and content control.

The multistakeholder framing of Internet freedom is also a way to elevate, preserve, or justify the privatization of governance whether through terms of service and private contractual agreements with consumers or through private contractual arrangements among network operators for interconnection. "Private-sector-led multistakeholder governance" is often the exact phrasing used. It is also sometimes very specifically linked to the privatization of human rights, the acknowledgment of the role that private companies play in establishing the conditions of civil liberties online, and the question of how to increase the legitimacy of this privatization of rights via transparency, accountability, government oversight, or other structures. For example, the private-sector-led GNI's "Principles on Freedom of Expression and Privacy" emphasize multistakeholder collaborative structures as a means to ensure private accountability for the promotion of human rights online.[41]

It is indeed still the case, as this author elaborated earlier in *The Global War for Internet Governance,* that "the multistakeholder Zeitgeist has elevated the concept to a value in itself or an end in itself without critically examining what this concept can obfuscate."[42] Nevertheless, the term accurately connotes that some technical governance areas involve the participation and direct oversight of multiple stakeholders. For example, ICANN's oversight of Internet domain names and numbers involves participation from corporations, civil society, and governments, albeit each with different authority over various functions. This implementation of multistakeholder governance can be critiqued in regard to whether there is the right balance of power among stakeholders in making decisions with public-interest implications and whether it shapes democratic freedom online, but it is an example of multistakeholder governance.

Freedom Realism and Cyber-Physical Rights

None of the conceptions of Internet freedom to date have accounted for cyber technology as it actually is, embedded in cars, medical devices, and industrial systems. Each evolutionary conception is completely content-centric, focused on issues of speech, access to knowledge, media freedom, or intellectual property. They are all concerned with communication between people rather than communication between things. Each perspective also reflects the economic objectives of stakeholder interests, whether promoting U.S. foreign policy or advancing the business models of multinational companies. Views of Internet freedom are completely immaterial to the descriptive reality that more things are connected than people. The growth of the Internet has also not equated to growth in freedom, with many areas of the world enacting systems of filtering, blocking, and surveillance as a means of political control.

Content Freedom Incommensurable with Reality

Internet freedom constructs have lacked correspondence with the lived reality of the actual state of digital freedom, not as one wants it to be but as it stands in practice. From a global perspective, real-world freedom, whether expressive or economic liberty, does not always match the promise of Internet freedom. Governments have shut down the Internet. The business models fueling the digital economy have become utterly dependent on the invasive collection of personal data. Concerted, targeted actions of troll armies have silenced voices. Oppressive systems of filtering and blocking have enacted highly efficient censorship.

Content freedom is on the decline. Freedom House, a Washington, DC–based research and advocacy institute focusing on democracy and human rights, conducts an annual "Freedom on the Net" review, among other freedom-index reports. The number of countries in the survey has expanded every year, so the annual comparison is not perfect; but the survey demonstrates a continuous annual decline in human rights online. Two-thirds of Internet users live in legal environments in which politically critical speech is censored, with China ranked as the worst offender.[43] Worse, "60% live in countries where ICT users were arrested or imprisoned for posting content on political, social, and religious issues."[44] The number of users accessing the Internet has increased, but the relative freedom of this access has declined.

Freedom online also has different meanings in different cultures. While "free and open" suggests unfettered access to information online, the user experience of this information access already varies considerably depending on geographical location. Under German law, information intermediaries must block access to Nazi content; content insulting members of a royal family is unlawful in Thailand and Malaysia; Brazil and other countries prohibit hate speech; in the United States, information intermediaries must follow the notice and takedown provisions of the DMCA for content that violates intellectual property rights. Private information intermediaries (e.g., social media companies) have detailed, if ever changing, terms of service that ban types of content from their sites. For example, Facebook states under its community standards for violence and graphic content, "We remove graphic images when they are shared for sadistic pleasure or to celebrate or glorify violence. We also remove extremely graphic videos, such as those depicting a beheading."[45]

The same technologies that enable access to knowledge and communicative expression can also be used for authoritarian purposes. Evgeny Morozov, in his 2011 book *The Net Delusion: The Dark Side of Internet Freedom,* provides a critique of linkages between the Internet and democracy objectives, noting how these objectives can "inadvertently embolden dictators and turn everyone who uses the Internet in authoritarian states into unwilling prisoners."[46] By the term "Net Delusion," Morozov is critiquing two approaches: cyber-utopian views that the Internet can vanquish authoritarianism, and Internet-centrism that pushes technological solutions without regard to context.[47]

The majority of human Internet users are not in the United States or even in so-called Western countries. They live in nondemocratic societies. China has the largest user base, with the number of people online exceeding the entire population of the United States. The experience of accessing the Internet in China is far different from accessing the Internet in Sweden, for example, and other democracies. Authoritarian governance approaches have increasingly sought greater control of information flows under the mantel of cyber sovereignty.[48] Governments view the cross-border and private, distributed architecture of the Internet as a threat to national sovereignty, even as they exploit this very infrastructure to engage in foreign intelligence gathering, launch cyberattacks, and seek to influence foreign elections. Governments advocating for tighter control and sovereign legal approaches do so under the guise of order and security, even while the underlying objectives are social control and regulation of the flow of content. For example, Russia cracks down on the on-line speech of lesbian, gay, bisexual and transgender citizens under the guise of preserving social order and protecting children.

Cyber-sovereignty approaches advocate for top-down government control of networks and multilateral rather than multistakeholder cooperation and nego-tiation in international policy approaches. These approaches not only philo-sophically depart from the private-sector-led multistakeholder model but materialize in tangible policy debates on the international stage. Conflicts be-tween multistakeholder and multilateral global approaches emerged, for exam-ple, during the 2012 World Conference on International Telecommunications that the ITU convened in Dubai. The meeting revisited an international tele-communications interconnection treaty addressing agreements about cross-border telecommunication. Countries interested in greater sovereignty sought to expand the agreements to regulate private Internet infrastructure agreements, in part to bring issues of content control under this multilateral treaty.

Powerful forces have an interest in keeping conceptions of freedom rooted in the free flow of content. It preserves revenue structures of private ordering and fuels the surveillance state. In focusing primarily on content, usage, and access, conceptions of Internet freedom have missed some of the most powerful forms of infrastructure-mediated control that either enhance or impede freedom of ex-pression. Control by co-opting infrastructure is already potent. Constructing freedom via arrangements of infrastructure should symmetrically follow. This is not to replace the need for freedom of expression but to augment it.

The free flow of information rests on a system of private surveillance capital-ism in which possibilities for individual privacy are becoming increasingly ten-uous. Governments then co-opt this infrastructure and associated data to enact surveillance and exert power over citizens. Tensions between openness and en-closure are high, with private companies increasingly using proprietary tech-nologies, rather than those based on open standards, for anticompetitive means. Trade-secrecy-protected, and therefore invisible, algorithms make decisions that have direct effects on human freedom. Governments increasingly tamper with global infrastructure—such as local DNS redirection—for censorship.

The forces in tension with Internet freedom are varied, but they are all forces of control: market forces geared toward *proprietary enclosure* rather than interoper-ability; public and private *censorship;* invasive *surveillance,* whether for online advertising monetization, political repression, intelligence-gathering purposes, or other law enforcement objective; *content manipulation,* such as social media bots and computational propaganda; and *cyber-sovereignty* models that seek to displace multistakeholder governance with nation-state cyber borders. This does not mean that the Internet does not hold the potential for greater speech rights. It means that Internet freedom, of any conceptualization, must consider how infrastructure tensions are now tied to both expressive and economic liberty.

Even while the Internet has created enormous opportunities for speech, innovation, and economic development, a critical realist perspective rooted in lived reality can help balance Internet freedom ideologies and uncritical convictions about a global free and open Internet. Throughout most of the world, the Internet is not free and open. The goal of restoring, or preserving, a free and open Internet (backward-looking idealization) should be replaced with the objective of progressively moving closer to freedom (forward-looking aspiration).

The Cyber-Physical World Transforms Freedom

The widespread embedding of digital technologies directly into objects and systems in the real world provides an opportunity to further emphasize direct connections between arrangements of technical architecture, freedom, and control. Some of these are positive liberties, meaning the power to do something; others are negative liberties, meaning freedom from something. In traditional communication contexts, freedom of association and expression are examples of positive liberties. Freedom from harassment or the right to be forgotten are examples of negative liberties. Many technology-policy approaches have to resolve tensions that exist among these various values.

Cyber-physical policy arenas—privacy, security, interoperability—speak to several dimensions of human rights that transform conceptions of digital freedom historically based on content and expressive freedom. Concerns about Internet freedom should probably always have integrated privacy to a greater extent. Privacy scholars and advocates certainly made a strong case for doing so. The boundary implications of the cyber-physical world will unquestionably foreground privacy as a value at play. The most personal spheres of human activity, work, and society interconnect at boundary objects that simultaneously reside in the real world and the digital world. The data-collection practices structurally underlying material control structures, as well as the firmly established revenue models that rely on pervasive data collection, mean that society is approaching a decision point about whether any possibility for a private sphere remains possible.

The reach of cyber-physical systems similarly elevates the importance of freedom from algorithmic discrimination. What were once concerns about discriminatory practices around content, such as the hidden decisions of search-engine algorithms, are now, as chapter 3 suggested, concerns about how data-driven algorithmic scoring affects employment decisions, credit ratings, insurance rates, law enforcement practices, and what is determined as one's political and economic value. Even more vitally, safety and human security become core rights considerations in the cyber-physical context. As chapter 4 explained, connected cars and connected medical devices, in particular, clearly indicate the dependence of human safety on encryption, authentication, data integrity, availability, and other dimensions of cybersecurity.

The right to innovate should have always been a component of Internet freedom. The focus on usage did not allow for this inclusion. Approaching human rights through a lens of infrastructure makes this connection obvious. Open standards that are freely published and not constrained by prohibitive intellectual property rights restrictions connect to the right to innovate, the ability to compete, and the market result of multiple manufacturers introducing interoperable products. The proprietary approaches in various Internet of things spheres, as well as the chaos of noninteroperable competing frameworks, encumber the freedom to innovate, especially for new market entrants. Chapter 5 has suggested that open standards, even within fragmented industry sectors, would help construct conditions for market innovation.

Novel Cyber-Physical Speech Problems: Is a 3D-Printed Gun a Speech Right?

Freedom should extend far beyond content-centric rights. At the same time, novel free-speech issues do arise in cyber-physical systems. Intersections with expressive freedom *emanate from* embedded systems and *arise within* these systems. The extent of security in IoT devices has direct consequences for the digital public sphere. The Mirai botnet demonstrated how DDoS attacks launched from insecure IoT devices directly affect conditions of speech on content intermediaries. If insecure home cameras can disrupt Twitter or a major media outlet, this is a significant free-speech concern.

Complicated speech issues also exist within cyber-physical systems them-selves, especially those that are not physical systems retrofitted to become cyber embedded (such as a door lock or cardiac monitor) but systems that are born cy-ber-physical, such as augmented reality and 3D printing. Is there a speech right to fabricate a gun from a 3D printer? The more precise question is whether a gun manufacturer has, in the United States, a First Amendment right to distribute blueprints for a 3D pistol that anyone can then print on a 3D printer. Does a pro-hibition on 3D-printed guns become prior restraint on free speech? An inventor and gun-rights advocate made printable-gun blueprints available online. The State Department demanded that the company—Defense Distributed—remove the blueprint on the grounds that it violated the Arms Export Control Act and the International Traffic in Arms Regulations. These are the same category of regulations that the U.S. government has employed over decades to restrict the international sale of strong encryption software. The affected business sued the government on First Amendment grounds, and the Department of Justice re-versed and settled the suit, even agreeing to pay the plaintiff's legal fees.[49] This and similar conflicts over speech versus safety issues in 3D printing are likely to continue. Technology continues to exceed the pace of law.

Augmented reality systems and wearable glasses raise more obvious speech questions because they have screens. A smartphone app or a wearable technol-ogy like glasses are usually the display screens for AR. As indicated by techno-logical investment patterns and patent filings, displays are moving to natural-world organic screens. Because augmented reality environments have a display interface, all of the content governance concerns that exist in the digital world exist in this cyber-physical interface.

Threats, defamation, and harassment arise in AR just as in traditional social media. Law enforcement and intelligence agencies seek information from AR companies in the same way they seek information from other intermediaries. Terms of service dictate, or should dictate, conditions of data collection, codes of behavior during platform use, and what counts as harassment. The privatization of governance, within the constraints of jurisdiction-specific statutes and social norms, applies in AR, as does the reality that these intermediaries are sites of conflict for competing values such as national security versus individual privacy. Commensurate with all embedded systems, AR has privacy implications in rela-tion to what data is collected about individuals, many of whom might not even be aware of the presence of the technology or the recordation of information.

Intellectual property complications arise. Some digital content superimposed in AR is protected by copyright but is then experientially combined with images and video captured from the physical world in real time. How does a recording of this experienced digital-physical nexus complicate intellectual property rights protections? What counts as a derivative work or a transformational use of copyrighted content? The question of fair use becomes more complicated. Terms of service for augmented reality systems often require users to grant the developer a nonexclusive royalty-free license to copy, to create derivative works, or to otherwise use content generated by users, such as images, video, and other content. In other words, those who take video and images might not have full copyright ownership over their own work.

Issues around free speech in augmented reality technologies are complicated. In the height of excitement around the augmented reality mobile game Pokémon Go, crowds of players overran private and public spaces. These impromptu gatherings created the same public challenges of an organized rally, producing litter, raising security concerns, creating traffic, and straining resources like public bathrooms. In response to the logistical challenges and safety concerns that these games created in public spaces, a Wisconsin municipality—the Milwaukee County Department of Parks, Recreation, and Culture—passed a local ordinance requiring the publishers of such games to apply for and acquire a special use permit to enable their apps to interact with public parks. The application pertained to large public events like bike races, rallies, religious gatherings, and also "virtual gaming," which it defined essentially as augmented reality experiences in which people interact with both a digital device and the surrounding natural environment, in this case a public park. The process required that the gaming company submit an application ninety days prior to an "event," obtain a certificate of insurance for at least $1 million liability, and assume responsibility for collection and removal of litter, among many other requirements and fees.[50]

Requiring permits for augmented reality usage does not seem reasonable, or feasible, because it treats an ongoing, real-time, individually engaged game as a finite event involving a fixed number of people at a specific time. It is difficult to anticipate how many individuals will use an application in a given spot and when they will do so.

AR permitting requirements also raise potential issues around prior restraint on speech. As such, the game developer Candy Lab filed a lawsuit against the

Milwaukee County Board of Supervisors and parks department in U.S. District Court claiming that the ordinance violated its free-speech rights. The lawsuit specifically claimed that the ordinance's attempt to regulate the company's right to publish augmented reality video games, constituting "a prior restraint on Candy Lab AR's speech, impermissibly restricts Candy Lab AR's speech because of its content, and is unconstitutionally vague such that Candy Lab AR does not have notice as to what speech must be approved by permit and which it can express without seeking a permit."[51] A U.S. District Court judge agreed with the company and granted a preliminary injunction in the case, which eventually resulted in a settlement in which the municipality agreed not to enforce the ordinance and paid legal fees to the company.

Even more complicated questions about speech rights are arising in cyber-physical systems—such as robots and virtual assistants—that inherently contain an artificial-intelligence-mediated voice. How do recordings of AI speech connect to the interacting person's speech rights? Under what conditions may law enforcement access this information? What counts as prior restraint on speech designed to be conveyed by a robot?

Speech complications at the boundary edge of the digital and physical world are just beginning. What is clear is that the political battles of the future—including the nature of freedom and what it means to be human—will continue to shift from the surface of digital content to the underlying material control structures.

Disruptions to Global Internet Governance

THE INTERNET IS IN A LIMINAL STATE. It is shifting from a communication network to a control network embedded in the physical world and increasingly co-opted as a proxy for political power. Everything is interconnected. There is nothing fixed about digital technology governance any more than there is anything fixed about technology itself. The cyber-physical disruption is a major technical and policy disruption. This structural transformation challenges prevailing Internet governance imaginaries and ideologies. What is the scope of cyber governance, considering intersections with issues and domains that previously had little connection to the digital world? What counts as multistakeholder governance when stakeholder communities are markedly changing? How are power structures shifting? What is the appropriate balance between interoperability and fragmentation? How are governing architectural principles now transformed? Cyber-physical systems prompt a rethinking of Internet governance scope, structures, institutions, and ideologies.

The Internet's Identity Crisis?

What is the thing being governed? Technology changes have always deposed everyday words and artifacts: horseless carriage, carbon copy, videotape, cassette tape, folding map, film, long-distance call, typewriter, telegram, and answering machine. The Internet is also transforming. The blurring of boundaries between the physical and virtual realms is also blurring understandings and affordances of the Internet itself.

Russian president Vladimir Putin has referred to the Internet as a "CIA Project."[1] The late United States senator Ted Stevens (R-Alaska) famously called it a series of tubes in the context of a discussion on net neutrality. These serve as amusing fodder for late-night comedy, but in reality, there really are divergent conceptions of what the Internet actually is. The Internet has constantly changed over its more than half-century history, arguably beginning with ARPANET. Notable transformations have included the 1990s rise of the web, its internationalization from a predominantly U.S. network to a global communication system, the twenty-first-century advent of social media, the global surge in mobile networks and smartphones, and now the Internet of things, in which everything from lighting systems to vacuum cleaners is directly connected to the Internet.

The stakes of the Internet's design and governance are high, but the thing itself being designed and governed is not always easy to define, partly because there is no *one* thing, one cloud, one network, one platform, or one governance structure. Definitions have politics. As the historian of technology Janet Abbate explains, "The ways in which historians define the Internet shape the geographic and temporal scope of our narratives, the activities we include or ignore, the dominance of certain countries and social groups and the marginality of others."[2] For example, technical-systems-based histories advantage developers of technology over users.[3] There have been many different historical and conceptual approaches to defining the Internet, none of them perfect in the contemporary context.

Already, the younger generation does not routinely even use the term "Internet." For example, some Facebook users are not cognizant that they are connected to the Internet. In 2012, researchers with an Asia Pacific think tank, LIRNEasia, noticed discrepancies in interviews conducted in Indonesia, in which individuals claiming not to use the Internet spoke about their Facebook usage.[4] Subsequent surveys in Africa and Asia found a significant percentage of Internet users who did not view online activities as being on the Internet.[5] The Internet has since its inception subverted or transformed such established categories as "space" and "friend" and "network."

Yet public policy about the Internet requires an understanding of what the thing being governed actually is. It is a complication that the Internet is sometimes discussed as fixed and taken for granted. As Evgeny Morozov rightly critiques, "There's something peculiar about this failure of our collective imagination to unthink 'the Internet.' It is no longer discussed as something contingent, as something that can go away; it appears fixed and permanent, perhaps even ontological—'the Internet' just is and it always will be."[6]

One surreal experience in technology policy discussions is to decipher the linguistic code-shifting, even in a closed room of like-minded experts, between calling technologies "cyber" when discussing international conflict or national security and calling technologies the "Internet" when discussing technical architecture or speech issues such as social media propaganda, censorship, access, or intellectual property.

The exact same technological infrastructure, albeit heterogeneous and always changing, is called something different and ascribed different meaning. These different framings—with different communities of interest, ideologies, and vocabularies—have coalesced with the global growth of digital networking technologies. Communities that use the term "cyber" often equate the term with security and especially national security. This usage perhaps follows the pre-Internet, 1948 Norbert Weiner conception of cybernetic control and communication, if not the word "cyberspace," coined by the science fiction writer William Gibson in his 1982 short story "Burning Chrome" and popularized in his 1984 book *Neuromancer.*

One reason to incorporate the broader "cyber" framing is because the IoT (Internet framing) is so often interpreted to mean consumer devices, which radically underrepresents and undertheorizes the ecosystems of sensor- and actuator-embedded material world that now exists across all sectors and in all spheres of life.

Using the term "cyber" as well as "Internet" also reflects on Joseph Nye's prescient concept of a cyber-regime complex, his application of regime theory in international relations to the cyber domain.[7] The Internet—as traditionally defined—is part of the broader cyber domain. This broader cyber-regime framing is even more appropriately applied to the cyber-physical world, because, as this book has argued, the traditional actors are different, the principles are different, the norms are different, and in many ways the rules are different. The technical architecture is also much more heterogeneous than what has historically defined the Internet as a communication network. Those who have a stake in viewing embedded, hybrid material-virtual systems as "just" an extension of the Internet (e.g., to preserve institutional or market power) will object to using the term "cyber-physical" at all.

In the contemporary era and in the context of policy, "cyber" often reduces to cyber war, cyber conflict, and cybersecurity and is used by military and government communities, as well as security researchers. The term "Internet" in the policy context refers more to global technical infrastructure, global multistakeholder governance, and issues of free speech, access, openness, and development. This has been a challenge because it has divided policy forums, advocacy, and scholarship into multiple tracks, even while addressing the exact same technical architecture, issues, institutions, and histories. A cultural and linguistic détente is necessary.

The cyber-physical transformation might present an opportunity to bring together the security and freedom and other communities. Already, some arenas use "Internet of things," while others use "cyber-physical systems"; and still others just place the word "smart" in front of whatever object is cyber embedded. Different still, the World Economic Forum calls it the "Fourth Industrial Revolution." The language this book has used, including "cyber-physical systems" and "Internet of things," is intentionally malleable to acknowledge all vernaculars and to accentuate the need for greater policy integration. This matches the descriptive reality that the same technological ecosystem is called different things, depending on stakeholder interest. Moving between "cyber" and "Internet" also helps to acknowledge the heterogeneity and fluidity that clearly exists. Nevertheless, many people with a stake in the terminology will strongly object to this fluidity.

What is the "Internet" in the context of cyber-physical systems? The Internet Society, the organizational home to some of the world's leading protocol designers and technologists, explains, "While it may seem like a simple question, defining the Internet isn't easy."[8] From an engineering standpoint, there is no one unitary network infrastructure. The Internet is, among other things, a collection of independent networks owned and operated by private companies. Some of these are large global network providers: AT&T, Comcast, China Mobile, Vodafone, Deutsche Telekom, and Verizon. Some are cloud-computing companies. Others are content distribution networks that operate massive networks that distribute and replicate content on servers around the world for redundancy and efficient access. Another class of network—such as Google's networks—are run by large content companies themselves. The distinct networks operated by these companies collectively make up the Internet's underlying backbone infrastructure. It is common to use the term "the public Internet," but this is a usage distinction signifying technologies accessed by the general public as opposed to a private or virtual private network used by a large corporate user of the Internet. There is no one network, and it certainly is not a publicly owned space or cloud or single platform.

As chapter 5 explained common architectural elements enable these distinct pieces to conjoin to become a global network of networks. This understanding is necessary both for public policy decisions and also to assess how public policy changes as the architecture moves into the context of cyber-physical systems. Private companies have historically agreed to interconnect their networks and to adhere to a common address space, common protocols, and common packet-switching architecture. Each "autonomous system," which at its most basic level is a collection of routers, has its own unique binary identifier, called an autonomous system number (ASN) and announces to the rest of the Internet the collection of IP addresses that are accessible in or through its system. The routers within these domains and between these systems form the circulatory system of the Internet and routing between these autonomous systems is handled by Border Gateway Protocol. The process of announcing available routes and addresses and exchanging information among networks is (sometimes problematically) based on trust among network operators that what they are announcing is accurate.

The physical interconnection takes place either bilaterally at one of the company's private facilities or at shared Internet exchange points (IXPs), enormous interconnection facilities scattered around the world. The underlying logical switching configuration, called packet switching, is based on a mesh networking configuration and the architectural approach of breaking transmission contents into small pieces (packets), appending a virtual address and other administrative overhead to the packet, and transmitting each packet to its end point over the most efficient path. When efforts to redesign the Internet recommend "mesh networking," it is important to note that the underlying architecture already is, essentially, mesh networking as opposed to the hierarchical and centralized circuit-switching approach of twentieth-century telecommunication networks.

The technical-architecture-based definition of the Internet is usually described as a network of networks based on a common set of standards known, in part, as TCP/IP.[9] TCP/IP is a suite of protocols including, among others: TCP, or Transmission Control Protocol, and IP, the Internet Protocol. Definitions of the Internet, early in its history, revolved particularly around IP. If a device could be reached (i.e., "PINGed") via the Internet Protocol, it was on the Internet; if it was not reachable via IP, it was not on the Internet.[10] The term "TCP/IP" evolved in common usage to represent an entire suite of protocols for various tasks, such as for file transfer, electronic mail, and the HTTPS standard that connects web browsers to websites. Having these openly available common standards was a revolutionary technical leap forward from previously proprietary environments that were controlled by different companies and in which users of one system could not exchange information with users of another system. There are hundreds of other core common standards that enable interoperability. Adhering to common standards enables thousands of different companies to produce the switches, routers, cables, wireless systems, applications, services, and devices that compose these networks.

A common name and number space is another defining historical characteristic of the Internet. Every device connected to the Internet, traditionally, has had a globally unique IP address, a unique binary number either permanently or temporarily assigned for a session. A domain name, such as wikipedia.org is translated into its associated IP address via the Domain Name System. A foundational infrastructure underlying the Internet, the DNS has received outsized policy, media, and scholarly attention, particularly the transition of power over certain functions from the United States to ICANN.

The technical definition of the Internet as based on common, open standards, packet switching, and a universal name and address space becomes complicated in the context of cyber-physical systems. On the one hand, the advent of cyber-physical systems and new entrants from different industries using standards with different governance norms and philosophies about openness is transforming various architectural layers of the Internet. More proprietary and heterogeneous architectures are arising. Machine-to-machine transactions do not necessarily require domain names, and systems of identifiers within Internet of things environments are often proprietary and then translated through a gateway. On the other hand, cyber-physical systems still rely on common core infrastructures of interconnection and interoperability. The exigencies and societal stakes of cyber-physical systems actually raise the stakes of moving forward with critical architectural improvements, especially around securing interconnection, routing, and addressing.

Human perception of the Internet is changing in a different way in the context of cyber-physical systems. In perhaps an obvious sense, humans consciously lose sight of technologies "as technologies" as they mature. At the 2015 World Economic Forum in Davos, Switzerland, Google CEO Eric Schmidt controversially predicted that "the Internet will disappear."

The Internet is becoming a background object that is difficult to cognitively disentangle from everyday objects. The "Internet" itself is also no longer universally viewed as high tech, although the new applications and gadgets it interconnects certainly are. This may be the normal course of history. A kitchen sink was once the height of modern technology but is not considered technology at all in contemporary society. As humans gradually acclimatize to new innovations, they no longer perceive these objects as "technology," and these innovations increasingly become concealed and contextualized within other objects.

As connectivity moves from screen-mediated devices and instead embeds in wearable technologies, appliances, cars, drones, walls, and the body, the Internet is receding further from human consciousness and moving from high tech to an essential background item diffusing into everyday life. The historian of science Steven Shapin explains, "It's common to think of technology as encompassing only very new, science-intensive things—ones with electronic or digital bits, for instance."[11] Digital technologies are now also becoming contextualized background objects.

Even in screen-mediated contexts, the underlying technical infrastructure of the Internet is already invisible. Humans observe primarily three things during routine Internet use: actual information, such as a text message or video; software applications, such as a search engine or social media; and the physical device, such as a phone or laptop, used to access content and applications. Routers, antennas, and satellite dishes are also sometimes visible, but 99 percent of infrastructure—fiber-optic cable, switching systems, server farms, coordinating institutions, companies, buildings—are absent from the immediate terrain of human perception. They are hidden, not intentionally concealed but nevertheless outside public view.

The massive underlying infrastructure of the Internet can therefore easily be taken for granted or not thought about at all. This condition perhaps explains strange popular-culture depictions of technology, such as smartphones shown working in disaster films despite molten lava consuming the Earth.

In other cases, technical infrastructure is intentionally hidden. Trade-secrecy laws conceal search-engine algorithms, making it difficult to comprehend and also to hold accountable the ways in which all of life's information is ordered.

Governments conceal surveillance infrastructures and systems of filtering and censorship. Anonymizing technologies like the Onion Router (TOR) obfuscate identities in the Dark Web. Malicious computer code and knowledge of system vulnerabilities sometimes remain concealed from view and stockpiled for cyber-offensive capability.

Despite technological changes and the phenomenological sense in which digital technologies are receding from view as they become taken for granted or seamlessly integrated into the material world, there is an ecosystem of technologies that collectively makes up the "Internet." Whether one sees these technologies or not, there are massive server farms in buildings, networks operated by independent companies, Internet exchange points where these network operators agree to conjoin, and a shared language of technical standards that create interoperability and enable everything from compression to encryption to error detection and correction. Whatever one calls this ecosystem, the end result is that data originating in one part of the world—whether from a connected lighting system or a laptop—can reach devices anywhere in the world.

Power Diffusion in Multistakeholder Governance

The heterogeneity and distributed nature of the technologies that collectively make up the Internet help to emphasize how governance of the Internet has never been a single-issue area. The question of "who should control the Internet" has always reflected a lack of understanding of the hundreds and hundreds of technical coordination areas necessary to keep networks operational.

A constellation of unique actors and institutions historically performed these roles. Private network operators make coordinating decisions about how to interconnect their networks and exchange packets. ICANN and the Internet Assigned Numbers Authority (IANA), along with Regional Internet Registries (RIRs), registrars, and DNS registries coordinate domain names and Internet addresses. Standards-setting institutions—W3C, IETF, IEEE, ITU, ETSI, and many others—develop the common protocols that facilitate interoperability. A combination of public and private institutions handle cybersecurity governance. Numerous CERTs around the world identify security flaws and issue advisories about patching vulnerabilities and handle emergencies.

Private intermediaries make decisions about conditions of privacy, speech, and safety via design and management approaches and via terms of service, subject to regulatory constraints in which they operate. Governments have authority over many cyber-policy areas ranging from security issues, cyber-offense strategy, privacy frameworks, and intellectual property rights enforcement. Governments also enact cyber governance via engaging in censorship, pervasive surveillance, blocking and filtering, and establishing laws—such as data localization—that profoundly affect both technical architecture and rights.

This messy balance of powers between the private sector, governments, and sometimes civil society has variously served as a check on private power and government power while keeping the Internet operational and allowing spaces for innovation and context-specific attention to human rights.

How does the cyber-physical disruption affect the distribution of Internet governance authority, which is already dispersed among many actors? Cyber-physical systems are changing both the actors and the arrangements of authority among actors. It also helps to emphasize that cyber governance is not about deliberation (people talking) but about praxis (companies doing, institutions coordinating, and governments regulating). The greater heterogeneity, pervasiveness, and issue complexity also should dispel calls for a single body to oversee everything, which usually reduces to a proposal to replace the multistakeholder distributed approach with multilateral United Nations oversight.

The considerable rearrangement to what counts as a technology company is the first significant influence shift. Yet many of these firms do not view themselves as technology companies. They may not participate in venues and forums that discuss digital policies. Furthermore, those who address digital technology policy, whether in traditional governance structures, think tanks, scholarship, or new global institutions, continue to focus primarily on content and network intermediaries like social media platforms and telecommunication companies rather than traditional companies that now raise the same types of civil liberties and national security issues as traditional tech companies, only with even more profound real-world implications. The stakeholders are different. Multistakeholder governance approaches in Internet policy have not yet caught up. There are new actors, new industries, and new public policy problems. The protean nature of firms has to be a backdrop of technology policy in the immediate future.

The arena of multistakeholder governance is private sector led, so this is a consequential change. Internet regulations have primarily focused on the Big 5 companies that are collectively called, especially in Europe, GAFAM. This is an acronym for Google (Alphabet Inc.), Apple, Facebook, Amazon, and Micro-soft. Because of the market reach and valuation of these companies, this atten-tion is appropriate. However, some of the private-industry sectors with more influence on areas such as privacy and security are cloud-computing compa-nies, microprocessor makers, back-end data-aggregation companies, and simi-lar behemoths in other countries, especially China. With the balance shift from content between people to communications between things, the private order-ing constructed by manufacturers of connected objects—from medical devices to automobiles—is becoming more consequential in cyber-governance arenas. Integrating these institutions in the traditional Internet governance institutions and venues—especially security and standards setting—is critical.

Another shift is that the already heterogeneous and distributed ecosystem of standards setting is becoming more varied and distributed. The IETF and W3C have had considerable de facto, expertise-driven authority over Internet direc-tions for decades. This influence will probably continue, but the multitude of standards-development efforts in the IoT space, as chapter 5 described, is creat-ing complexity and competition. It is not yet clear which standardization efforts will take hold. The standardization arena has always involved dozens of domi-nant players, but what once involved a clearer demarcation of territorial juris-diction has given way to multiple competing efforts within a single space. The already contentious norm of cooperation *within* institutions is giving way to the need for cooperation and coordination *among* institutions.

The power of ICANN, real and imagined, also shifts somewhat. Because ICANN is a multistakeholder organization and because of the global acrimony that led to the transition away from U.S. contractual oversight of ICANN, ques-tions about management of names and numbers and specifically the DNS have dominated discussions about multistakeholder Internet governance. The IANA functions at the heart of this concern involve administration of globally unique identifiers such as allocation of Internet addresses, assignment of technical pro-tocol parameters, and administration of and authority over changes to the root zone file mapping top-level domains into associated IP addresses. Authority over these functions long rested with the U.S. Commerce Department's National Tel-ecommunications and Information Administration (NTIA), administered under a contract with ICANN, the private, not-for profit corporation founded in 1998 under a contract with the U.S. government to coordinate Internet names and numbers. The stated intention was always to transition U.S. oversight entirely, which became a decades-long controversy involving international pressure and U.S. resistance until certain accountability safeguards were put in place. In 2014, under the Obama administration, the NTIA announced that the transition would definitively proceed; the transition occurred in 2016 and essentially involved turning over authority to ICANN itself. The transition occurred, and the Internet continued to operate, albeit with pressure from some quarters in the United States to reverse the transition and with some people in the international community still critical of both ICANN and perceived U.S. power.[12]

This area, the administration of Internet names and numbers and the Domain Name System, has always only been one facet of global cyber coordination, albeit an important one involving questions of domain name speech and trademark issues, among many other public-interest concerns. The cyber-physical disruption places this area in perspective as only one component within the much-larger functional arena of technical coordination. ICANN itself stresses that the Internet of things is not specifically in its mandate. Viewing the Internet as a control network connecting digitally embedded objects, however, creates a shift in the role and significance of the DNS ecosystem and institutions. Cyber-physical systems—whether a connected medical device, consumer IoT appliance, or industrial control system sensor—do not rely on domain names in the same way human communications do.

The meaning of IP addresses changes, as well. Proprietary architectures often employ ad hoc identifiers rather than end-to-end IP address usage. It has not been atypical, historically, for multiple devices to share a single universal IP address (e.g., via Network Address Translation to conserve IP addresses). But in the IoT environment, there are sometimes completely proprietary addressing schemes, different in kind from sharing of globally unique IP addresses. Even considering these arrangements, because of the massive numbers of cyber-physical devices connected to the public Internet, IP addresses will be important, and moving to the IPv6 standard will be vitally important to accommodate address demand. But cyber-physical systems move the architecture further away from an end-to-end universal address space made up of globally unique identifiers.

The more pronounced privacy, national security, and consumer-safety implications of cyber-physical systems also raise questions about how the balance of power shifts between governments and private industry. This balance already differs by region, but generally many of the policy issue areas have been private sector led. This is shifting. The sweeping effect of the European Union privacy regulation (GDPR) on private-industry data-collection and disclosure practices is one example. Regulatory agencies that address consumer safety and consumer protection are inherently relevant to cyber-embedded system security, privacy, and safety. Agencies with national security portfolios have a critical interest in both cyber-physical defense and the role of these systems in foreign-intelligence and cyber-offense capability. Brazil, Australia, and other countries already have national IoT strategies. Indeed, national cyber strategies must encompass cyber-physical systems.

Based on the insufficient state of privacy, security, and interoperability in the IoT, as well as the implications for human safety and societal stability, the prevailing philosophy of a private-sector-led governance structure has to be on the table for debate. Paradigmatic governmental responsibility for national security and for human safety clearly reaches into the cyber realm. The complication, as discussed throughout this book, is how to do this without creating disincentives for innovation and technological progress.

One rational argument suggests that the existing ecosystem of Internet governance institutions, such as ICANN, standards bodies including the IETF, and registries, in conjunction with private industry and governments, subsume cyber-physical systems as a natural trajectory and expansion.[13] In reality, there is increasing heterogeneity and complexity and indications that many shifts in power are inevitable.

Local Objects Are a Global Internet Governance Concern

The local and the global are increasingly intertwined, even though cyber-embedded material objects seem especially local. A motion-detecting video-surveillance system embedded in a doorbell can stream this video anywhere in the world. A hacker can potentially access a U.S. traffic-control system from North Korea. A coffeemaker can be switched on from anywhere in the world. Local objects are no longer merely local.

The Internet's logical architecture is already border agnostic and not bounded by physical location. The physical infrastructure (e.g., fiber-optic cable, satellite antennas, interconnection points, embedded objects) resides within borders, but the flow of data and the coordination of this data crosses borders in complicated ways involving decentralized, mesh topologies and border agnosticism.

A single transaction originating and terminating in one country can traverse an Internet exchange point in another country before being routed back to its destination. Content distribution networks replicate, cache, and distribute data onto servers located around the world, for performance, security, resiliency, or other purpose. The replication and distribution of content brings it close to end points, and decisions about flow optimize a variety of parameters such as traffic, bandwidth, storage, and latency calculations. DNS queries resolving domain names into binary IP addresses are another example of logical transactions that are not necessarily tied to geography. The location of root servers, DNS resolution providers, and registries is not tied to borders. Even many country-code top-level domains (ccTLDs) do not have a local presence requirement, meaning that an entity anywhere in the world can register a domain name with that country. For example, Canada (.ca) and Norway (.no) have local presence requirements; the Bahamas (.bs) and Switzerland (.ch) do not. As another example, VPNs allow someone to access a resource (e.g., a website) via a secure tunnel through a VPN server, which can be located in another country.

Collectively, these and many more systems that work together to create the global Internet cross borders—and all in different ways. How transnational companies do business accentuates this geographical distribution. There is no natural connection between where data is stored, where a company is headquartered, where a domain name is registered, where customer-service personnel are located, or where customers are located. Some information transmissions, of course, also leave the Earth via satellite communications. If there are logical borders on the Internet, they are the borders between autonomous systems, mediated by Border Gateway Protocol. This is why bordered, jurisdictional approaches to governance of the Internet so frequently have inherent conflicts and especially why governments seek to exert or regain control through attempts to force the distributed technology of the Internet, or the flow of data over these technologies, to stay within national borders. These mandates that tamper with technical arrangements in a way that asserts localization are part of two trends: the assertion of cyber-sovereignty models of Internet governance (as opposed to private-sector-led multistakeholder governance) by China and other countries with authoritarian cyber approaches and also the "turn to infrastructure for Internet governance," in which Internet infrastructure is co-opted for some extraneous purpose and control is in the service of state power.[14]

When governments are faced with Internet policy problems located outside their jurisdictional reach, they increasingly seek to impose modifications, via private intermediaries, to technical arrangements and architecture. Data localization requirements are one example, involving policy attempts to enact a range of prohibitions on where and how companies store customer data. Local DNS redirection is another mechanism for superimposing sovereignty on cross-border technologies via technical modifications.[15] Governments tamper with the universal name and number directory of the Internet to locally impose censorship, such as banning social media in some countries or blocking illegal material in others. Some of these efforts could be called intraterritoriality, efforts to reconcentrate distributed global systems within sovereign borders. Data localization requirements, local DNS redirection, and associated calls for Internet sovereignty as an ideological competitor to the multistakeholder model of Internet governance do not match the way cross-border technology works in practice. As such, they can create architectural instability and produce a new set of tensions around access to knowledge, privacy, law enforcement, intelligence, speech rights, and national sovereignty.

The distributed, border-agnostic characteristics of various cyber technologies create opportunities to exert special forms of control across borders. Control by extraterritoriality, for the purposes of this book, refers to influence or disruption exerted beyond the jurisdiction in which the originating actor is situated. Rather than intending to comply with a precise legal definition, this more generally represents a feature of cyber infrastructure—the many ways in which networked technologies do not neatly map onto borders and the ways in which cross-border power can be exerted from a distance. It is not about applicable law but about reach and distributed architecture, as well as attempts to constrain this reach.

Control of the local is also control of the global. What happens within national borders can have cascading effects far beyond these borders. Regional policies have global control consequences, such as the way in which the European Union's GDPR, a regional framework, has had global implications for how transnational companies do business, how law enforcement access to data across borders occurs, and even how the architecture of the Internet is configured. On this latter point, an example is how the GDPR is directly shaping the technological affordances of the WHOIS system of website registrants and what information is permitted to be publicly accessible in light of a strong European Union privacy directive.[16] The WHOIS system, which dates back to 1982, is a freely available, searchable, global directory from which anyone can look up the name and other personal information of the person who registered a particular domain name, unless the person registered via a proxy. This personal information is captured by registrars at the time a person registers a domain name. The question of whether someone should be able to register a domain name anonymously has been a policy question for decades. Transparency and disclosure of this information serves interests such as law enforcement, combating terrorism, and identifying those who engage in cyberbullying, hate speech, piracy, spam, and defamation. Anonymity favors values of freedom of expression and the ability of individuals to disseminate information without fear of imprisonment or other punishment in authoritarian contexts. The introduction of the GDPR called this entire system into question because of its rules and obligations on the collection and use of personal data, as well as its data-minimization principle requiring that data collection be limited to the purpose for which it is collected. This is an example of local constraints affecting the global system.

The ability to extend beyond the local to the global is even more powerful, especially the use of cross-border attacks and breaches for political or economic purposes. The Russian influence campaign and email hacking during a U.S. presidential campaign is a specific example of the broader politicization and exploitation of Internet infrastructure and how this reaches across borders. One of the most infamous cases of cross-border politicization of Internet infrastructure was the massive DDoS attack on Estonia in 2007. Estonian government servers, banking systems, news, and other sites were disrupted over a three-week period in a politically motivated DDoS attack. Officials in the city of Tallinn had relocated a statue of a World War II–era Soviet soldier from a park, angering Russian minorities, who responded with street protests and scattered incidents of looting. This political tension simultaneously manifested itself online when DDoS attacks disabled critical information infrastructures. Prior to the actual cyberattack, Russian-language online forums were reportedly discussing the expected attack on Estonia's digital systems.[17]

One way these global control struggles unfold is through cross-border conflicts between competing values, laws, and economic forces. In "Bits and Borders," the legal scholar Jennifer Daskal explains that "the cross-border effects of competing jurisdictional claims are in many ways more contested, fraught, and consequential than Goldsmith and Wu recognized"[18] (in the latter authors' influential 2006 book *Who Controls the Internet? Illusions of a Borderless World*).[19] Law enforcement access to data housed by a transnational company in another jurisdiction is a prime example. The legal scholar Anupam Chander similarly explains how Internet trade conflicts arise from tensions between local principles and the Internet's cross-border characteristics.[20]

Technology companies must comply with the local statutory contexts in which they operate. This became clear in the year 2000. The French court case *LICRA v. Yahoo!* ruled that the ability of French citizens to purchase Nazi memorabilia through the Yahoo! platform was illegal, even though the U.S. company's servers were located within the borders of the United States and within a culture of strong constitutional free-speech protections. As subsequent cases have borne out, sorting out jurisdiction is complicated by the distributed architecture of technology, and companies have to deal with a patchwork of regulatory environments.

Control related to extraterritoriality therefore takes three forms: the ways in which local action has global consequences; the ability to reach across borders digitally for a political or economic purpose; and the ways in which conflicts over competing spheres of influence materialize in conflicts over control of cross-border technologies. The actors are not only governments but private companies, networks of terrorists, nongovernmental institutions, and even individuals.

These traditional control features of extraterritoriality raise several immediate concerns and questions in regard to cyber-physical systems. What types of local arrangements of cyber-material technology and law have cascading effects for people in other jurisdictions? In reference to the Mirai botnet, the inability to secure a digital thing locally can have global effects when that device is used to launch attacks targeting a site located elsewhere. Local policies, such as the European privacy frameworks, can affect the design and operation of digital objects requiring compliance in order to sell into the European market. What types of cross-border jurisdictional conflicts, such as law enforcement requests for data, arise around cyber-physical systems, and how can or should they be resolved? Perhaps most consequentially, the feature of extraterritoriality that enables reaching across borders raises an entire new domain of concern around foreign surveillance, hacking, election interference, and cyber warfare that reaches across borders and directly into industrial systems, homes, and transportation systems. This feature of extraterritoriality, extended to cyber-physical systems, creates a condition in which someone wanting to directly exert physical influence (changing a temperature, turning off a light, altering an object constructed by a 3D printer) does not have to be anywhere near the system.

Cyber Policy Entanglements with Everything

As everything in society becomes interconnected and digitally mediated, the scope of Internet governance enlarges. Internet governance has always involved coordination and policy formulation around the technologies that underpin the digital economy, the public sphere, and every industry sector. Because of the importance of digital information systems to the economy and society, governments have recognized Internet governance as a global policy concern on par with other critical cross-border issues such as terrorism and food security. Despite this importance, cyber policy is often a stand-alone issue that is primarily related to the public sphere and the digital economy.

Reframing the Internet as a material control network rather than a communication network helps to illuminate cyber intersectionality with other public policy areas that previously have had minimal connections to digital policy. Many other entanglements speak to how the scope of Internet governance transforms because of the cyber-physical transformation. As already addressed, some of these areas involve energy policy, consumer protection, risk and insurance markets, labor policy, and health-care and medical policy. Democracy is completely intertwined with cyber policy, as attempts to interfere with elections around the world have made clear. Without the political will to acknowledge and address such interference as an existential threat, it will potentially become more potent by exploiting the embedded material systems such as transportation infrastructure, home systems, and even voting machines.

Environmental policy and cryptocurrency governance are two policy entanglements that are less obvious than the ones already addressed. Environmental connections with governance of the Internet have usually focused on content and usage and how information and communication technologies can support sustainable development. The United Nations, via its Millennium Development Goals initiative, has advocated for the integration of information technologies into development efforts to help improve health and education, to ameliorate poverty, and also to promote environmental sustainability.[21] In this context, Internet-policy connections to environmental sustainability focus on the dissemination of knowledge, as well as the management of natural resources via GPS and geographical information systems. It also includes technologically mediated responses to natural disasters. The Internet Society has, more specifically, advocated for the application of Internet technologies to sustainable development and environmental protection.[22] Most of these discussions have focused on development in emerging markets, which are confronted simultaneously with rapid technological change and critical needs for greater security around water, health, and food. They are also areas that, because of lower levels of infrastructure, face more devastation when a natural disaster hits.

The emerging context of ubiquitous sensor networks and the mass data collection of cyber-physical system sensor data profoundly escalates what is possible in data collection around natural resources like water, food, and energy sources as well as climate and weather patterns. Cyber-embedded devices already make positive contributions to environmental protection and energy conservation. The connected technologies and sensor networks of smart cities and smart buildings facilitate greater energy efficiency and increase prospects for enhanced management of natural resources. Everyday light switches in offices, factories, and homes automatically switch off when occupants leave the vicinity. Cyber-physical technologies promote environmental sustainability.

At the same time, the mass proliferation of processing and data collection by cyber-physical system sensors and networks contributes to the energy consumption of digital systems. From cooling-system behemoths in sprawling server farms to call-center facilities to Internet exchange points, what appears sustainable or "green" at end points (e.g., going paperless) actually involves massive energy consumption. There is growing recognition of the impact of e-waste on both health and the environment, particularly the toxic waste in discarded electronic devices like phones, switches, and digital display technologies. As everyday objects embed electronic components, e-waste increases.

Digital control systems manage waste-management and water-treatment facilities and power plants. The cybersecurity protections in these systems have consequences for environmental protection and health. In 2000, a computer attack resulted in millions of liters of raw sewage intentionally released at a Queensland, Australia, sewage-treatment plant into rivers, parks, and hotel grounds.[23] The attack was carried out by a disgruntled employee who had worked for the contracting firm that installed the SCADA sewage-control system and was retaliating after the local municipality rejected him for a permanent position with the public water-treatment facility.[24] This was both a public-health issue and an environmental-security issue. In the contemporary era of cyber-connected physical systems, the environmental risks of attacks on critical infrastructure are potentially catastrophic. In some low-lying areas, for example, an attack on a hydroelectric dam would be devastating. Cyber policy links directly to environmental concerns.

Cyber policy and currency policy have also converged, particularly with the rise of cryptocurrency. In 1790, Alexander Hamilton explained the need for a central bank, "a National Bank is an Institution of primary importance to the prosperous administration of the Finances, and would be of the greatest utility in the operations connected with the support of the Public Credit."[25] The Bitcoin creator's (or creators')[26] original case for a peer-to-peer currency system in 2008 was to remove this role of a trusted institution and replace it with, essentially, mathematics: "What is needed is an electronic payment system based on cryptographic proof instead of trust, allowing any two willing partners to transact directly with each other without the need for a trusted third party."[27]

There are, as of this writing, thousands of cryptocurrencies, with Bitcoin being the most prominent. Taking the long view of history, there is nothing unique about monetary systems constantly changing. There is not a single currency on Earth that existed two thousand years ago. Some linguistic terms still exist, such as the "shekel" of thousands of years ago, but the modern currency system of the Israeli shekel is a twentieth-century contemporary revival of the term. Currencies that no longer exist include those that were recently replaced by the Euro, such as the Austrian schilling, German Deutsche Mark, and Italian lira, as well as those that were lost as dominant empires waned, such as the ancient Roman denarius and other currencies.

Yet there are radical differences between traditional currency and cryptocurrency. Most cryptocurrencies are not linked to a nation-state and so exist completely across borders. They also have no tangible presence in the real world. They exist entirely online and depend on the global infrastructure of the Internet. Most relevant to discussions of Internet governance, cryptocurrencies are not administered by central authorities. Entities such as the Federal Reserve in the United States serve as central banks regulating systems of currency and other core economic features. There is no central authority regulating cryptocurrency, nor is there a single cryptocurrency. The tracking and introduction of new currency is overseen by the technology itself—fueled by cryptography and blockchain—rather than by a trusted centralized authority.

Cryptocurrencies are decentralized systems but have deep connections to cyber governance questions.[28] There are many questions: Who sets the standards for these systems? What transparency is necessary to legitimate the public-interest issues constructed by the technologies? Are the underlying technologies actually secure, and what happens if cryptography is overpowered by advancements in processing power? There are many other questions.

Cryptocurrency also intersects with other cybersecurity areas. Ransomware attacks often demand payment in Bitcoin. Cryptocurrencies are similarly used to carry out anonymous Dark Web transactions. Types of unlawful exchanges using cryptocurrency include illegal drug trade, illegal weapons trade, trade in endangered animals, child pornography, and human trafficking. The use of traditional currencies online, which are subject to regulatory oversight and authentication protections, to transact illegal trade in the Dark Web would undo the anonymization that criminals seek for such unlawful activities. Those who make transactions using cryptocurrencies like Bitcoin have a degree of anonymization that is not possible using nation-state-controlled currency. Cryptocurrencies are also used for perfectly legitimate transactions.

The rapid ascent of cyber-only currency perhaps best exemplifies the metamorphosis of the Internet away from its traditional role as a communication network for accessing knowledge and exchanging information between people to a system that is deeply embedded in all social and economic processes, material and virtual, and now including the production and circulation, not only use, of currency. It also serves as an example of the need for retooling Internet governance systems to encompass these transformations. The undeniable rise of cryptocurrencies represents a major transformation in how modern societies operate and interact and, as such, should be a major topic of cyber policy, as well as monetary, environmental, and law enforcement policy. Yet the design, coordination, and regulation of cryptocurrency is not only outside of stable cyber governance regimes but also outside of traditional governance structures.

Cryptocurrency also intersects directly with the Internet of things, particularly around "cryptojacking." Cryptocurrency is "mined"—in other words "earned"—by cryptomining software that solves complex mathematical problems necessary for validating transactions. Massive processing power is required to perform these calculations. Cryptojacking is the practice of exploiting vulnerabilities in devices to install malware that hijacks processing power to perform these cryptographic calculations. Cryptojacking is a serious problem, mirroring the effects of other cybersecurity attacks such as disrupting operations and degrading network performance. IoT devices, especially those with weak security, are targets of cryptojacking incursions.[29]

Everything is interconnected. Cyber policy touches every public-interest area, no longer relegated to the digital information realm only but the natural world, currency, biology, labor, safety, democracy, and every other public policy sphere. It may eventually be necessary and more accurate to state that there is no longer cyber policy because it folds directly into every other policy arena.

Updating Core Architectural Principles

As the Internet has emerged as a transformational and global communication network, one dominant set of architectural design principles has historically shaped the technology and has served as a useful and productive force shaping rapid growth and innovation. The Internet Society has referred to these principles as "Internet invariants," described as conditions that must be maintained for the Internet to thrive.[30] Taken together, these principles form the basis of an aspirational hope for preserving (or building) what is usually referred to as a "free and open Internet." Part of what has maintained some of these characteristics over decades is a stable system of Internet governance centered around a combination of private-sector decisions, expert design communities, and global coordinating institutions and shaped initially by democratic societies and especially the United States.

The idea behind a fixed set of fundamental design principles is that technology continually changes, but what has made the Internet the Internet and what have served as the technological affordances enabling growth and innovation are these Internet invariants. The Internet Society has described the core principles as (1) global reach/integrity, (2) general purpose, (3) permissionless innovation, (4) accessibility, (5) interoperability and mutual agreement, (6) collaboration, (7) reusable (technical) building blocks, and (8) no permanent favorites.

Universality is an underlying theme. Most pertinent, interoperability designed into systems is what creates the potential for universality. Any manufacturer can invest in the development of products with the assurance that their technical features—whether addressing, compression, error checking, formatting, or encryption—are compatible with other products connected to the same digital network. The technical principle of permissionless innovation enables developers to introduce new services, devices, and software without having to entreat a gatekeeper for permission, such as setting up a new social media platform without having to ask permission of an intermediary or regulatory agency. The potential for anyone to innovate and connect to the system results in the principle of no permanent favorites because new entrants, in theory, can develop innovative products that compete in interconnected markets. This also speaks to the principle of global reach, the expectation that anyone anywhere in the world, or at least any device anywhere in the world, has the capacity to reach any other device. Universality is also served by the principle of the Internet being a general-purpose system that accommodates many different applications, from email to web hosting to digital video services.[31]

These aspirational values have indeed helped to shape the Internet's trajectory, such as the availability of open standards contributing to innovation. As explained, the reality of how technology is designed, implemented, and regulated has not always lived up to this aspirational vision. Even while the Internet continues to grow rapidly, half the world's population still does not have access.[32] Where there is access, there are disparities in access speeds and interconnection infrastructure, language barriers, censorship regimes, protocol fragmentation, and proprietary enclosure. Private-industry trends toward proprietary enclosure and authoritarian control approaches by China, Russia, and many other countries controvert the idea of a free and open Internet. Values of openness and enclosure coexist in the global Internet environment. There is regional and cultural malleability: a successful Internet in Thailand embeds the normative value of prohibiting speech that insults the monarch; in the United States, this type of prohibition would constitute a free-speech abridgement.

Even in culturally specific contexts, values shaping technology are in constant conflict. Inherent tensions arise between individual privacy rights and law enforcement, such as in the question of law enforcement access to an encrypted iPhone. Conflicts arise between freedom of expression and intellectual property rights, such as content-takedown determinations in YouTube. Some tensions reflect increasing incongruity between Westphalian notions of nation-states and a distributed technical architecture that crosses borders and is coordinated by nonstate actors and new transnational institutions. Contention over values may just be a feature of global architecture.

The very idea of invariant principles is predicated on the idea that technologies change, usage contexts change, and industries change. The cyber-physical disruption is instantiating profound changes in technological architecture and usage contexts. Governance contexts are changing. Stakeholders are changing.

More is at stake, not just economically and socially, but for human safety and national security.

Setting aside global norm heterogeneity and just focusing on Western democracies, architectural principles are not fixed. Neither should they be fixed. The transformation of the Internet from a network between people to a network enmeshed in the real, physical world provides an opportunity to revisit what are called invariant architectural principles. They may no longer be ideally suited to the emerging problems, contexts, and stakeholder interests of the modern era. The public-interest issues arising in cyber-physical systems inform a different set of values than the public-interest concerns around the Internet when it was primarily a system for communication and the exchange of information between humans.

New architectural principles are needed to coincide with the demands of the contemporary moment. *Privacy* and *security* take primacy as values for the design of cyber technologies. Architectural principles, even with a recognition of the values in tension depending on context, have to prioritize privacy-enhancing design and creating strong security frameworks at every layer of technology. The real-world dependencies on connected systems critically require *stability, reliability, availability, integrity,* and *authentication.* The pervasive and intimate nature of always-on data collection around real-world activities elevates privacy as a core contemporary architectural value.

Older architectural principles are challenged. The ability to interconnect billions and billions of objects—from health devices to industrial control systems—depends on the global reach of digital technologies. But the question relative to cyber-physical trends is whether universality-enabling principles should retain a privileged status. In speech and access-to-knowledge contexts, universality is advantageous, at least in democratic contexts. Fragmentation often has unsalutary effects on speech and access to knowledge for a communication network, even while some forms of technical fragmentation are necessary for protecting data. But in the context of the Internet as a control network connecting the material world, fragmentation at certain layers may become an important aspirational principle shaping technical architectures that promote the values of security and privacy. Open standards within each unique sector and in the core of network infrastructure are important for accountability, security, and competition, but the aspiration for every conceivable object interoperating at the application and data layer is not as clear.

Monocultures are not necessary or desirable. But there are obvious disadvantages to interoperability between China's system of facial recognition and social scoring and cyber-embedded heart monitors. Energy-grid sensors in the United States should not be easily accessible in Russia. Cyber-physical system firewalling is not necessarily problematic but can serve as a check on widespread cybersecurity attacks and mass data-collection practices.

The principle of permissionless innovation is also less clear. Should this apply in an environment involving direct physical-world vulnerabilities rather than content-centric risk? The converse of permissionless innovation is the precautionary principle, defined and critiqued by Adam Thierer as "the belief that new innovations should be curtailed or disallowed until their developers can prove that they will not cause any harm to individuals, groups, specific entities, cultural norms, or various existing laws, norms, or traditions."[33] Thierer and Adam Marcus argue that, in the case of 3D printing as well as other emerging technologies, "precautionary principle-based regulation can also have profound macroeconomic consequences by discouraging the sort of entrepreneurialism that fuels economic growth and competitive advantage."[34] This concern is, in some ways, a straw-man argument because the question is not whether entrepreneurial innovation should be curtailed in additive manufacturing but how the results of the innovation comply with real-world regulatory constraints such as gun ownership or liability and risk around potential harm. In other words, it is not the innovation but the spectrum of uses.

Even if permissionless innovation is a default value, the stakes of embedded objects suggest that there should be exceptions carved out in critical societal areas. Having precautionary, ex ante regulations about the safety of connected objects like driverless cars and weapons is soundly reasonable and a reminder of the importance to move from theoretical debates about principles to the question of what regulation, industry efforts, and technical standards are needed in each specific context.

The Internet itself has had no intrinsic Heideggerian essence described by some narrative or waiting to be discovered. The technology has constantly changed, and its ontology has been interpretably flexible. In the same way that underlying technologies change, the Internet's technical evolution has reflected a historically specific set of values, or principles, arising in particular social, economic, and political contexts. The cyber-physical milieu is one such context.

8

The Cyber-Physical Policy Moment

THE DIFFUSION OF CYBERSPACE INTO THE physical world is part of a long trajectory. The Internet has already turned fifty, if one views its inception as the late-1960s U.S. milestone when the first packets were exchanged among university research sites over its predecessor network, ARPANET. To place the Internet's provenance in historical context, in 1968, the Vietnam War was raging and Gordon Moore founded a novel technology company called Intel in Mountain View, California, in an area that would later be known as Silicon Valley. The founders of Google and Facebook were not yet born, and NASA was still preparing the Apollo 11 mission to attempt the first lunar landing in history. The Greenwich Village Stonewall riots foreshadowing the inception of the gay rights movement in the United States were still a year away, and abortion was illegal in much of the country. The Internet's first coordinating body—the Network Working Group—was convened to develop protocols for communicating over ARPANET, and that same year, Martin Luther King Jr. was assassinated.

In the context of the Cold War, the United States was introducing new institutions to advance science and technology, including the Advanced Research and Projects Agency (ARPA), founded as a reaction to the Soviet Union's successful launch of the first artificial Earth satellite, Sputnik.[1] During the period of national crisis over the Soviet preeminence in satellite technology, U.S. President Dwight Eisenhower founded ARPA to be a "fast response mechanism . . . to ensure that Americans would never again be taken by surprise on the technological frontier."[2] This political aspiration is retrospectively chilling a half century later, in light of calculated Russian cyber influence via troll farms, bots, social media influence campaigns, and hacking.

Fifty years is an eternity in Internet time. Even a decade seems interminably long. The span between 2005 and 2015 alone engendered immense technological, social, and economic change online. In 2005, Mark Zuckerberg had recently launched "TheFacebook"—as it was originally called—at Harvard. On February 14, 2005, the domain name YouTube.com was activated. Twitter launched in 2006, and Apple released the first-generation iPhone in 2007. In 2013, the U.S. government charged Edward Snowden with violating the Espionage Act for releasing classified documents about the National Security Agency's expansive surveillance program. By 2015, the number of Chinese Internet users exceeded twice the entire population of the United States, with a significant percentage accessing the Internet from mobile phones.

Another sea change is that Internet governance has become a critical global political concern, comparable in importance to other global collective-action problems such as climate change and poverty. Once-esoteric technical concerns—network protocols, cybersecurity, routing, and interconnection—have become geopolitical concerns. Arrangements of technology connect to foreign intelligence, censorship, national security, cyber war, digital theft of intellectual property, and what counts as privacy and freedom of expression online. The proliferation of high-profile incidents from Stuxnet to Snowden have drawn public attention to connections between digital technologies and politics. Political control now requires control of infrastructure.

This global policy attention to digital technologies also reflects the enormous economic stakes of cyberspace.[3] The Internet contributes trillions in U.S. dollars to the global economy, and the potential value of the Internet of things alone could reach an estimated $11 trillion by 2025.[4] More importantly, every sector of the economy from financial services to transportation depends on the Internet for basic transactions and operations. An Internet outage is now also a significant disruption of the digital economy.

The Internet has challenged the business models of entire industries, from music to print journalism to transportation. Technological change and associated globalization have contributed to the loss of jobs in manufacturing and other industries in advanced economies. At the same time, the Internet has also created entirely new industries and economic opportunities and given rise to some of the most powerful companies in the world. The proliferation of cyber-physical systems will further impel transformations of industries and jobs.

Technology giants such as Apple, Facebook, Google (Alphabet), and Microsoft occupy the upper echelon of multinational companies in market capitalization, and Alibaba and other Chinese companies are following suit in their reach, power, and market capitalization. In the summer of 2018, Apple became the first company in history to reach a market value of $1 trillion.

By many measures, the Internet represents a phenomenal achievement in human history, transforming the way societies communicate, learn, conduct business, shop, and function. It has created new opportunities for expression and commerce, even while simultaneously facilitating unprecedented levels of government surveillance and censorship and new forms of cybercrime, harassment, and digital terrorism.

The history of technology has always been the history of change. *The blurring boundaries between offline and online worlds is a seismic one.* In 1962, Thomas Kuhn's *The Structure of Scientific Revolutions* portrayed the scientific process as relatively calm periods of knowledge accretion punctuated by crisis-induced revolutions.[5] The controversial shift from a geocentric view of the universe to a heliocentric one is the best example of how experts continue operating within their epistemological paradigm, even in the face of incontrovertible anomalies. Those who believed that the sun revolved around the Earth were unable, even when faced with scientific evidence, to shift their ideological and religious beliefs to accept that the Earth could be revolving around the sun. Most techno-scientific shifts are much subtler but also involve adherence to systems of belief. Part of Kuhn's lasting contribution was to address the cultural and historical influences on understanding, as well as the problem of different knowledge communities having irreconcilable worldviews and how communities, after recognizing a shift, see a different world than they previously pictured.

The diffusion of digital technologies into the material world represents a major societal transformation. Yet it will be difficult to view the Internet as anything other than a communication network accessed through screens. There is now a different Internet world than previously understood. The growth and success of the Internet can convey a sense of inevitability that it will continue on a trajectory moving toward expressive freedom and economic growth. Cyberspace melding into the physical world calls into question all assumptions that applied to human communication systems, including the trajectory of the Internet itself.

All of the policy issues in two-dimensional digital space have leapt into three-dimensional real-world space and have added new concerns around physical safety and everyday human activity. Digital technologies are inside of the material world. So must digital technology policy move inside of the physical world. The integration of the physical world and the virtual world is changing what it means to be human and transmuting conceptions of human rights. This book has provided many specific recommendations around privacy, security, and interoperability and has offered provocations for how Internet freedom and Internet governance have to be rethought through the lens of the cyber-physical nexus. There are also cross-cutting themes that help orient and hopefully draw attention to the need for urgent policy attention in this space: policy should move from a content focus to an infrastructure lens; cybersecurity has to now be viewed as one of the most pressing human rights issues; there is a critical need for clarification about liability in the cyber-physical space; and to achieve the trust and human rights protections necessary for cyber-physical innovation, all stakeholders are responsible.

An Infrastructure-Based Policy Lens

Policy attention needs to shift from digital content to digital infrastructure. Much of cyber policy focuses on content, whether speech rights, fake news, cyberbullying, or intellectual property rights. Many of the levers of control in cyberspace are now conflicts around infrastructure. Emphasizing infrastructure governance questions in no way minimizes the importance of the technology debates unfolding at the level of content. Computational propaganda, social media privacy, content censorship, consumer data protection, and theft of intellectual property are critical society-wide problems. Problems around content and problems around infrastructure are actually the opposite sides of the same coin. The Mirai botnet exploiting the IoT to attack major information platforms, the Equifax data breach, and Russian social media influence campaigns have much in common.

The technological reality of cyber-embedded real-world things complicates and augments control struggles, often behind the scenes of public view but with heightened social and economic repercussions. It has also created control levers that are much more directly enmeshed in the physical world. These cyber-physical control struggles are playing out in many arenas: (1) through the enactment of technical design; (2) via private intermediation; (3) via cross-border, extraterritorial conflict; (4) at points of transduction where one form of energy is converted into another; and (5) by the mediation of debates over cybersecurity. The mediation of conflict at these points of control in emerging terrains of cyber-physical systems will determine political power in the digital age and shape the future of everything from what counts as human privacy to the prospects for the stability of democratic systems.

To suggest that modes of infrastructure control create public-interest concerns in cyber-physical systems is not to suggest that arrangements of Internet infrastructure have not always been entangled with economic and political power. Quite the contrary. The concept of infrastructure-based control of content has a well-developed history,[6] including, relative to Internet governance, the author's infrastructure-based notion of content control, that "battles over the control of information online are often fought at the level of Internet infrastructure," whether the use of the DNS for intellectual property rights enforcement or DDoS attacks that disrupt the flow of content.[7] Infrastructure is not only exploited for content control but also increasingly tampered with for content control, such as regulatory efforts to modify technical architecture to require data localization within national borders, often under the guise of protecting privacy.

Control of the material world via digital technologies once primarily stemmed from dependencies on adjacent information systems that inform real-world interactions (rather than direct physical control via embedded cyber technologies). It has long been the case that actions in the digital world, such as a modification to a digital control system or data file, can have the effect of changing conditions in the material world. Health-care providers depend on information systems for scheduling, medical records, insurance authorizations, and payment systems. When a ransomware attack disrupts such a system, medical providers are unable to perform scheduled procedures or otherwise function. In this conventional example, nothing in the information systems directly connects to the material world, such as implants, diagnostic equipment, or physical treatment devices, but the ability to function in the real world directly depends on information from the digital world.

Mechanisms of control over the flow of communication are features of cyberspace. As Ron Deibert and Rafal Rohozinski explained in "Liberation vs.

Control: The Future of Cyberspace" (2010), "these control mechanisms are growing in scope and sophistication as part of a general paradigm shift in cyberspace governance and an escalating arms race in cyberspace."[8] In 1998, long before Facebook, Twitter, and smartphones, the law professor Lawrence Lessig's article "Laws of Cyberspace" warned about "pushing the architecture of the Internet from an architecture of freedom to an architecture of control."[9] This admonition, given the time in which it was written, was concerned with freedom of expression and the possible role of the state in constraining freedom. Other, more postmodern approaches, such as Alexander Galloway's *Protocol: How Control Exists after Decentralization* (2004), follow Lessig in dispelling conceptions of the Internet as an inherently uncontrolled and liberatory technological platform. Galloway suggests that the Internet's underlying technical architecture, which he groups into a unitary category "protocol," is a totalizing control apparatus, a type of control emanating from extreme technical organization rather than limitations on individual freedom or decisions.[10] In the real world, of course, technology is not homogeneous. Neither is it fixed. It is heterogeneous, fluid, always changing, historically specific, and therefore able to be shaped.

Although the ways in which cyber technologies directly infiltrate and control the material world represent a newer epoch in the Internet's history, this view of the Internet as a control network was actually presaged in the years immediately after World War II. Twenty years prior to ARPANET and a decade before Sputnik, the MIT professor Norbert Weiner set out to develop a program of control theory with his 1948 book *Cybernetics: Or Control and Communication in the Animal and the Machine.* Almost four decades prior to the advent of the personal computer, he suggested that "the modern ultra-rapid computing machine was in principle an ideal central nervous system to an apparatus for automatic control; and that its input and output need not be in the form of numbers or diagrams but might very well be, respectively, the readings of artificial sense organs, such as photoelectronic cells or thermometers, and the performance of motors or solenoids."[11] The formulation of his work included the notion of learning machines, the role of feedback mechanisms in control, and the fundamental inseparability of control engineering and communication engineering. The reality of cyber-physical systems, to some extent, matches this imagining. The Internet is dissipating into previously offline physical spaces. Technology policy has to catch up to this major technological transformation.

Cybersecurity as the Great Human Rights Issue of Our Time

The need for strong cybersecurity is the common denominator of the most consequential public interest concerns of the present era. Privacy depends upon cybersecurity technologies. National security and the functioning of critical societal and industrial infrastructure require strong cybersecurity. Cybersecurity is increasingly connected to the legitimacy of democratic elections. Cybersecurity is necessary for human safety. Trust in financial systems and the stability of the global economic system depend upon cybersecurity.

Those who developed encryption standards in the 1970s, whether for securing financial data or for preserving the confidentiality of government communication, could never have predicted that cryptography would not be ubiquitously deployed everywhere well into the twenty-first century. Powerful forces have worked against strong end-to-end encryption. Both the economic business models that rely on extensive personal data collection and the intelligence agency and law enforcement need for pervasive surveillance are in direct tension with encryption and other security technologies.

A societal shift toward greater cybersecurity is necessary for progress. Cyber-embedded medical devices are bringing health benefits to millions of people. Wearable technologies are allowing the elderly to independently remain in their own homes. Energy sensors help conserve natural resources. Autonomous vehicles improve safety and productivity in industrial settings. Consumer IoT devices create conveniences and efficiency in homes. The potential for human flourishing is tremendous. But these innovations are inverting public policy priorities. Privacy concerns, while always significant, are no longer relegated to the data activities that individuals choose to transact online, such as retail purchases or personal messages, or the information collected by third parties about these transactions. Privacy issues now infiltrate all human activity that was previously viewed as offline but that is now interconnected, including biological measurements and home activities. The stability of every industry sector now depends on networks of sensors and actuators, so that an Internet outage is an outage of society and the economy. Cyber conflict has moved into cyber-physical objects. Human safety depends on the stable performance of cyber-embedded objects. Security is lagging behind product development, and there are technological constraints and market disincentives for building strong security into systems.

Security is not anywhere near sufficient. Interoperability standards for cyber-physical system security are in a chaotic state and often involve competing, closed standards monocultures. The lack of adequate security, privacy, and interoperability in the Internet of things is a society-wide concern. IoT security vulnerability is also a political failure, with government interests often contrary to strong cybersecurity, whether stockpiling/hoarding knowledge of vulnerabilities for cyber-offense capability rather than sharing them with manufacturers or preferring weak security for surveillance purposes rather than requiring/promoting security frameworks that provide greater security but make it more difficult to carry out government surveillance.

These problems put more than just the cyber-physical world at risk. Exploiting home appliances to carry out attacks places the entire Internet and digital economy at risk. The security of financial systems, information systems, and social media is only as robust as the security of cyber-physical systems. Trust in the digital economy depends on trust in all digital technologies.

Even while the very operation of embedded sensor and actuator systems relies structurally on extensive and continuous data collection, imperatives of security and privacy require mechanisms of data minimization that set reasonable expectations about data not being shared beyond its immediate purpose. Cyber-physical risk requires greater privacy and security by design, device upgradeability and life-cycle management, and maximum transparency and disclosure about everything from data breaches to vulnerability discoveries to privacy and security practices. A range of external inducements including government procurement policies, clear liability frameworks, third-party certification, and insurance risk markets can spur actions lacking inherent market incentives. Already-difficult debates, especially about encryption back doors and zero-day vulnerability stockpiling, rise in importance and consequence.

Intermediary Liability in the High-Risk Era

Cyber governance is highly privatized. Private industry owns and operates the majority of intermediating infrastructure. Third-party networks and systems facilitate the flow, exchange, manipulation, and aggregation of data between end points, whether these end points are humans or connected objects.

These private companies determine a range of public-interest concerns about privacy, speech, interoperability, consumer safety, and security. They enact discretionary censorship to block information or accounts if usage violates a company's terms of service—such as portrayals of violence, hate-speech harassment, or immorality. As such, a significant theme in Internet governance has always been the public policy role of private actors. Rebecca MacKinnon, in *Consent of the Networked: The Worldwide Struggle for Internet Freedom*, describes these information intermediaries as "the new digital sovereigns" who will have to "recognize that their own legitimacy—their social if not legal license to operate—depends on whether they too will sufficiently respect citizens' rights."[12] The proliferation of connected material devices heightens the consequences of issues of private sovereignty and legitimacy.

The international-relations scholar Joseph Nye also discusses cyber power in terms of this diffusion of control away from the state: "Some observers welcome this trend as marking the decline of the sovereign state that has been the dominant global institutions since the Peace of Westphalia in 1648. They predict that the Information Revolution will flatten bureaucratic hierarchies and replace them with network organizations. More governmental functions will be handled by private markets as well as by nonprofit entities."[13]

Private intermediation also directly serves the interests of governments, which are unable to enact surveillance or block data directly. They do so via delegated surveillance and delegated censorship. Government surveillance does not happen sui generis. It requires cooperation from private entities—social media platforms, search engines, transactional sites—that serve as information intermediaries.

The constitutional law scholar Jack Balkin was an early theorist examining the nature and consequences of this private ordering. Information intermediaries and their data-driven business models facilitate both infrastructures of free expression and the digital surveillance state.[14] The implication is not only that private companies control speech and other conditions but that the only way for the state to exert control is via intermediaries. As Balkin summarizes, "The largest owners of private infrastructure are so powerful that we might even regard them as special-purpose sovereigns. They engage in perpetual struggles for power for control of digital networks with nation states, who, in turn, want to control and coopt these powerful players."[15]

The levers of control within private intermediaries are numerous. Terms of service agreements with users establish rules for behavior online, including what counts as harassment, hate speech, and violence and what information is allowed to be posted and when content or accounts will be terminated. The technological affordances of these systems, such as whether they require unique physical or logical identifiers, also shape rights. Privatized governance also occurs via coordination and management of systems. Internet service providers have the ability, should they choose, to throttle back (i.e., discriminate against) specific content, sites, or classes of traffic. This capacity is at the heart of the net-neutrality question of whether they should be legally prohibited from doing so. The question extends to cyber-physical systems and whether intermediaries should have the legal right to block or slow down traffic from embedded systems that compete with their core offerings.

Much of the power of private intermediaries emanates from massive data-collection and monetization practices that underpin business models based on interactive advertising. As Balkin vividly describes it, big data is Soylent Green—the fictional wafer meant to ameliorate food scarcity via covert cannibalism. Hence, Balkin analogizes that "Big Data is Soylent Green. Big Data is People."[16] It is this data collection that enables business models to succeed but also creates significant privacy concerns and enables governments, by extension, to enact invasive surveillance.

The privatization of governance extends overwhelmingly into cyber-physical intermediaries, which have the same power to block devices or accounts that violate private contractual usage agreements, shape conditions of privacy, and carry out governance functions that were once the domain of the state. They control embedded objects with intellectual property restrictions such as standards-based patents and copyrighted software.

Intermediary liability is a policy question central to concerns about control by private ordering. The global Internet governance tradition, generally, is for information intermediaries to not be liable for the content passing through their systems. How should liability shift when the data mediated is not a social media post but information with life-and-death consequences in the real world? As businesses connect digitally embedded material objects to a greater extent than merely screen-mediated devices, questions arise: What is an intermediary in the era of cyber-physical systems? Under what conditions should intermediaries now be liable for data passing through or hosted by them when that data affects not freedom of expression but potentially someone's life? How these questions around private intermediation settle—including the descriptive preliminary question of what even counts as intermediation in cyber-physical systems— will shape a variety of policy debates.

The rising stakes of digital security and stability challenge a sacrosanct regulatory tradition. Although regulatory requirements vary by jurisdiction, information intermediaries generally have had legal immunity from liability for the information passing through their infrastructure, especially in the U.S. context. Certain quid pro quo conditions apply, such as the obligation of notice and takedown procedures around intellectual property rights infringement. Generally, though, social media companies, information-aggregation sites, and other content intermediaries are not liable for the content that others post in these platforms. As such, Facebook has immunity from liability in cases in which a subscriber is sexually harassed or threatened.

In the United States, the roots of legally excepting companies from responsibility for the content passing through them lies with Section 230 of the Communications Decency Act. Section 230 provides that "interactive computer services" are not liable for content published or transmitted by others on these services. Intermediaries are generally not legally treated as a speaker or publisher of content that others post or send on their platforms. Furthermore, under the Good Samaritan provision of Section 230, if these intermediaries voluntarily choose to restrict access to information, such as Twitter deleting a post or suspending an account because of violent, indecent, or harassing content, the intermediary is not liable for these actions "whether or not this material is constitutionally protected."[17]

Social media companies and other content intermediaries voluntarily establish terms of service that set (or at least purport to set) the conditions of speech over their platforms, such as in regard to hate speech, violence, harassment, pornographic content, and cyberbullying. In addition to these voluntary terms of service that navigate different questions related to freedom of expression and subscriber safety, intermediaries are subject to various nation-specific content regulations to which they must adhere if operating in the relevant jurisdiction. Intermediaries traverse different cultural and legal contexts and have to respond directly to government requests around hate speech, Holocaust denials, state secrets, defamation, and blasphemy. For example, speech that is legal in the United States could be classified as illegal hate speech in Brazil or violate decency laws in many countries. Other than the complexities of navigating jurisdictionally specific content laws and setting terms of service that comport with the entities' corporate social values, in the United States especially, intermediaries have been generally immune from liability to content produced by their users.

This potent combination of immunity from liability for the content traversing these platforms and immunity from liability for deleting or otherwise controlling this content has given information intermediaries tremendous power. This gate-keeping function amounts to a form of privatized governance determining conditions of privacy, safety, and expression. But it has also served as a spur to entrepreneurial innovation and investment and contributed to the associated rapid introduction of new platforms. Stated simply, shifting to content-intermediary liability would create a disincentive to innovation and risk. The Center for Democracy & Technology succinctly summarizes how the rationale for protecting content intermediaries from liability lies at the nexus of speech rights, risk, and innovation: "Protections for intermediaries from liability for users' content are necessary to a vibrant, innovative Internet. These legal protections allow internet access providers, content hosts, social networks, and others to support a robust online environment for free expression without worrying about potential liability for the material stored on or moving across their networks. Without them, services would be much less willing to accept user-generated content for fear of potential civil and criminal liability."[18]

Even in the realm of content and communications among people, pressure has mounted to hold companies legally accountable for the data they intermediate. These platforms are not neutral to content. They sort, prioritize, monetize, and curate content and establish policies about what speech is permitted and who or what is prohibited. What accountability and liability should apply for data breaches? Should social media companies be held accountable for inappropriate data sharing and political interference? Should transactional sites be liable for sex trafficking, child pornography, and other illegal content and transactions on these platforms? Should video repositories be liable for intellectual property rights violations or for hate speech? There has always been pressure to establish legal accountability for intermediaries, even while providing immunity from liability has been vital for speech to flourish and innovation to occur.[19]

The contemporary complication is the question of what counts as an intermediary in the burgeoning cyber-physical industries. It is not always entirely clear. When Bill Clinton became president of the United States, Amazon, eBay, Facebook, Google, Twitter, and YouTube did not yet exist, never mind Alibaba, Baidu, Instagram, or Uber. At that time, intermediaries were online systems such as UseNet discussion boards, file-sharing platforms, and email services. The shift to cyber-physical intermediaries is another such transformation. In general, intermediaries are companies that do not necessarily provide content, like a media company, but facilitate transactions, interactions, or the exchange of information among those who generate or access this data. These companies are search engines, social media platforms, content-aggregation sites, financial intermediaries, transactional intermediaries, trust intermediaries, and advertising intermediaries. *They are now also cyber-physical intermediaries.* Even augmented reality systems can cause physical harm and raise questions about what type of liability arises around information when overlaid on the material world.[20]

Calls for rethinking intermediary liability are emerging from many stakeholders, with the exception of the companies involved. The Internet Society, whose historical traditions have normatively favored a light-touch regulation of flows of content on the Internet, has even called for the creation of "an accountability regime, including liability provisions to ensure that those entities that collect, compile and manipulate data are liable for its abuse and its security, not the users."[21]

The risk factors in cyber-physical intermediating systems are different in kind from those that arise in information intermediaries. Harms shift from psychological or economic damage to real property damage and physical injury. The case for liability of these intermediaries is much clearer, in principle. However, there are a number of complicating principles that make liability and accountability extremely challenging. With consideration of infrastructure heterogeneity and the layered architectures on which data flows, exactly who is responsible for harms? Is it the software developer, the system designers, the manufacturer of the end object, the back-end data analysis, or the components added along the supply chain? Some of the intermediary services cross borders. Data originates from many sources. There are numerous stakeholders involved in the design, development, implementation, maintenance, and operation of cyber-physical systems.

Some decisions that can lead to real property damage and personal harm involve artificial intelligence and machine learning. In the case of cyber-physical things, an object like a self-driving car will have to make a split-second decision between hitting a baby in a stroller or injuring the passengers in the car. A common thought experiment in ethics, and in discussions about autonomous vehicles, is the "trolley problem." An observer sees a trolley careening toward multiple people tied up on the trolley's path and has to make a split-second decision. The observer can do nothing and allow the trolley to hit these people, or pull a lever and direct the trolley to a side track where it will kill only one person. Such experiments are no longer hypothetical scenarios in the age of autonomous vehicles. Someone has to decide initially, and sometimes this decision in practice is influenced by machine learning.

The need for liability in the cyber-physical realm is obvious but complicated. There is an immediate and critical need for regulatory clarification about responsibility and the assignment of liabilities. This issue will also have to connect to the possible evolution of enforcement of certification and standardization mechanisms. Clarification is critical not only for protection of people and property but for innovation and investment. For example, companies should not be dissuaded from disclosing vulnerabilities because of the threat of class-action lawsuits, even in cases in which no harms have occurred. The complications around cyber-physical liability are significant and exceeding the pace of law. This is an area for urgent attention.

Cybersecurity and Corporate Governance

Another crucial development is the intensifying oversight role and importance of corporate officers and boards in addressing security and privacy. All companies are now tech companies that collect digital data about customers and that offer services and physical products that are directly embedded with cyber capability. They are also large users of the Internet of things, whether operating warehouses with industrial IoT infrastructure or office buildings with cyber-connected security systems. This integration of cyber-physical systems into all firms is an opportunity to improve the broader cybersecurity milieu because of corporate incentives to reduce liability and risk (and reputational and financial damage) and to ensure compliance with rapidly changing legal contexts. Because many cybersecurity vulnerabilities and breaches originate in third-party networks of suppliers and business partners, corporate attention to cybersecurity extends to the security practices of these partners and therefore has cascading effects.

The issues faced by boards in particular—from finance to risk to strategy—now have crucial cybersecurity dimensions. Digital issues such as data privacy, data breaches, cyber policy around risk management, and theft of intellectual property have risen to the top of board agendas. Every corporate asset—whether a cyber-physical asset or digital only—connects in some way to a network that exposes private business data, customer data, and trade secrets to hackers all over the world. Privacy and security problems can disrupt operations or result in financial loss. They can create reputational harm and loss of investor confidence and can involve actual liability.

In fairly recent history, responsibility for cybersecurity was relegated to IT departments. The stakes have escalated responsibility for cyber risk management, operations, and strategy above these departments and into executive leadership, usually at the level of general counsel, compliance officer, and chief information and security officer (CISO), as well as fiduciary responsibility at the corporate-board level. Regular updates from the CISO to the board on cybersecurity is increasingly becoming standard practice. It is a company-wide issue. In some cases, boards have at least one director with cybersecurity expertise to serve as a liaison and adviser. Boards have an agenda-setting and oversight function to ensure that there is a cybersecurity strategy that follows best practices, that the company has a transparent data-privacy policy, and that there are procedures for cybersecurity breach response and notification. Once a company goes through the process of passing the bar for obtaining cyber insurance, this usually means that security best practices have been implemented.

Any director on any board, corporate or nonprofit, should be able to answer, at a minimum, ten simple questions about the firm's cybersecurity: (1) Is there a data-privacy policy, including a data breach notification policy, and how is that communicated and to whom? (2) Is there a formal cybersecurity policy that includes a response plan, business continuity strategy, and details about access rules and how data is collected, handled, and stored (and for how long)? (3) What executive oversees cybersecurity in the organization? (4) Does the organization have cyber liability insurance? (5) How are employees educated about cybersecurity and privacy issues? (6) Does the organization conduct a regular IoT device inventory and security assessment? (7) Given the complex and continually changing regulatory contexts, what is the ongoing strategy for staying abreast of and in compliance with regulations? (8) How secure are the networks of business partners and other third parties that connect directly to the company's networks? (9) What is the overall cybersecurity budget? (10) What is the director's overall level of confidence in the state of the organization's cybersecurity? Many of these questions should sound obvious, but these and many more questions have not yet become standard practice to ask. The security and privacy afforded to society directly depends on these corporate practices.

Rejecting Dystopian Imaginings

Examining the public-interest dilemmas accompanying the rise of cyber-physical systems and calling for all-hands-on-deck action on cybersecurity and privacy are neither dystopian nor disheartening. It is precisely because Internet of things innovations are so exciting and promising for human advancement and economic development that these issues profoundly matter. Trust in a secure and stable Internet of everything is a prerequisite. There is a generational moment to shape the constitution of this future.

No one action alone can sufficiently address the privacy, security, and interoperability concerns emerging in cyber-physical systems. Global discussions around "norm setting" can focus too exclusively on government action and make undue assumptions about how trustworthy governments are to comply with norms. Regulation alone is not sufficient to address security and privacy because law so often trails behind technological change and because of barriers of technological complexity that can impede meaningful policy formulation.

Viewing cyber policy merely through the lens of traditional governance structures and laws is wholly insufficient. Technical infrastructure—its design, privatization, cross-border characteristics, materialization, and securitization—are co-opted for political and economic objectives. Understanding this technical architecture is a prerequisite for cyber policy because governments can do little without turning to private companies and intermediating architecture.

Voluntary industry self-regulation is inadequate in itself because there is not always an endogenous incentive structure to naturally induce strong security measures. Watchdog functions by major retailers and insurance companies and certifications by third parties are part of the solution. Advocacy groups are often effective influencers of policy formulation. While none of these solutions is in itself sufficient to address cyber-physical policy concerns, all of these together have the capacity to effect change.

How concerned is society about privacy and security issues in the Internet of things? The truth is that people going about their lives in connected cars and connected cities are both concerned and unconcerned. For example, the "2018 CIGI-Ipsos Global Survey on Internet Security and Trust," which reached more than twenty-five thousand Internet users in twenty-five countries, included a set of questions about public perceptions about the IoT. Questions gauging individuals' concern about Internet-connected devices (e.g., cars) produced mixed, even contradictory, results. On the one hand, 77 percent of respondents were concerned about being monitored. Conversely, 53 percent said, "It doesn't really bother me that almost everything seems to be connected to the Internet."[22]

Individual human agency holds the most potential to enact change. Cyber-physical systems create several conditions that, on the surface, could be construed to diminish citizens' influence. Systems often operate autonomously from human intervention. Notice and consent are not always possible. People are not necessarily aware of the presence and affordances of ambient cyber-embedded devices or aware of cybersecurity vulnerabilities. Those who are not actually "online" are now affected by breaches and by technological change. Unplugging is no longer possible because so many products, including cars, inherently collect data. But a multitude of individual actions—market choices, pressure on policymakers, staying abreast of cyber-policy issues, keeping software upgraded, participating in policy discussions, and many other choices—collectively have impact.

Ultimately, shaping human rights and security in the cyber-physical world is now an enormous collective-action problem in which all are vulnerable and all are responsible.

Each groundbreaking transformation of the Internet is accompanied by predictions of either its demise or the world's. Thus far, neither has happened. The Tesla and SpaceX CEO, Elon Musk, has ominously described artificial intelligence as a "fundamental existential risk for human civilization."[23] Musk, who has had unusually high involvement in technological innovation in his various positions, has also described AI as summoning demons. His concern is not as much technology out of control and morphing into autonomous living hybrid systems but rather AI taking the instructions of its designers to the extreme. The example most commonly used is the notion that AI programs designed to maximize the stock price of defense companies could optimize its instructions by starting a war.

In 1995, long before the birth of smartphones, Google, or Wi-Fi, the inventor of Ethernet, Robert Metcalfe, predicted that the Internet would "soon go spectacularly supernova and, in 1996 catastrophically collapse."[24] Because he was the respected founder of the network switch company 3Com and had invented a major local area networking standard, the media and industry took his predictions quite seriously. The network obviously did not collapse, and since that time, the number of human users online has grown from forty million to billions and transformed, to varying degrees, every facet of society. This growth and transformation will continue.

The merging of cyberspace with the physical world is clearly here, even if this chapter is still in its infancy. Connected sensors and actuators are in everything, including the flesh. Being human and being digital are now physically intertwined. The Internet has had many chapters. Its leap from the digital world to the physical world is an extraordinary one.

Epilogue

The week I completed this book, a five-year-old boy received his first 3D-printed prosthetic arm, at a Home Depot in Annapolis, Maryland, not far from my home in Washington, DC. A wonderful sales associate created the prosthetic arm on a Dremel 3D printer using blueprints he downloaded from an organization called Enabling the Future, a group of volunteers around the world who use their 3D printers to fabricate free artificial upper limbs for people in need.[25] The beaming smile on the boy's face is a reminder that building digital trust and security is ultimately about people. The cyber-physical nexus is a human space.

NOTES

Chapter 1. After the Internet

1. Transcript of interview by Dr. Sanjay Gupta, "Dick Cheney's Heart," CBS, October 20, 2013. Accessed at https://www.cbsnews.com/news/dick-cheneys-heart/.
2. FDA Safety Communication, "Cybersecurity Vulnerabilities Identified in St. Jude Medical's Implantable Cardiac Devices and Merlin@home Transmitter," January 9, 2017. Accessed at https://www.fda.gov/MedicalDevices/Safety/AlertsandNotices/ucm535843.htm.
3. Ibid.
4. ICS-CERT, "Advisory: Primary Stuxnet Indicators," September 29, 2010.
5. See, for example, David E. Sanger, "Obama Order Sped Up Wave of Cyberattacks against Iran," *New York Times,* June 1, 2012.
6. See, for example, Sara Ashley O'Brien, "Widespread Cyberattack Takes Down Sites Worldwide," CNN, October 21, 2016.
7. Kyle York, "Dyn Statement on 10/21/2016 DDoS Attack," Dyn, October 22, 2016. Accessed at http://dyn.com/blog/dyn-statement-on-10212016-ddos-attack/.
8. Francesca Musiani, Derrick Cogburn, Laura DeNardis, and Nanette Levinson, eds., *The Turn to Infrastructure in Internet Governance,* Palgrave Macmillan, 2016.
9. See Laura DeNardis, "The History of Internet Security," in Karl de Leeuw and Jan Bergstra, eds., *The History of Information Security: A Comprehensive Handbook,* Elsevier, 2007, pp. 681–704.
10. US-CERT, "Alert (TA16-288A): Heightened DDoS Threat Posed by Mirai and Other Botnets," October 14, 2016. Accessed at https://www.us-cert.gov/ncas/alerts/TA16-288A.
11. Ibid.
12. Department of Justice Office of Public Affairs, "Justice Department Announces Charges and Guilty Pleas in Three Computer Crime Cases Involving Significant DDoS Attacks: Defendants Responsible for Creating 'Mirai' and Clickfraud Botnets, Infecting Hundreds of Thousands of IoT Devices with Malicious Software," December 13, 2017. Accessed at

https://www.justice.gov/opa/pr/justice-department-announces-charges-and-guilty-pleas-three-computer-crime-cases-involving.

13. See, for example, Garrett M. Graff, "How a Dorm Room Minecraft Scam Brought Down the Internet," *Wired,* December 13, 2017.

14. For example, Cisco projects that there will be 26.3 billion IP-connected devices by 2020. See "Cisco Visual Network Index Predicts Near-Tripling of IP Traffic by 2020," June 7, 2016. Accessed at https://newsroom.cisco.com/press-release-content?type=press-release&articleId=1771211.

15. As the philosopher of science Donna Haraway wrote before the widespread use of the web, "the boundary between physical and non-physical is very imprecise for us." Donna Haraway, "A Cyborg Manifesto: Science, Technology, and Socialist-Feminism in the Late Twentieth Century," in *Simians, Cyborgs and Women: The Reinvention of Nature,* Routledge, 1991, p. 149.

16. Google, "The Google Self-Driving Car Project Is Now Waymo." Accessed December 16, 2017, at https://www.google.com/selfdrivingcar/.

17. See, for example, the ITU's global and regional information and communications technology data by various usage categories from 2005 to 2016. Accessed February 12, 2017, at https://www.itu.int/en/ITU-D/Statistics/Documents/facts/ICTFactsFigures2016.pdf.

18. *Merriam Webster,* s.v. "bot." Accessed March 2, 2017, at https://www.merriam-webster.com/dictionary/bot.

19. *Webster's Dictionary Unabridged Second Edition,* s.v. "bot," 1860.

20. Onur Varol, Emilio Ferrara, Clayton Davis, Filippo Menczer, and Alessandro Flammini, "Online Human-Bot Interactions: Detection, Estimation, and Characterization," ICWSM 2017.

21. "Update: Russian Interference in 2016 U.S. Election, Bots, and Misinformation," *Twitter Public Policy Blog,* September 28, 2017. Accessed at https://blog.twitter.com/official/en_us/topics/company/2017/Update-Russian-Interference-in-2016—Election-Bots-and-Misinformation.html.

22. According to Krebs on Security, "Target Hackers Broke in Via HVAC Company," February 5, 2014. Accessed at https://krebsonsecurity.com/2014/02/target-hackers-broke-in-via-hvac-company/.

23. Target, "A Message from CEO Gregg Steinhafel about Target's Payment Card Issues," December 20, 2013. Accessed at https://corporate.target.com/discover/article/Important-Notice-Unauthorized-access-to-payment-ca.

24. See also Target's data-breach FAQ. Accessed March 2, 2018, at https://corporate.target.com/about/shopping-experience/payment-card-issue-FAQ#q5961.

25. See, for example, Yochai Benkler, *The Wealth of Networks: How Social Production Transforms Markets and Freedom,* Yale University Press, 2006; Manuel Castells, *Communication Power,* Oxford University Press, 2009; and Lee Rainie and Barry Wellman, *Networked: The New Social Operating System,* MIT Press, 2012.

26. Andrew Feenberg, *Questioning Technology,* Routledge, 1999, p. 131.

27. Langdon Winner, "Do Artifacts Have Politics?" *Daedalus,* Vol. 109, No. 1, 1980, p. 134.

28. Susan Leigh Star, "The Ethnography of Infrastructure," *American Behavioral Scientist,* Vol. 43, No. 3, 1999, pp. 377–378.

29. Geoffrey Bowker and Susan Leigh Star, "How Things (actor-net)Work: Classification, Magic and the Ubiquity of Standards," 1996. Accessed at http://citeseerx.ist.psu.edu/viewdoc/download?doi=10.1.1.464.2715&rep=rep1&type=pdf.

30. Laura DeNardis and Mark Raymond, "The Internet of Things as a Global Policy Frontier," *UC Davis Law Review,* Vol. 51, No. 2, 2013, pp. 475–497.

31. Bruno Latour, "On Technical Mediation—Philosophy, Sociology, Genealogy," *Common Knowledge,* Vol. 3, No. 2, 1994, p. 36.

Chapter 2. The Cyber-Physical Disruption

1. Gilles Deleuze, "Postscript on the Societies of Control," *October,* Vol. 59, Winter 1992, p. 4.

2. Opening statement of the Hon. Michael C. Burgess, "The Internet of Things: Exploring the Next Technology Frontier," hearing before the Subcommittee on Commerce, Manufacturing, and Trade of the Committee on Energy and Commerce, U.S. House of Representatives, March 24, 2015. Accessed at https://energycommerce.house.gov/hearings/internet-things-exploring-next-technology-frontier/.

3. Rose Schooler, Intel, prepared statement, ibid.

4. Thomas S. Kuhn, *The Structure of Scientific Revolutions,* University of Chicago Press, 1962.

5. Boston Consulting Group, "Winning in IoT: It's All about the Business Processes," January 2017. Accessed at https://www.bcg.com/en-us/publications/2017/hardware-software-energy-environment-winning-in-iot-all-about-winning-processes.aspx.

6. Rajeev Alur, *Principles of Cyber-Physical Systems,* MIT Press, 2015, p. 1.

7. NIST, "Framework for Cyber-Physical Systems Release 1.0," May 2016. Accessed at https://pages.nist.gov/cpspwg/.

8. For a political examination of primarily consumer IoT, see, for example, Philip N. Howard, *Pax Technica: How the Internet of Things May Set Us Free or Lock Us Up,* Yale University Press, 2015.

9. Internet Society, "IoT Security for Policymakers," April 19, 2018. Accessed at https://www.internetsociety.org/resources/2018/iot-security-for-policymakers/.

10. Gartner Group, "Gartner Says 8.4 Billion Connected Things Will Be in Use in 2017, Up 31 Percent from 2016," February 7, 2017. Accessed at https://www.gartner.com/newsroom/id/3598917.

11. For example, Cisco projects that there will be 26.3 billion IP-connected devices by 2020. See Cisco, "Cisco Visual Network Index Predicts Near-Tripling of IP Traffic by 2020," June 7, 2016. Accessed at https://newsroom.cisco.com/press-release-content?type=press-release&articleId=1771211. See also Gartner Group's projection of 20 billion devices by 2020, November 10, 2015. Accessed at http://www.gartner.com/newsroom/id/3165317.

12. United Nations, Department of Economic and Social Affairs, Population Division, "The World's Cities in 2016," 2016, p. 1.

13. See, for example, the IDC report "IDC Forecasts Shipments of Wearable Devices to Nearly Double by 2021 as Smart Watches and New Product Categories Gain Traction," December 21, 2017, which estimated the number of wearable device shipments in

2017 at 113.2 million. Accessed at https://www.idc.com/getdoc.jsp?containerId=pr US43408517.

14. FDA, "FDA Approves Pill with Sensor That Digitally Tracks If Patient Has Ingested Their Medicine," November 13, 2017. Accessed at https://www.fda.gov/NewsEvents/ Newsroom/PressAnnouncements/ucm584933.htm.

15. Rio Tinto, "Rio Tinto's Autonomous Haul Trucks Achieve One Billion Tonne Milestone," January 30, 2018. Accessed at http://www.riotinto.com/media/media-releases-237_23991.aspx.

16. Industrial Internet Consortium, "Industrial Internet of Things Volume G4: Security Framework," 2016. Accessed at https://www.iiconsortium.org/pdf/IIC_PUB_G4_ V1.00_PB-3.pdf.

17. Mark Purdy and Ladan Davarzani, "The Growth Game-Changer: How the Industrial Internet of Things Can Drive Progress and Prosperity," Accenture Strategy Report, 2015. Accessed at https://www.accenture.com/_acnmedia/Accenture/Conversion-Assets/ DotCom/Documents/Global/PDF/Dualpub_18/Accenture-Industrial-Internet-Things-Growth-Game-Changer.pdf.

18. Description of "Total Farm Automation" system provided by the company AMS Galaxy USA. Accessed April 11, 2018, at https://www.amsgalaxyusa.com/total-barn-automation-1/.

19. See, for example, W. W. Rostow, "Is There Need for Economic Leadership? Japanese or U.S.?," *American Economic Review,* Vol. 75, No. 2, 1985, pp. 285–291.

20. Klaus Schwab, "The Fourth Industrial Revolution: What It Means, How to Respond," World Economic Forum, January 14, 2016. Accessed at https://www.weforum.org/ agenda/2016/01/the-fourth-industrial-revolution-what-it-means-and-how-to-respond/.

21. Ibid.

22. See Alfred D. Chandler Jr., *The Visible Hand: The Managerial Revolution in American Business,* Harvard University Press, 1977.

23. MakerBot Replicator+ User Manual. Accessed May 9, 2018, at https://www.makerbot. com/img/replicator/Replicator+_User_Manual.pdf.

24. Peter Cooper, "Aviation Cybersecurity—Finding Lift, Minimizing Drag," Atlantic Council, November 7, 2017. Accessed at http://www.atlanticcouncil.org/publications/ reports/aviation-cybersecurity-finding-lift-minimizing-drag.

25. See Thomas P. Caudell and David W. Mizell, Boeing Computer Services, "Augmented Reality: An Application of Heads-Up Display Technology to Manual Manufacturing Processes," *IEEE Proceedings on the Twenty-Fifth Hawaii International Conference on System Sciences,* Vol. 2, January 7–10, 1992.

26. Steve Ditlea, "Augmented Reality," *Popular Science,* January 2, 2002.

27. Arlington National Cemetery, "ANC Policy Regarding Pokémon Go and Other Smartphone Gaming," June 1, 2016. Accessed at https://www.arlingtoncemetery.mil/News/ Post/3752/ANC-Policy-regarding-Pokemon-Go-other-smartphone-gaming.

28. Kuwait News Agency, "Vital Landmarks, Locations off Limits to Pokémon Go Users," July 15, 2016.

29. Duvall, Washington, Duvall Police Department Facebook posting, July 10, 2016, https:// www.facebook.com/Duvall.Police.Department/photos/a.585641684854128. 1073741828.581937435224553/1044284952323130/?type=3.

30. For example, augmented-reality glasses and headsets assumed a prominent presence at the 2018 consumer electronics show (CES 2018) in Las Vegas.

31. Mark Lemley and Eugene Volokh, "Law, Virtual Reality, and Augmented Reality," *University of Pennsylvania Law Review,* Vol. 166, No. 5, 2018, p. 1055.

32. Michael Froomkin, "Introduction," in Ryan A. Calo and Michael Froomkin, eds., *Robot Law,* Edward Elgar, 2016, p. 1.

33. Ibid., p. 6.

34. Karen Rose, Scott Eldridge, and Lyman Chapin, "The Internet of Things: An Overview," Internet Society, October 2015.

35. See, for example, Rebecca Crootof, "The Killer Robots Are Here: Legal and Policy Implications," *Cardozo Law Review,* Vol. 36, 2015, pp. 1837–1915.

36. Langdon Winner, *Autonomous Technology: Technics-out-of-Control as a Theme in Political Thought,* MIT Press 1977, p. 13.

37. For example, the European Telecommunications Standards Institute (ETSI) uses the term "M2M" and launched a OneM2M standards initiative with partners in 2012. For more information, see ETSI, "ETSI Worldwide." Accessed March 7, 2018, at http://www.etsi.org/about/what-we-do/global-collaboration/onem2m.

38. Ines Robles, "Routing over Low Power and Lossy Networks (ROLL) on a Roll," *IETF Journal,* April 24, 2018. Accessed at https://www.ietfjournal.org/rol-on-a-roll/.

39. Carsten Bormann, Mehmet Ersue, and Ari Keranen, "Terminology for Constrained-Node Networks," RFC 7228, May 2014, p. 3.

40. ITU, ITU-T Recommendation Y.2060, "Overview of the Internet of Things," June 15, 2012.

Chapter 3. Privacy Gets Physical

1. FBI, "Consumer Notice: Internet-Connected Toys Could Present Privacy and Contact Concerns for Children," Alert Number 1-071717-PSA, July 17, 2017. Accessed at https://www.ic3.gov/media/2017/170717.aspx.

2. For information about COPPA, see FTC, "Protecting Your Child's Privacy Online." Accessed May 22, 2018, at https://www.consumer.ftc.gov/articles/0031-protecting-your-childs-privacy-online.

3. For technical information about the Foscam camera vulnerability, see CERT Coordination Center, Carnegie Mellon University Software Engineering Institute, "Foscam IP Camera Authentication Bypass Vulnerability," CERT-CC Vulnerability Note VU#525132, original release date March 3, 2014. Accessed at https://www.kb.cert.org/vuls/id/525132.

4. FTC, "Vizio to Pay $2.2 Million to FTC," February 6, 2017. Accessed at https://www.ftc.gov/news-events/press-releases/2017/02/vizio-pay-22-million-ftc-state-new-jersey-settle-charges-it.

5. *Federal Trade Commission et al. v. Vizio, Inc.,* Case No. 2:17-cv-00758 (D. N.J. Feb. 6, 2017). Accessed at https://www.ftc.gov/system/files/documents/cases/170206_vizio_2017.02.06_complaint.pdf.

6. FTC, "Electronic Toy Maker VTech Settles FTC Allegations That It Violated Children's Privacy Law and the FTC Act," January 8, 2018. Accessed at https://www.ftc.gov/news-

events/press-releases/2018/01/electronic-toy-maker-vtech-settles-ftc-allegations-it-violated.

7. See, for example, the California state law (Decision 11-07-056) designed "to protect the privacy and security of the electricity usage data" of energy customers. July 28, 2011.

8. See, for example, Laura DeNardis and Andrea Hackl, "Internet Governance by Social Media Platform," *Telecommunications Policy,* Vol. 39, No. 9, 2015, pp. 761–770.

9. Cambridge Analytica, "Cambridge Analytica and SCL Elections Commence Insolvency Proceedings and Release Results of Independent Investigation into Recent Allegations," May 2, 2018. Accessed at https://ca-commercial.com/news/cambridge-analytica-and-scl-elections-commence-insolvency-proceedings-and-release-results-3.

10. Mark Zuckerberg, response to Cambridge Analytica incident, Facebook online public posting, March 21, 2018. Accessed at https://www.facebook.com/zuck/posts/10104712037900071.

11. Ronald J. Deibert, *Black Code: Inside the Battle for Cyberspace,* Signal, 2013, p. 60.

12. Statement of Daniel Castro, Vice President, Information Technology and Innovation Foundation, "The Internet of Things: Exploring the Next Technology Frontier," hearing before the Subcommittee on Commerce, Manufacturing, and Trade of the Committee on Energy and Commerce, U.S. House of Representatives, March 24, 2015. Accessed at https://energycommerce.house.gov/hearings/internet-things-exploring-next-technology-frontier/.

13. For example, Senator Chuck Schumer submitted a letter to smart TV manufacturers calling for additional security measures, expressing concern that "for a TV to secretly function as a spy-cam would violate a fundamental expectation of privacy in the American home." See, for example, Ramsey Cox, "Schumer Warns Consumers Their TVs Could Be Spying on Them," *The Hill,* August 7, 2013. Accessed at http://thehill.com/blogs/floor-action/senate/315963-schumer-warns-consumers-their-tvs-could-be-spying-on-them?mobile_switch=standard.

14. Danielle Citron, "Protecting Sexual Privacy in the Information Age," in Marc Rotenberg, Julia Horwitz, and Jeramie Scott, eds., *Privacy in the Modern Age: The Search for Solutions,* New Press, 2015, p. 47.

15. See, for example, South Eastern Centre Against Sexual Assault and Family Violence (SECASA) official submission to the Australian "Enquiry into the Impact of New and Emerging ICTs by the Parliamentary Joint Committee on Law Enforcement," January 24, 2018. Accessed at https://www.aph.gov.au.

16. See examples in Nellie Bowles, "Thermostats, Locks and Lights: Digital Tools of Domestic Abuse," *New York Times,* June 23, 2018.

17. See, for example, Diana Freed, Jackeline Palmer, Diana Minchala, Karen Levy, Thomas Ristenpart, and Nicola Dell, "'A Stalker's Paradise': How Intimate Partner Abusers Exploit Technology," *CHI '18: Proceedings of the ACM SIGCHI Conference on Human Factors in Computing Systems,* ACM, 2018.

18. *N.P. v. Standard Innovation Corp.,* Case No. 1:16-cv-8655 (N.D. Ill. filed Sept. 12, 2016).

19. See Janice Hopkins Tanne, "FDA Approves Implantable Chip to Access Medical Records," *BMJ,* Vol. 329, no. 7474, 2004, p. 1064. Accessed at https://www.ncbi.nlm.nih.gov/pmc/articles/PMC526112/.

20. For a personal account of Warwick's experience and experimentation with the human-implantable silicon chip in the late 1990s, see Kevin Warwick, "Cyborg 1.0," *Wired,* February 1, 2000.

21. Three Square Market, "32M Microchips Employees Company-Wide," July 21, 2017. Accessed at https://32market.wordpress.com/2017/07/21/32m-microchips-employees-company-wide/.

22. BiChip home page: http://www.bichip.com.

23. Internet of Things Privacy Forum, "Clearly Opaque: Privacy Risks of the Internet of Things," May 2018, p. 2. Accessed at https://www.iotprivacyforum.org/wp-content/uploads/2018/06/Clearly-Opaque-Privacy-Risks-of-the-Internet-of-Things.pdf.

24. See, for example, Liz Sly, Dan Lamothe, and Craig Timberg, "U.S. Military Reviewing Its Rules after Fitness Trackers Exposed Sensitive Data," *Washington Post,* January 29, 2018; "Fitness App Strava Lights Up Staff at Military Bases," BBC News, January 29, 2018.

25. Letter from eight Democratic members of the U.S. House of Representatives Committee on Energy and Commerce to James Quarles, CEO of Strava, January 31, 2018. Accessed at https://democrats-energycommerce.house.gov/sites/democrats.energycommerce.house.gov/files/documents/Strava%20Briefing%20Request.2018.01.31.pdf.

26. James R. Clapper, "Statement for the Record: Worldwide Threat Assessment of the US Intelligence Community," U.S. Senate Armed Services Committee, February 9, 2016, p. 1. Accessed at https://www.armed-services.senate.gov/imo/media/doc/Clapper_02-09-16.pdf.

27. BBC, "Chinese Man Caught by Facial Recognition at Pop Concern," April 13, 2018. Accessed at https://www.bbc.com/news/world-asia-china-43751276.

28. John Cowley, "Beijing Subway to Install Facial Recognition as Fears Grow of China Surveillance Powers," *The Telegraph,* June 19, 2018.

29. Christina Zhao, "Jaywalking in China: Facial Recognition Surveillance Will Soon Fine Citizens via Text Message," *Newsweek,* March 27, 2018.

30. Michel Foucault, *Discipline and Punish: The Birth of the Prison,* trans. Alan Sheridan, Vintage Books, 1977.

31. Ibid., p. 203.

32. European Parliamentary Research Service, Scientific Foresight Study, "Ethical Aspects of Cyber-Physical Systems," June 2016, p. 67. Accessed at https://euagenda.eu/upload/publications/untitled-70446-ea.pdf.

33. The 1997 MCI "Anthem" television ad can be viewed on YouTube. Accessed May 24, 2018, at https://www.youtube.com/watch?v=ioVMoeCbrig. For a contemporary analysis of this ad, see Lisa Nakamura, *Cybertypes: Race, Ethnicity, and Identity on the Internet,* Routledge, 2002.

34. See, for example, Danielle Citron, *Hate Crimes in Cyberspace,* Harvard University Press, 2016.

35. Lisa Nakamura, "Gender and Race Online," in Mark Graham and William H. Dutton, eds., *Society and the Internet: How Networks of Information and Communication are Changing Our Lives,* Oxford University Press, 2014, p. 81.

36. Joy Buolamwini and Timnit Gebru, "Gender Shades: Intersectional Accuracy Dispari-
    ties in Commercial Gender Classification," *Proceedings of Machine Learning Research,*
    Vol. 81, 2018, pp. 1–15.
37. See, for example, Chris Jay Hoofnagle, "Big Brother's Little Helpers: How ChoicePoint
    and Other Commercial Data Brokers Collect and Package Your Data for Law Enforce-
    ment," *North Carolina Journal of International Law and Commercial Regulation,*
    Vol. 29, 2003, pp. 595–637.
38. Danielle Keats Citron and Frank Pasquale, "The Scored Society: Due Process for
    Automated Predictions," *Washington Law Review,* Vol. 89, 2014, pp. 1–33.
39. FTC, "Internet of Things: Privacy and Security in a Connected World," January 2015,
    p. ii. Accessed at https://www.ftc.gov/system/files/documents/reports/federal-trade-
    commission-staff-report-november-2013-workshop-entitled-internet-things-privacy/
    150127iotrpt.pdf.
40. Samuel D. Warren and Louis D. Brandeis, "The Right to Privacy," *Harvard Law Review,*
    Vol. 4, No. 5, 1890, p. 193.
41. DHS, "Privacy Policy Guidance Memorandum," December 29, 2008, p. 3. Accessed at
    https://www.dhs.gov/sites/default/files/publications/privacy_policyguide_2008-01_0.
    pdf.
42. Helen Nissenbaum, presentation at the "Digital Identities, Privacy and Security
    Issues" panel at the "State of the Field Workshop on the Digital Transformation," at the
    Columbia University School of International and Public Affairs, June 15, 2018.
43. Joel R. Reidenberg, N. Cameron Russell, Alexander J. Callen, Sophia Qasir, and
    Thomas B. Norton, "Privacy Harms and the Effectiveness of the Notice and Choice
    Framework," *I/S: A Journal of Law and Policy for the Information Society,* Vol. 11,
    No. 2, pp. 485–524.
44. Steve Mann, Jason Nolan, and Barry Wellman, "Sousveillance: Inventing and Using
    Wearable Computing Devices for Data Collection in Surveillance Environments,"
    Surveillance & Society, Vol. 1, No. 3, 2003, pp. 331–355.
45. See Helen Nissenbaum, *Privacy in Context: Technology, Policy, and the Integrity of
    Social Life,* Stanford University Press, 2009.
46. Julie E. Cohen, "What Privacy Is For," *Harvard Law Review,* Vol. 126, 2013, p. 1905.
47. Otonomo, "About Us." Accessed May 23, 2018, at https://otonomo.io/about-us/.
48. U.S. National Science and Technology Council, "National Privacy Research Strategy,"
    June 2016. Accessed at https://www.nitrd.gov/PUBS/NationalPrivacyResearchStrategy.
    pdf.
49. "Internet Architecture Board Comments to United States National Telecommunications
    and Information Administration Request for Comments: 'The Benefits, Challenges, and
    Potential Roles for the Government in Fostering the Advancement of the Internet
    of Things,'" May 27, 2016. Accessed at https://www.iab.org/wp-content/IAB-uploads/
    2016/05/ntia-iot-20160525.pdf.
50. From the text of the European Union General Directive Privacy Regulation, p. 199/13.

Chapter 4. Cyber-Physical Security

1. US-CERT, "Alert (TA18-074): Russian Government Cyber Activity Targeting Energy and Other Critical Infrastructure Sectors," March 15, 2018. Accessed at https://www.us-cert.gov/ncas/alerts/TA18-074A.
2. Ibid.
3. ICS-CERT, "Alert IR-ALERT-H-16-056-01: Cyber-Attack against Ukrainian Critical Infrastructure," February 25, 2016. Accessed at https://ics-cert.us-cert.gov/alerts/IR-ALERT-H-16-056-01.
4. Ibid.
5. Natalia Zinets, "Ukraine Hit by 6,500 Hack Attacks, Sees Russian 'Cyberwar,'" Reuters, December 29, 2016.
6. Gordon Goldstein, "Cyber War—Bigger than Ever—Is Here to Stay," *Washington Post,* March 18, 2016.
7. Charles Perrow, *Normal Accidents: Living with High-Risk Technologies,* Princeton University Press, 1984, p. 3.
8. *U.S. v. Robert Tappan Morris,* Case No. 89-CR-139 (N.D.N.Y. May 16, 1990).
9. See Mark Eichin and Jon Rochlis, "With Microscope and Tweezers: An Analysis of the Internet Virus of November 1988," Massachusetts Institute of Technology, November 1988.
10. White House, "Foreign Policy: Statement from the Press Secretary [on NotPetya]," February 15, 2018. Accessed at https://www.whitehouse.gov/briefings-statements/statement-press-secretary-25/.
11. US-CERT, "Alert (TA14-098A): OpenSSL 'Heartbleed' Vulnerability," original release date April 8, 2014.
12. CERT Coordination Center, Carnegie Mellon University Software Engineering Institute, Vulnerability Note VU#584653, "CPU Hardware Vulnerable to Side-Channel Attacks," original release date January 3, 2018. Accessed at https://www.kb.cert.org/vuls/id/584653.
13. Target, "Target Provides Update on Data Breach and Financial Performance," January 10, 2014. Accessed at http://pressroom.target.com/news/target-provides-update-on-data-breach-and-financial-performance.
14. Yahoo!, "An Important Message to Yahoo Users on Security," September 22, 2016. Accessed at https://investor.yahoo.net/releasedetail.cfm?releaseid=990570.
15. Yahoo!, "Yahoo Security Notice," December 14, 2016. Accessed at https://help.yahoo.com/kb/SLN27925.html.
16. Equifax, "Equifax Announces Cybersecurity Firm Has Concluded Forensic Investigation of Cybersecurity Incident," October 2, 2017. Accessed at https://www.equifaxsecurity2017.com/2017/10/02/equifax-announces-cybersecurity-firm-concluded-forensic-investigation-cybersecurity-incident/.
17. Equifax, "Equifax Releases Details on Cybersecurity Incident, Announces Personnel Changes," September 15, 2017. Accessed at https://www.equifaxsecurity2017.com/2017/09/15/equifax-releases-details-cybersecurity-incident-announces-personnel-changes/.

18. US-CERT, "Alert (TA18-106A): Russian State-Sponsored Cyber Actors Targeting Network Infrastructure Devices," original release date April 16, 2018. Accessed at https://www.us-cert.gov/ncas/alerts/TA18-106A.

19. Ronald J. Deibert, *Black Code: Inside the Battle for Cyberspace,* Signal, 2013.

20. President's Commission on Critical Infrastructure Protection, "Overview Briefing," Washington, DC, June 1997.

21. U.S. government, *The National Strategy to Secure Cyberspace,* Washington, DC, February 2003.

22. Commission on Enhancing National Cybersecurity, *Report on Securing and Growing the Digital Economy,* December 2016, p. 90. Accessed at https://www.nist.gov/sites/default/files/documents/2016/12/02/cybersecurity-commission-report-final-post.pdf.

23. A list of attacks believed by DHS and the FBI to be carried out by North Korean government-sponsored cyber actors is available on the US-CERT website: "HIDDEN COBRA—North Korean Malicious Cyber Activity." Accessed July 17, 2018, at https://www.us-cert.gov/HIDDEN-COBRA-North-Korean-Malicious-Cyber-Activity.

24. Microsoft, "Microsoft Security Bulletin MS17-010—Critical: Security Update for Microsoft Windows SMB Server (4013389)," March 14, 2017. Accessed at https://docs.microsoft.com/en-us/security-updates/SecurityBulletins/2017/ms17-010.

25. See, for example, the statement of the UK National Health Service, "Statement on Reported NHS Cyber Attack." Accessed April 20, 2018, at https://digital.nhs.uk/article/1491/Statement-on-reported-NHS-cyber-attack.

26. White House, "Press Briefing on the Attribution of the WannaCry Malware Attack to North Korea," December 19, 2017. Accessed at https://www.whitehouse.gov/briefings-statements/press-briefing-on-the-attribution-of-the-wannacry-malware-attack-to-north-korea-121917/. See also the op-ed of Homeland Security Advisor Thomas P. Bossert, "It's Official: North Korea Is Behind WannaCry," *Wall Street Journal,* December 18, 2017.

27. See, for example, Nicole Periroth and David E. Sanger, "Hackers Hit Dozens of Countries Exploiting Stolen N.S.A. Tools," *New York Times,* May 12, 2017.

28. "Dragonfly: Western Energy Sector Targeted by Sophisticated Attack Group," *Threat Intelligence* (blog), Symantec, October 20, 2017. Accessed at https://www.symantec.com/blogs/threat-intelligence/dragonfly-energy-sector-cyber-attacks.

29. For detailed attack techniques, see US-CERT, "Alert (TA18-074A): Russian Government Cyber Activity."

30. See "Car Hacked on 60 Minutes," video, CBS News, February 6, 2015. Accessed at http://www.cbsnews.com/news/car-hacked-on-60-minutes/.

31. See, for example, "How a Fish Tank Helped Hack a Casino," *Washington Post,* July 21, 2017; Thomas Freeman, "Genius Hackers Used a Vegas Casino's Fish Tank Thermometer to Steal High Rollers' Personal Information," *Maxim,* April 16, 2018.

32. Grant Ho, Derek Leung, Pratyush Mishra, Ashkan Hosseini, Dawn Song, and David Wagner, "Smart Locks: Lessons for Securing Commodity Internet of Things Devices," Berkeley Technical Report No. UCB/EECS-2016-11, March 12, 2016. Accessed at https://www2.eecs.berkeley.edu/Pubs/TechRpts/2016/EECS-2016-11.pdf.

33. ICS-CERT, "Advisory (ICSMA-17-241-01): Abbott Laboratories' Accent/Anthem, Accent MRI, Assurity/Allure, and Assurity MRI Pacemaker Vulnerabilities," original release date August 29, 2017.

34. U.S. Government Accountability Office, "Technology Assessment: Internet of Things," May 2017. Accessed at https://www.gao.gov/assets/690/684590.pdf.

35. Animas, letter to One Touch Ping Pump users, "Important Information about the Cybersecurity of Your OneTouch Ping Insulin Infusion Pump," September 27, 2016.

36. Testimony of Bruce Schneier, "Understanding the Role of Connected Devices in Recent Cyber Attacks," hearing before the Subcommittee on Communications and Technology and the Subcommittee on Commerce, Manufacturing, and Trade of the Committee on Energy and Commerce, U.S. House of Representatives, November 16, 2016. Accessed at http://docs.house.gov/meetings/IF/IF17/20161116/105418/HHRG-114-IF17-Wstate-SchneierB-20161116.pdf.

37. "Joint Statement from the Department of Homeland Security and Office of the Director of National Intelligence on Election Security," October 7, 2016. Accessed at https://www.dhs.gov/news/2016/10/07/joint-statement-department-homeland-security-and-office-director-national.

38. DHS and FBI, "GRIZZLY STEPPE—Russian Malicious Cyber Activity," JAR-16-20296, December 29, 2016. Accessed at https://www.us-cert.gov/sites/default/files/publications/JAR_16-20296A_GRIZZLY%20STEPPE-2016-1229.pdf.

39. Ethan Zuckerman, Hal Roberts, Ryan McGrady, Jillian York, and John Palfrey, "Distributed Denial of Service Attacks against Independent Media and Human Rights Sites," Berkman Center for Internet and Society, December 2010.

40. "Internet Society 2018 Action Plan." Accessed December 12, 2018, at https://www.internetsociety.org/action-plan/2018/.

41. NIST, "Draft NISTIR 8200: Interagency Report on Status of International Cybersecurity Standardization for the Internet of Things (IoT)," February 2018. Accessed at https://csrc.nist.gov/CSRC/media/Publications/nistir/8200/draft/documents/nistir8200-draft.pdf.

42. DHS, "Strategic Principles for Securing the Internet of Things," November 2016. Accessed at https://www.dhs.gov/sites/default/files/publications/IOT%20fact%20sheet_11162016.pdf.

43. President's Commission on Enhancing National Cybersecurity, "Report on Securing and Growing the Digital Economy," December 2016, p. 90. Accessed at https://www.nist.gov/sites/default/files/documents/2016/12/02/cybersecurity-commission-report-final-post.pdf.

44. ENISA, "Baseline Security Recommendations for the IoT in the Context of Critical Information Infrastructures," November 2017, p. 7. Accessed at https://www.enisa.europa.eu/publications/baseline-security-recommendations-for-iot/at_download/fullReport.

45. Article 29 Data Protection Working Party, "Opinion on the Recent Developments in the Internet of Things," September 16, 2014, p. 3. Accessed at http://ec.europa.eu/justice/article-29/documentation/opinion-recommendation/files/2014/wp223_en.pdf.

46. GSMA, "IoT Security Guidelines: Overview Document," October 31, 2017, p. 5. Accessed at https://www.gsma.com/iot/gsma-iot-security-guidelines-complete-document-set/.

47. U.S. Commission on Enhancing National Cybersecurity, "Report on Securing and Growing the Digital Economy," December 2016, p. 7. Accessed at https://www.nist.gov/sites/default/files/documents/2016/12/02/cybersecurity-commission-report-final-post.pdf.

48. DHS, "Strategic Principles."

49. GSMA, "IoT Security Guidelines."

50. NTIA, "Stakeholder-Drafted Documents on IoT Security," July 13, 2018. Accessed at https://www.ntia.doc.gov/IoTSecurity.

51. IoT Security Foundation, "Establishing Principles for Internet of Things Security," September 2015. Accessed at https://iotsecurityfoundation.org/wp-content/uploads/2015/09/IoTSF-Establishing-Principles-for-IoT-Security-Download.pdf.

52. Cloud Security Alliance, "New Security Guidance for Early Adopters of the Internet of Things (IoT), April 2015. Accessed at https://downloads.cloudsecurityalliance.org/whitepapers/Security_Guidance_for_Early_Adopters_of_the_Internet_of_Things.pdf.

53. DHS, "Strategic Principles."

54. NIST, "Framework for Cyber-Physical Systems: Volume 1, Overview, Version 1.0," June 2017, p. 10. Accessed at https://nvlpubs.nist.gov/nistpubs/SpecialPublications/NIST.SP.1500-201.pdf.

55. For a comprehensive assessment of IoT standards, see NIST, "Draft NISTIR 8200."

56. Bruce Schneier, "The Internet of Things Is Wildly Insecure—and Often Unpatchable," *Wired,* January 6, 2014.

57. Internet Society, "IoT Security for Policymakers," April 19, 2018. Accessed at https://www.internetsociety.org/resources/2018/iot-security-for-policymakers/.

58. See detailed technical explanations in Hannes Tschofenig and Stephen Farrell, "Report from the Internet of Things Software Update (IoTSU) Workshop 2016," RFC 8240, September 2017.

59. Internet Society, "IoT Security for Policymakers."

60. ENISA, "Baseline Security Recommendations for IoT in the Context of Critical Information Infrastructures," November 2017. Accessed at https://www.enisa.europa.eu/publications/baseline-security-recommendations-for-iot.

61. See, for example, the 2017 proposed Cyber Shield Act in the United States, which would involve the Department of Commerce establishing a voluntary IoT cybersecurity certification system.

62. Sarah Young, "Amazon, Target, and Walmart Stop Selling CloudPets Toys over Security Issues," *Consumer Affairs,* June 6, 2018.

63. See, for example, the requirements proposed in U.S. Senate Bill 1691, the "Internet of Things Cybersecurity Improvement Act of 2017," introduced on August 1, 2017, to ensure minimal cybersecurity standards in devices purchased by the federal government.

64. See, for example, Internet Society, "Collaborative Security: An Approach to Tackling Internet Security Issues," April 2005. Accessed at https://www.internetsociety.org/wp-content/uploads/2015/04/Collaborative-Security.pdf.

65. OTA, "The Enterprise IoT Security Checklist," 2018. Accessed at https://otalliance.org/system/files/files/initiative/documents/enterprise_iot_checklist.pdf.

66. Ibid.

67. Ibid.

68. Homeland Security Advisor Tom Bossert disclosed that the United States retains 10 percent of vulnerabilities it discovers, in White House, "Press Briefing on the Attribution of the WannaCry Malware Attack to North Korea," December 19, 2017. Accessed at ht-

tps://www.whitehouse.gov/briefings-statements/press-briefing-on-the-attribution-of-the-wannacry-malware-attack-to-north-korea-121917/.

69. See Brad Smith, "The Need for Urgent Collective Action to Keep People Safe Online: Lessons from Last Week's Cyberattack," *Microsoft on the Issues: The Official Microsoft Blog,* May 14, 2017. Accessed at https://blogs.microsoft.com/on-the-issues/2017/05/14/need-urgent-collective-action-keep-people-safe-online-lessons-last-weeks-cyberattack/.

70. Bill Marczak and John Scott-Railton, "The Million Dollar Dissident: NSO Group's iPhone Zero-Days Used against a UAE Human Rights Defender," Citizen Lab, August 24, 2016. Accessed at https://citizenlab.ca/2016/08/million-dollar-dissident-iphone-zero-day-nso-group-uae/.

71. Apple security update, original release date January 23, 2017. Accessed at https://support.apple.com/en-us/HT207130.

72. See, for example, "Israeli Accused of Trying to Sell Stolen Spyware for $50 Million," Bloomberg, July 5, 2018.

73. US-CERT, "Alert (TA16-250A): The Increasing Threat to Network Infrastructure Devices and Recommended Mitigations," September 6, 2016. Accessed at https://www.us-cert.gov/ncas/alerts/TA16-250A.

74. Rob Joyce, "Improving and Making the Vulnerability Equities Process Transparent Is the Right Thing to Do," White House, November 15, 2017. Accessed at https://www.whitehouse.gov/articles/improving-making-vulnerability-equities-process-transparent-right-thing/.

75. White House, "Vulnerabilities Equities Policy and Process for the United States Government" (unclassified), November 15, 2017. Accessed at https://www.whitehouse.gov/sites/whitehouse.gov/files/images/External%20-%20Unclassified%20VEP%20Charter%20FINAL.PDF.

76. James B. Comey, statement before the Senate Select Committee on Intelligence, "Counterterrorism, Counterintelligence, and the Challenges of Going Dark," July 8, 2015. Accessed at https://www.fbi.gov/news/testimony/counterterrorism-counterintelligence-and-the-challenges-of-going-dark.

77. Laura DeNardis, "The Internet Design Struggle between Surveillance and Security," *IEEE Annals of the History of Computing,* Vol. 37, No. 2, 2015.

78. Prepared statement of Dr. Natha P. Myhrvold, Vice President, Advanced Technology and Business Development, Microsoft, "The Threat of Foreign Economic Espionage to U.S. Corporations," Serial No. 65, hearings before the Subcommittee on Economic and Commercial Law of the Committee on the Judiciary, U.S. House of Representatives, April 29 and May 7, 1992, p. 379.

79. Ibid.

80. Ibid.

81. Chertoff Group, "The Ground Truth about Encryption and the Consequences of Extraordinary Access," 2016, p. 1. Accessed at https://www.chertoffgroup.com/files/238024-282765.groundtruth.pdf.

82. Joseph Lorenzo Hall, Apratim Vidyarthi, and Benjamin C. Dean, "Security Research: Four Case Studies," CTD, December 2017. Accessed at https://cdt.org/files/2017/12/2017-12-15-Importance-of-Security-Research.pdf.

Chapter 5. Interoperability Politics

1. "Hardening the Internet" was the title of the Technical Plenary of the IETF 88 meeting of the Internet Engineering Task Force in Vancouver, BC, Canada, in November 2013.

2. Stephen Farrell and Hannes Tschofenig, "Pervasive Monitoring Is an Attack," RFC 7258, May 2014.

3. IAB, "IAB Statement on Internet Confidentiality," November 14, 2014, https://www.iab.org/2014/11/14/iab-statement-on-internet-confidentiality/.

4. See Laura DeNardis, "The Internet Design Tension between Surveillance and Security," *IEEE Annals of the History of Computing,* Vol. 37, No. 2, 2015, pp. 72–83.

5. Janet Abbate, *Inventing the Internet,* MIT Press, 1999, p. 179.

6. Hannes Tschofenig, Jari Arkko, David Thaler, and Danny McPerhson, "Architectural Considerations in Smart Object Networking," RFC 7452, March 2015, p. 17.

7. See, for example, Knut Blind, *The Economics of Standards: Theory, Evidence, Policy,* Edward Elgar, 2004.

8. Laura DeNardis, *Protocol Politics: The Globalization of Internet Governance,* MIT Press, 2009.

9. Brenden Kuerbis and Milton Mueller, "Securing the Root," in Laura DeNardis, ed., *Opening Standards: The Global Politics of Interoperability,* MIT Press, 2011.

10. See, for example, Sandra Braman, "Internet RFCs as Social Policy: Network Design from a Regulatory Perspective," *Proceedings of the American Society for Information Science and Technology,* Vol. 46, No. 1, 2009, pp. 1–29.

11. Corrine Cath and Luciano Floridi, "The Design of the Internet's Architecture by the Internet Engineering Task Force (IETF) and Human Rights," *Science and Engineering Ethics,* Vol. 23, No. 2, 2017, pp. 449–468.

12. DeNardis, "Internet Design Tension."

13. For an extensive account of the social and economic consequences of algorithms, see Frank Pasquale, *The Black Box Society: The Secret Algorithms That Control Money and Information,* Harvard University Press, 2015.

14. David C. Clark, "Control Point Analysis," paper presented at TPRC, September 10, 2012. Accessed at https://ssrn.com/abstract=2032124.

15. Lawrence Lessig, "The Laws of Cyberspace," Berkman-Klein Center for Internet and Society, 1998, p. 3. Accessed at https://cyber.harvard.edu/works/lessig/laws_cyberspace.pdf.

16. ITU, ITU-T Recommendation Y.2060, "Overview of Internet of Things," June 2012.

17. The Bluetooth core specifications are available on the Bluetooth Special Interest Group site. Accessed December 14, 2018, at https://www.bluetooth.com/specifications/bluetooth-core-specification.

18. Nandakishore Kushalnagar, Gabriel Montenegro, and Christian Schumacher, "IPv6 over Low-Power Wireless Personal Area Networks (6LoWPAN): Overview, Assumptions, Problem Statement, and Goals," RFC 4919, August 2007.

19. Tim Winter, ed., "RPL: IPv6 Routing Protocol for Low-Power and Lossy Networks," RFC 6550, March 2012.

20. Patrik Fältström, "Market-Driven Challenges to Open Internet Standards," *Global Commission on Internet Governance Papers Series,* No. 33, CIGI, 2016, p. 7.

21. All W3C standards and drafts can be accessed online at http://www.w3.org/TR/.

22. IEEE, "IEEE P2413—Standard for an Architectural Framework for the Internet of Things." Accessed January 10, 2018, at https://standards.ieee.org/develop/project/2413.html.

23. Ibid.

24. Zigbee Alliance, "The Zigbee Alliance and Threat Group Address IoT Fragmentation with the Availability of the Dotdot Specification over Thread's IP Network," December 12, 2017. Accessed at https://www.zigbee.org/zigbee-alliance-and-thread-group-address-iot-industry-fragmentation-with-dotdot-over-thread/.

25. W3C, "W3C Begins Standards Work on the Web of Things to Reduce IoT Fragmentation," February 24, 2017. Accessed at https://www.w3.org/2017/02/media-advisory-wot-wg.html.en.

26. Open Connectivity Foundation, "Unlocking the Internet of Things," April 12, 2018. Accessed at https://openconnectivity.org/blog/unlocking-internet-things.

27. ENISA, "Baseline Security Recommendations for the IoT in the Context of Critical Information Infrastructures," November 2017. Accessed at https://www.enisa.europa.eu/publications/baseline-security-recommendations-for-iot/at_download/fullReport.

28. Dave Thaler and Bernard Aboba, "What Makes for a Successful Protocol?," RFC 5218, July 2018.

29. Danny Bradbury, "Grab a Fork! Unravelling the Internet of Things Standards Spaghetti," *The Register,* August 2, 2017. Accessed at https://www.theregister.co.uk/2017/08/02/iot_standards_spaghetti/.

30. John Deere, "License Agreement for John Deere Embedded Software." Accessed April 10, 2018, at https://www.deere.com/privacy_and_data/docs/agreement_pdfs/english/2016-10-28-Embedded-Software-EULA.pdf.

31. For an extensive treatment of the economic and political effects of open standards, see Laura DeNardis, ed., *Opening Standards: The Global Politics of Interoperability,* MIT Press, 2011.

32. IAB and IESG, "IAB and IESG Statement on Cryptographic Technology and the Internet," RFC 1984, August 1996.

33. All of the Internet RFCs are freely accessible on the IETF.org website.

34. See Zigbee Alliance membership page at http://www.zigbee.org/zigbeealliance/join/.

35. See W3C Web of Things standards work at https://www.w3.org/WoT/.

36. See IEEE architectural framework for the IoT at http://grouper.ieee.org/groups/2413/.

37. See information about the ISO/IEC Reference Architecture for the IoT at https://www.iso.org/standard/65695.html.

38. See the IIC Industrial Internet Reference Architecture at https://www.iiconsortium.org/IIRA.htm.

39. Andree Toonk, "Popular Destinations Rerouted to Russia," BGPmon, December 12, 2017. Accessed at https://bgpmon.net/popular-destinations-rerouted-to-russia/.

40. This governance process of interconnection, addressing, and routing is explained in detail in Laura DeNardis, *The Global War for Internet Governance,* Yale University Press, 2014.

41. "The 32-bit AS Number Report," updated daily by the Internet engineer Geoff Huston. Accessed May 24, 2018, at http://www.potaroo.net/tools/asn32/.

42. John Hawkinson and Tony Bates, "Guidelines for Creation, Selection, and Registration of an Autonomous System (AS)," RFC 1930, March 1996.

43. For more technical information, see "A Border Gateway Protocol 4 (BGP-4)," RFC 4271, 2006.

44. Kotikalapudi Sriram, Doug Montgomery, Danny McPherson, Eric Osterweil, and Brian Dickson, "Problem Definition and Classification of BGP Route Leaks," RFC 7908, June 2016.

45. Toonk, "Popular Destinations Rerouted."

46. Tschofenig et al., "Architectural Considerations."

47. For elaboration on the reasons to apply the Internet Protocol in cyber-physical environments, see Kushalnagar, Montenegro, and Schumacher, "IPv6 over Low-Power Wireless Personal Area Networks (6LoWPAN)."

48. The history of IPv6 is addressed in DeNardis, *Protocol Politics.*

49. Thomas Hughes, *American Genesis: A History of the American Genius for Invention,* Penguin Books, 1989, pp. 462–463.

50. For example, the IEEE formed a quantum computing working group, NIST convened a workshop on quantum computing and cryptography, ETSI formed a working group on quantum-safe cryptography. See, for example, ETSI, "Quantum-Safe Cryptography (QSC)," July 2016. Accessed at https://www.etsi.org/deliver/etsi_gr/QSC/001_099/001/01.01.01_60/gr_QSC001v010101p.pdf.

51. See, for example, Melanie Swan, *Blueprint for a New Economy,* O'Reilly Media, 2015; and Michael Crosby, Nachiappan, Pradan Pattanayak, Sanjeev Verman, and Vignesh Kalyanaraman, "Blockchain Technology: Beyond Bitcoin," *Applied Innovation Review,* No. 2, June 2016.

52. This theme is developed in Laura DeNardis, "One Internet: An Evidentiary Basis for Policy Making on Internet Universality and Fragmentation," *Global Commission on Internet Governance Paper Series,* No. 38, CIGI, 2016.

53. Dame Wendy Hall, private conversation with the author.

54. "Two forces are in tension as the Internet evolves. One pushes toward interconnected common platforms; the other pulls toward fragmentation and proprietary alternatives." Kevin Werbach, "The Centripetal Network: How the Internet Holds Itself Together, and the Forces Tearing It Apart, *University of California Davis Law Review,* Vol. 42, 2008, p. 343.

Chapter 6. The Internet Freedom Oxymoron

1. See Kent Walker, Google Senior Vice President and General Counsel, "Preserving a Free and Open Internet (Why the IANA Transition Must Move Forward)," *Google Blog,* September 26, 2016. Accessed at https://blog.google/topics/public-policy/preserving-free-and-open-internet/.

2. Julius Genachowski, "Preserving a Free and Open Internet," *FCC Blog,* December 1, 2010. Accessed at https://www.fcc.gov/news-events/blog/2010/12/01/preserving-free-and-open-internet.

3. Hillary Rodham Clinton, "Remarks on Internet Freedom," February 15, 2011. Previously but no longer accessible on the U.S. State Department website.

4. Daniel Costa-Roberts, "Saudi Court Sentences Man to 10 Years, 2,000 Lashes for Atheist Tweets," *PBS NewsHour,* February 27, 2016. Accessed at http://www.pbs.org/newshour/rundown/saudi-court-sentences-man-to-10-years-2000-lashes-for-atheist-tweets/.

5. Committee to Protect Journalists, "2015 Prison Census: 199 Journalists Jailed Worldwide," December 1, 2015.

6. Tom Standage, *The Victorian Internet: The Remarkable Story of the Telegraph and the Nineteenth Century's On-Line Pioneers,* Walker, 1998, pp. xiii–xiv.

7. See, for example, Susan J. Douglas, *Inventing American Broadcasting: 1899–1922,* Johns Hopkins University Press, 1987; and Hugh R. Slotten, *Radio and Television Regulation: Broadcast Technology in the United States, 1920–1960,* Johns Hopkins University Press, 2000.

8. Andrew L. Russell, "Rough Consensus and Running Code and the Internet-OSI Standards War," *IEEE Annals of the History of Computing,* July–September, 2006, p. 56.

9. Paulina Borsook, "How Anarchy Works," *Wired,* October 1, 1995. Accessed at https://www.wired.com/1995/10/ietf/.

10. Susan Harris, ed., "The Tao of IETF—A Novice's Guide to the Internet Engineering Task Force," RFC 3160, August 2001.

11. David Clark, "A Cloudy Crystal Ball, Visions of the Future," plenary presentation, *Proceedings of the Twenty-Fourth Internet Engineering Task Force: Massachusetts Institute of Technology, NEARnet, Cambridge, July 13–17, 1992,* Corporation for National Research Initiatives, 1992, p. 539. Accessed at http://www.ietf.org/proceedings/prior29/IETF24.pdf.

12. Telecommunications Act of 1996. Full original text available at http://transition.fcc.gov/Reports/tcom1996.txt.

13. Peter H. Lewis, "Protest, Cyberspace-Style, for New Law," *New York Times,* February 8, 1996.

14. See the biography of John Perry Barlow on the Electronic Frontier Foundation website at https://homes.eff.org/~barlow/.

15. John Perry Barlow, "A Declaration of the Independence of Cyberspace," EFF, February 8, 1996. Accessed at https://projects.eff.org/~barlow/Declaration-Final.html.

16. Ibid.

17. *Reno v. American Civil Liberties Union,* 521 U.S. 844 (1997). Accessed at http://www.law.cornell.edu/supremecourt/text/521/844#writing-USSC_CR_0521_0844_ZO.

18. See, for example, Aimée Hope Morrison, "An Impossible Future: John Perry Barlow's 'Declaration of the Independence of Cyberspace,'" *New Media & Society,* Vol. 11, February–March 2009, pp. 53–71.

19. For a detailed account of the SOPA/PIPA reaction and implications, see Laura DeNardis, *The Global War for Internet Governance,* Yale University Press, 2014, pp. 2–14.

20. Alexis Ohanian, on Bloomberg Television's *InBusiness with Margaret Brennan,* January 4, 2012.

21. See, for example, the letter to Congress submitted by eighty-three prominent Internet engineers, including the TCP/IP inventor, Vinton Cerf, warning that the potentially catastrophic bill would "risk fragmenting the Internet's Domain Name System," "engender censorship," create "fear and uncertainty for technological innovation," and "seriously harm the credibility of the United States in its role as a steward of key Internet infrastructure." "An Open

Letter from Internet Engineers to the US Congress," EFF, December 15, 2011. Accessed at https://www.eff.org/deeplinks/2011/12/internet-inventors-warn-against-sopa-and-pipa.

22. The full text and video of Secretary Clinton's "Remarks on Internet Freedom" speech, made January 21, 2010, at the Newseum in Washington, DC, are available on C-SPAN at https://www.c-span.org/video/?291518-1/secretary-clinton-remarks-internet-freedom.

23. See, e.g., Adam Thierer, "Hillary Clinton's Historic Speech on Global Internet Freedom," *The Technology Liberation Front* (blog), January 21, 2010. Accessed at http://techliberation. com/2010/01/21/hillary-clintons-historic-speech-on-global-internet-freedom/. See also "Secretary Clinton Speech Makes Global Internet Freedom Foreign Policy Priority," *CDT Blog,* January 21, 2010. Accessed at https://www.cdt.org/blogs/brock-meeks/secretary-clinton-speech-makes-global-internet-freedom-foreign-policy-priority.

24. See the Bureau of Democracy, Human Rights, and Labor, U.S. Department of State, "Internet Freedom," program statement. Accessed June 13, 2017, at https://www.state. gov/j/drl/internetfreedom/index.htm.

25. Madeline Carr, "Internet Freedom, Human Rights and Power," *Australian Journal of International Affairs* Vol. 67, No. 5, 2013, p. 622. Accessed at https://doi.org/10.1080/ 10357718.2013.817525.

26. Richard Fontaine and Will Rogers, "Internet Freedom: A Foreign Policy Imperative in the Digital Age," Center for a New American Security, June 2011, p. 5.

27. United Nations Human Rights Council, "The Promotion, Protection and Enjoyment of Human Rights on the Internet," A/HRC/RES/20/8, July 16, 2012, p. 3. Accessed at http:// www.ohchr.org/EN/HRBodies/HRC/RegularSessions/Session20/Pages/ResDecStat.aspx.

28. For an extensive examination of this topic, see Shawn M. Powers and Michael Jablonski, *The Real Cyber War: The Political Economy of Internet Freedom,* University of Illinois Press, 2015.

29. Pablo Chavez, Senior Policy Counsel, "Promoting Free Expression on the Internet," *Google Public Policy Blog,* May 20, 2008. Accessed at https://publicpolicy.googleblog. com/2008/05/promoting-free-expression-on-internet.html.

30. EFF, "EFF Resigns from Global Network Initiative," October 10, 2013. Accessed at https://www.eff.org/press/releases/eff-resigns-global-network-initiative.

31. Rebecca MacKinnon, *Consent of the Networked: The Worldwide Struggle for Internet Freedom,* Basic Books, 2012, p. xxiv.

32. Rebecca MacKinnon, Nathalie Marechal, and Priya Kumar, "Corporate Accountability for a Free and Open Internet," *Global Commission on Internet Governance Paper Series,* No. 45, CIGI, December 2016. Accessed at https://www.cigionline.org/publications/ corporate-accountability-free-and-open-internet.

33. Marvin Ammori, *On Internet Freedom,* Elkat Books, 2013, Kindle loc. 249 of 1830.

34. See, for example, FCC, "Preserving the Open Internet: Final Rule," *Federal Register,* Vol. 76, No. 185, September 23, 2011. Accessed at https://www.federalregister.gov/ documents/2011/09/23/2011-24259/preserving-the-open-internet.

35. Comments of Comcast Corporation before the FCC, In the matter of Restoring Internet Freedom, WC-Docket No. 17-108, July 17, 2017. Accessed at http://update.comcast. com/wp-content/uploads/sites/33/securepdfs/2017/07/2017-07-17-AS-FILED-Comcast-2017-Open-Internet-Comments-and-Appendices.pdf.

36. United Nations Human Rights Council, "Promotion, Protection and Enjoyment of Human Rights on the Internet."

37. Working Group on Internet Governance, "Report of the Working Group on Internet Governance," 2005. Accessed at https://www.wgig.org/docs/WGIGREPORT.pdf.

38. For a detailed and critical examination of multistakeholder governance, see Mark Raymond and Laura DeNardis, "Multistakeholderism: Anatomy of an Inchoate Global Institution," *International Theory,* Vol. 7, No. 3, 2015, pp. 572–616.

39. U.S. Commerce Department, "NTIA Announces Internet to Transition Key Internet Domain Name Functions," March 14, 2014. Accessed at https://www.ntia.doc.gov/press-release/2014/ntia-announces-intent-transition-key-internet-domain-name-functions.

40. Jari Arkko and Andrew Sullivan, "NTIA Assessment of the IANA Stewardship Transition Proposal," *IETF Blog,* June 9, 2016, https://www.ietf.org/blog/2016/06/ntia-assessment-of-the-iana-stewardship-transition-proposal/.

41. GNI, "GNI Principles on Freedom of Expression and Privacy," 2018. Accessed March 24, 2019, at https://globalnetworkinitiative.org/wp-content/uploads/2018/04/GNI-Principles-on-Freedom-of-Expression-and-Privacy.pdf.

42. DeNardis, *Global War for Internet Governance,* p. 238.

43. Freedom House, "Freedom on the Net 2016," November 2016. Accessed at https://freedomhouse.org/sites/default/files/FOTN_2016_BOOKLET_FINAL.pdf.

44. Ibid.

45. Facebook, "Community Standards," section on violence and graphic content. Accessed September 15, 2017, at https://www.facebook.com/communitystandards#violence-and-graphic-content.

46. Evgeny Morozov, *The Net Delusion: The Dark Side of Internet Freedom,* Perseus Books, 2011, p. 320.

47. Ibid., p. xvii.

48. Laura DeNardis, Gordon Goldstein, and David Gross, "The Rising Geopolitics of Internet Governance: Cyber Sovereignty v. Distributed Governance," paper presented at Columbia University School of International and Public Affairs, November 30, 2016.

49. For more information about this case, see *Defense Distributed v. U.S. Department of State,* 838 F. 3d 451 (5th Cir. 2016).

50. Milwaukee County Parks, "2018 Special Event Permit Application," 2018. Accessed at http://county.milwaukee.gov/ImageLibrary/Groups/cntyParks/permits/SpecialEventPermit Application.pdf.

51. From the complaint filed in the United States District Court for the Eastern District of Wisconsin, *Candy Lab, Inc. v. Milwaukee County,* Case No. 2:17-cv-00569-JPS (E.D. Wis. filed April 21, 2017). Accessed at https://www.documentcloud.org/documents/3878598-CandyLabARLawsuit.html.

Chapter 7. Disruptions to Global Internet Governance

1. Ewen MacAskill, "Putin Calls Internet a 'CIA Project' Renewing Fears of Web Breakup," *The Guardian,* April 24, 2014. Accessed at http://www.theguardian.com/world/2014/apr/24/vladimir-putin-web-breakup-internet-cia.

2. Janet Abbate, "What and Where Is the Internet? (Re)defining Internet Histories," *Internet Histories,* Routledge, 2017, pp. 1–2.

3. Ibid., p. 3.

4. Rohan Samarajiva, "Facebook = Internet?," LIRNEasia, May 17, 2012. Accessed at http://lirneasia.net/2012/05/facebook-internet/.

5. Leo Mirani, "Millions of Facebook Users Have No Idea They're Using the Internet," *Quartz,* February 9, 2015. Accessed at https://qz.com/333313/milliions-of-facebook-users-have-no-idea-theyre-using-the-internet/.

6. Evgeny Morozov, *To Save Everything, Click Here: The Folly of Technological Solutionism,* Public Affairs, 2013, p. 12.

7. Joseph S. Nye Jr., "The Regime Complex for Managing Global Cyber Activities," *Global Commission on Internet Governance Paper Series,* No. 1, CIGI, May 2014.

8. Internet Society, "About the Internet." Accessed April 16, 2018, at https://www.internetsociety.org/internet/.

9. See Vinton Cerf and Robert Kahn, "A Protocol for Packet Network Intercommunication," *IEEE Transactions on Communications,* Vol. COM-22, No. 5, May 1974, pp. 637–648. See also "Internet Protocol," RFC 791, September 1981. In 1991, David Clark and other Internet pioneers called TCP/IP the "magnetic center of Internet evolution." David Clark, Lyman Chapin, Vinton Cerf, Robert Braden, and Russ Hobby, "Towards the Future Internet Architecture," RFC 1287, December 1991.

10. Clark et al., "Towards the Future Internet Architecture."

11. Steven Shapin, "What Else Is New? How Uses, Not Innovations, Drive Human Technology," *New Yorker,* May 14, 2007.

12. See, for example, the NTIA notice of inquiry on "International Internet Policy Priorities," in *Federal Register,* Vol. 83, No. 108, June 5, 2018, p. 26038, which includes the question, "Should the IANA Stewardship Transition be unwound? If yes, why and how? If not, why not?" Additionally, Senator Ted Cruz has continued to be a vocal proponent for rolling back the transition, if that were possible.

13. See, for example, Virgilio A. F. Almeida, Danilo Doneda, and Marilia Monteiro, "Governance Challenges for the Internet of Things," *IEEE Internet Computing,* Vol. 19, No. 4, 2015, pp. 56–59.

14. Laura DeNardis and Francesca Musiani, "Governance by Infrastructure," in Francesca Musiani, Derrick Cogburn, Laura DeNardis, and Nanette Levinson, eds., *The Turn to Infrastructure in Internet Governance,* New York: Palgrave Macmillan, 2016, pp. 3–21.

15. Samantha Bradshaw and Laura DeNardis, "The Politicization of the Internet's Domain Name System: Implications for Internet Security, Universality, and Freedom," *New Media & Society,* Vol. 20, No. 1, 2016, pp. 332–350.

16. Samantha Bradshaw and Laura DeNardis, "Privacy by Infrastructure: The Unresolved Case of the Domain Name System," *Policy & Internet,* January 15, 2019.

17. Gadi Evron, "Battling Botnets and Online Mobs: Estonia's Defense Efforts during the Internet War," *Georgetown Journal of International Affairs,* Vol. 9, No. 1, 2008, pp. 121–126.

18. Jennifer Daskal, "Borders and Bits," *Vanderbilt Law Review,* Vol. 71, No. 1, 2018, p. 181.

19. Jack Goldsmith and Tim Wu, *Who Controls the Internet? Illusions of a Borderless World,* Oxford University Press, 2006.

20. Anupam Chander, "Principles for Trade 2.0," in Mira Burri and Thomas Cottier, eds., *Trade Governance in the Digital Age: World Trade Forum,* Cambridge University Press, pp. 17–44.

21. United Nations Development Program, "Mozambique National Human Development Report 2008: The Role of Information Communication Technology in Achieving the Millennium Development Goals." Accessed at http://hdr.undp.org/sites/default/files/mozambique_nhdr_2008_ict.pdf.

22. Internet Society, "The Internet and Sustainable Development," June 5, 2015. Accessed at https://www.internetsociety.org/resources/doc/2015/the-internet-and-sustainable-development/.

23. Parliament of the Commonwealth of Australia, Parliamentary Joint Committee on the Australian Crime Commission, *Cybercrime,* March 2004.

24. A technical account of the attack is available in Marshall Abrams and Joe Weiss, "Malicious Control System Cyber Security Attack Case Study—Maroochy Water Services, Australia," MITRE Corporation, August 2008. Accessed at https://www.mitre.org/sites/default/files/pdf/08_1145.pdf.

25. Alexander Hamilton, "Final Version of the Second Report on the Further Provision Necessary for Establishing Public Credit (Report on a National Bank)," December 13, 1790. Accessed at the National Archives Hamilton Papers Repository, https://founders.archives.gov/documents/Hamilton/01-07-02-0229-0003.

26. Incredibly, the question of who invented Bitcoin is not publicly known. The legend is that it was invented by a person or people called "Satoshi Nakamoto." Not surprisingly, governments have expressed concerns about whether foreign governments were in fact the originators of Bitcoin and whether the technology could be weaponized in the future. Nakamoto released the Bitcoin software code in 2009 but stopped communicating with the early community of developers and stopped contributing to the Bitcoin project, at least under that name, in 2011. For a complete history of the origin of Bitcoin, see Nathaniel Popper, *Digital Code: Bitcoin and the Inside Story of the Misfits and Millionaires Trying to Reinvent Money,* Harper, 2015.

27. See the 2008 white paper by the person or people known as Sotoshi Nakamoto, "Bitcoin: A Peer-to-Peer Electronic Cash System." Accessed at https://bitcoin.org/bitcoin.pdf.

28. Primavera de Filippi and Benjamin Lovelock, "The Invisible Politics of Bitcoin: Governance Crisis of a Decentralised Infrastructure," *Internet Policy Review,* Vol. 5, No. 3, 2016.

29. US-CERT, "Security Tip ST18-002: Defending against Illicit Cryptocurrency Mining Activity," June 26, 2018. Accessed at https://www.us-cert.gov/ncas/tips/ST18-002.

30. Internet Society, "Internet Invariants: What Really Matters," February 3, 2012. Accessed at https://www.internetsociety.org/internet-invariants-what-really-matters.

31. Laura DeNardis, "One Internet: An Evidentiary Basis for Policy Making on Internet Universality and Fragmentation," *Global Commission on Internet Governance Paper Series,* No. 38, CIGI, 2016.

32. According to ITU indicators, 3.2 billion people had Internet access by 2015. ITU, "ICT Facts and Figures—The World in 2015," 2015. Accessed at http://www.itu.int/en/ITU-D/Statistics.

33. Adam Thierer, *Permissionless Innovation: The Continuing Case for Comprehensive Technological Freedom,* Mercatus Center at George Mason University, 2016, p. 1.

34. Adam D. Thierer and Adam Marcus, "Guns, Limbs, and Toys: What Future for 3D Printing?," *Minnesota Journal of Law, Science & Technology,* Vol. 17, No. 2, 2016, p. 818.

Chapter 8. The Cyber-Physical Policy Moment

1. Janet Abbate, *Inventing the Internet,* MIT Press, 2009, p. 36.
2. Katie Hafner and Matthew Lyon, *Where Wizards Stay Up Late: The Origins of the Internet,* Simon and Schuster, 1996, p. 14.
3. The political and economic stakes of Internet governance are elaborated in Laura De-Nardis, Gordon Goldstein, and David A. Gross, "The Rising Geopolitics of Internet Governance: Cyber Sovereignty v. Distributed Governance," Columbia School of International and Public Affairs working paper, November 2016. Accessed at https://sipa.columbia.edu/sites/default/files/The%20Rising%20Geopolitics_2016.pdf.
4. James Manyika, Michael Chui, Peter Bisson, Jonathan Woetzel, Richard Dobbs, Jacques Bughin, and Dan Aharon, "Unlocking the Potential of the Internet of Things," McKinsey Global Institute, June 2015. Accessed at http://www.mckinsey.com/business-functions/digital-mckinsey/our-insights/the-internet-of-things-the-value-of-digitizing-the-physical-world.
5. Thomas S. Kuhn, *The Structure of Scientific Revolutions,* University of Chicago Press, 1962. See also his early book *The Copernican Revolution,* Harvard University Press, 1957.
6. See, for example, James R. Beniger, *The Control Revolution: Technological and Economic Origins of the Information Society,* Harvard University Press, 1986; Ronald Diebert, John Palfrey, Rafal Rohozinski, and Jonathan Zittrain, eds., *Access Denied: The Practice and Policy of Global Internet Filtering,* MIT Press, 2008.
7. Laura DeNardis, "Hidden Levers of Internet Control: An Infrastructure-Based Theory of Internet Governance," *Journal of Information, Communication & Society,* Vol. 15, No. 5, 2012, p. 721.
8. Ronald Deibert and Rafal Rohozinski, "Liberation vs. Control: The Future of Cyberspace," *Journal of Democracy,* Vol. 21, No. 4, 2010, p. 48.
9. Lawrence Lessig, "The Laws of Cyberspace," paper presented at Taiwan Net '98, Taipei, April 1998.
10. Alexander R. Galloway, *Protocol: How Control Exists after Decentralization,* MIT Press, 2004, p. 142.
11. Norbert Weiner, *Cybernetics; or, Control and Communication in the Animal and the Machine,* MIT Press, 1947, p. 26.
12. Rebecca MacKinnon, *Consent of the Networked: The Worldwide Struggle for Internet Freedom,* Basic Books, 2012, p. 165.
13. Joseph S. Nye Jr. *The Future of Power,* Public Affairs, 2011, pp. 113–114.
14. Jack Balkin, "The Future of Expression in the Digital Age," *Pepperdine Law Review,* Vol. 36, No. 2, 2009, pp. 427–444.
15. Jack Balkin, "Free Speech in the Algorithmic Society: Big Data, Private Governance, and New School Speech Regulation," *UC Davis Law Review,* Vol. 51, 2017, pp. 1153.
16. Ibid., p. 1157.
17. From the text of Title 47, Section 230, United States Code, enacted as part of the Communications Decency Act, in turn a component of the Telecommunications Act of 1996.

18. CDT, "Intermediary Liability." Accessed June 2, 2018, at https://cdt.org/issue/free-expression/intermediary-liability/.

19. See, for example, Jack M. Balkin, "Information Fiduciaries and the First Amendment," *UC Davis Law Review,* Vol. 49, No. 4, 2016, pp. 1183–1234.

20. Tech Policy Lab, "Augmented Reality: A Technology and Policy Primer," September 2015, p. 6. Accessed at http://techpolicylab.org/wp-content/uploads/2016/02/Augmented_Reality_Primer-TechPolicyLab.pdf.

21. Internet Society, "Top Ten Recommendations for the Future of the Internet," 2018. Accessed June 1, 2018, at https://future.internetsociety.org/recommendations/.

22. CIGI-Ipsos, "2018 CIGI-Ipsos Global Survey on Internet Security and Trust," 2018. Accessed at http://www.cigionline.org/internet-survey-2018.

23. Elon Musk, closing plenary remarks at the National Governors' Association Summer Meeting, Providence, RI, July 15, 2017. Accessed at https://www.nga.org/cms/video/2017/sm/closing-plenary.

24. Robert M. Metcalfe, "From the Ether," *InfoWorld,* December 4, 1995.

25. For video coverage of the encounter, see "3D Printer Prosthetics at Home Depot," *Capital Gazette,* July 27, 2018. For more information about the volunteer organization, see enablingthefuture.org.

ACKNOWLEDGMENTS

Even before finishing *The Global War for Internet Governance* in 2013, a question loomed large in my mind: How will the Internet of things complicate Internet governance and what will it mean for the future of human rights? For me, embarking on any project commences with the feedback of my long-time intellectual home—the Yale Information Society Project (ISP). This book began in earnest with an "ideas lunch" and talk at Yale Law School and conversation with mentor Jack Balkin and the Yale ISP community.

I wish to extend a very special thank-you to the Hewlett Foundation Cyber Initiative team and to program director Eli Sugarman for influencing and so generously supporting my research.

I was also fortunate to spend two years from 2014 to 2016 serving as the Director of Research for the Global Commission on Internet Governance, during which time I engaged with an incredible group of thinkers and traveled the world examining cyber policy concerns from Stockholm to Seoul and The Hague to Amman. It was during many international discussions that my long-held concern about IoT governance crystallized. I wish to thank the twenty-five members of the Commission and also the fifty scholars who contributed original research supported by the MacArthur Foundation and program officer Eric Sears. I am most especially grateful to the Centre for International Governance Innovation (CIGI) for inviting and supporting my participation and for my continued affiliation as a Senior Fellow.

Thank you to Yale University Press and especially senior editor Joseph Calamia, whose development notes and suggestions strengthened this book immensely. Thanks also to the anonymous peer reviewers for their insightful recommendations.

I am grateful to have had the opportunity to present the research and ideas leading to this book over several years at some of the world's greatest institutions of learning, receiving feedback and invaluable ideas, especially at the Council on Foreign Relations, the Royal Society in London, Harvard Law School, the University of Salerno in Italy, the University of San Andres in Buenos Aires, the Aspen Forum, Cyber Week in Tel Aviv, the Hague Cyber Norms Conference, the American Bar Association, the Ohio State University, the Center for Democracy & Technology, the Global Internet Governance Academic Network (GigaNet) Symposium, the Humanities Lab at American University, the Internet Governance Forum (IGF) in Guadalajara, Mexico, the Cosmos Club, the Brookings Institution, the Cyber 360 Cybersecurity Conclave in Bangalore, University of Oklahoma, Cycon, Colgate University, Yale Law School, Columbia University, the University of Maryland Center for International Security Studies, University of Virginia, the Michigan State University Quello Center, and beyond. I am especially grateful to Anupam Chander for not only influencing my thinking but organizing a thought-provoking research symposium at UC Davis, "The Law of the Future: From rDNA to Robots."

My sincere appreciation for my fellowship at the Columbia University School of International and Public Affairs and for the support of Dean Merit Janow.

I am most grateful for the tremendous institutional support and intellectual encouragement of Provost Daniel Myers, Jeffrey Rutenbeck, President Sylvia Burwell, and the faculty, staff, administration, doctoral students, and research assistants at American University, far too numerous to list but foremost in my appreciation.

The Internet Governance Lab at American University has become a vibrant intellectual community for me, and I wish to thank the faculty fellows, postdoctoral fellows, doctoral fellows, staff, and especially my co-faculty directors and dear friends Derrick Cogburn and Nanette Levinson for sharing this journey with me.

A special thank-you to my writing collaborators Mark Raymond, Samantha Bradshaw, Jen Daskal, and Francesca Musiani, who all have had a profound influence on my thinking.

Much of this book was written sitting across from my writing partner and friend Aram Sinnreich and I am grateful for his influence on my work.

I am truly appreciative for the support of such a rich landscape of dear friends and loved ones, far too numerous to list, from many chapters of my life, American University, the Yale ISP, the Cosmos Club, St. Paul's Lutheran Church in Washington, DC, and my neighborhood in Chevy Case, DC.

It is difficult to imagine life or this book without the love of my wonderful family, the DeNardis clan, the Smiths, and the Slaters. A special thanks to my brilliant and kind mother, Gail Hansen DeNardis, who has proofread and commented on every book I've ever written, including this one. Thank you.

Finally, I wish to thank and acknowledge my wife, Deborah Smith, who has supported, loved, and inspired me for more than twenty-five years and who continues in her quest to stop me from using five-syllable words. I am already excited about the next project.

INDEX